BASICS OF LICENSING:
International Edition

Danny Simon
Greg Battersby

Kent Press

This publication is designed to provide accurate and authoritative information in regard to the subject matter covered. It is sold with the understanding that the publisher is not engaged in rendering legal, accounting or other professional services. If legal or other professional assistance is required, the services of a competent professional person should be sought.

–From a *Declaration of Principles* jointly adopted by a Committee of the American Bar Association and a Committee of Publishers and Associations

© 2014 Kent Press— All Rights Reserved.

Printed in the United States of America

ISBN 978-0-9830963-9-9

To Susan – 44 years of marriage and now over 35 books. I don't know how you withstood either, but I couldn't imagine life without you.

-Greg

To the things that mean the most – my wife Carey for her love and friendship, my daughter Jane who lights up my life, and my faithful stuffed champions Dorothy and Doggie Arf Arf for their steadfast support.

-Danny

About The Authors

Greg Battersby holds an A.B. (bio-chemistry) from Seton Hall University and a J.D. from Fordham University School of Law. He is a member of the New York and Connecticut Bars and is admitted to practice as a patent attorney before the United States Patent and Trademark Office. He is managing member of The Battersby Law Group, LLC, 25 Poplar Plain Road, Westport, CT 06880 (203) 454-9646 which specializes in intellectual property and licensing law with a particular emphasis on merchandising law and toy licensing. Mr. Battersby has been a guest lecturer at the Franklin Pierce Law School, University of Connecticut Law School and Quinnipiac Law School. He has been a Vice President and member of the Board of Directors of The New York Intellectual Property Law Association. Since 1995, he has served as General Counsel for the International Licensing Industry Merchandisers' Association ("LIMA") and was inducted into its Hall of Fame in 2009 and remains the only practicing lawyer in the Hall. He has also been an officer and member of the Board of Directors of the New York Intellectual Property Law Association ("NYIPLA").

Greg is a prolific author, having written more than 35 books on various licensing and IP topics, including the seminal book on the law of merchandising entitled *The Law of Merchandise & Character Licensing,* which was originally published in 1985 and is updated annually by West Publishing. He is a founder and executive editor of *The Licensing Journal* and the *IP Litigator*, both published by Aspen and for the last six years has been the legal columnist for *Total Licensing*. He has written more than 50 articles on various licensing and IP topics and given more than 200 talks on the subject before a wide range of audiences, including the INTA, LES, AIPLA and other organizations. He has been qualified as an expert in more than thirty actions on licensing related matters.

Greg turned a passion for baseball into a business, having invented a computerized video baseball/softball pitching simulator for which he has received 13 U.S. patents and numerous international ones. In his spare time, he created and now runs a company called ProBatter Sports, which manufactures and sells these simulators to a wide range of customers including a dozen Major League teams and more than 400 colleges and commercial training facilities.

Danny Simon is a thirty plus year veteran of the licensing industry with expertise in all phases of the merchandising and licensing process. Having built the licensing division for Lorimar Productions, 20th Century Fox and Carolco Pictures, he opened his own licensing agency in 1992 in Los Angeles, CA, called The Licensing Group, Ltd.

Danny has been a pioneer in the area of entertainment licensing, with a focus on material geared to the teen plus market. Beginning with the television program DALLAS, he was among the first to license adult, prime-time television entertainment and, with DYNASTY, he was the first to apply branding techniques to television shows. He also developed successful licensing programs for M*A*S*H, Fall Guy, Alf, Rambo, Terminator 2: Judgment Day, Mortal Kombat, Baywatch, U.S. Secret Service, Arnold Schwarzenegger and David Hasselhoff.

He has also succeeded in feature film development. With MORTAL KOMBAT, he produced the first ever film adaptation of a video game. He's a partner in an entertainment development company that sold the rights to the MATT HELM book series to DreamWorks, where it is currently in development as a motion picture.

For the past 18 years Danny has taught a continuing college level course on entertainment licensing at UCLA. He's a founding member of LIMA and has been its president and a two-time member of its Board. With Greg Battersby, he developed and serves as Co-Dean of LIMA's Certificate of Licensing Studies program.

Danny also is a regular lecturer on a variety of licensing topics around the world and serves as an international licensing consultant, providing consulting services to the Hong Kong Trade Development Council and other international groups.

He has been qualified as an expert witness on licensing issues in over 20 different litigations.

Over the years Danny has written many articles on the subject of licensing for various licensing magazines. He is a regular contributor to the book *Licensing Update*, published annually by Aspen, and also writes a monthly column on entertainment licensing for *The Licensing Journal*.

About the Contributors

Francesca Ash became involved in the licensing industry in 1978 when she co-organized the first-ever character merchandising conference and exhibition. In the 1980s she became the first non-American officer of LIMA — a position she held for two years. Acknowledged as an expert in licensing on a worldwide basis, in 2003 she co-founded Total Licensing and currently is responsible for publishing Total Licensing magazine, a worldwide publication with readers in over 100 countries. In addition, she publishes Total Art Licensing, Total Licensing Australia, Total Licensing UK and co-publishes The Total Licensing Report. In 2014, she will be responsible for the launch of Total Licensing's latest magazine, Total Brand Licensing. Francesca regularly addresses seminars and conferences around the world

Eric Belloso began his professional career with LCI (Leisure Concept International and after 4 Kids Entertainment) in London in 1995. Since then, Mr. Belloso has worked as Licensing Manager for companies such as BRB Internacional in Spain, BKN International in Paris and Viacom Consumer Products in London, developing properties including the Spanish national football (soccer) team, David the Gnome, Rugrats, Pokémon, Dangerous Dinosaurs and Star. Mr. Belloso set up his own company in 2003 consulting with different FMCG companies involved in the entertainment business, including Clear Channel Entertainment (part of Live Nation) in the live show business, Sony Pictures Home Entertainment in the DVD market and Sony Computer Entertainment (PlayStation) in the video game business. Beginning in 2007, Mr. Belloso also became International Business Development Director at Zinkia, managing all facets of the business (TV, toys, licensing strategy, licensing agents, internet and virtual world) for the series Pocoyó and taking the lead with respect to the brand in Latin America and China. He joined Exim Licensing Group in 2010 to head the international exploitation of their first property (BondiBand) and also developed and implemented, from 2012, the licensing and commercial worldwide strategy for Kandor Graphics, an animated studio based in Granada that launched the 3D feature film "Justin and the Knights of Valour." As of April 2014, he has been hired by Planeta Junior as DreamWorks Brands Director.

Dalia Benbassat, VP of Corporate Relations and Executive Associate at Tycoon Enterprises, is a graphic artist by profession and has developed a long standing career in licensing beginning in 1996 when she joined the Tycoon Group. She started in Equity Promotions, becoming involved in the development and sale of promotional premiums, then progressively became engaged in licensing services by becoming head of Promotions for Tycoon Enterprises in 2001, then Director of Licensing a few years after. Dalia has been directly involved in sound licensing successes with brands such as Pokémon, the new Star Wars saga, Shrek, and Yugioh!, and has worked via Tycoon for major studios including 20th Century Fox, Turner, Sesame Workshop, Marvel Entertainment and Rovio Mobile. Since 2006, she has been in charge of corporate relations and in-bound licensing at Tycoon and has participated in several International Licensing forums and seminars and currently acts as VP of Promarca (Mexico's Licensing Association).

Roger Berman is President of ZenWorks Co., Ltd., a licensing consultancy and agency in Tokyo, Japan. He has been active in Japanese, East Asian, and international licensing for over 25 years. His creative content management and development experience is wide-ranging, covering property categories such as publishing (Peter Rabbit, Paddington Bear, Eric Carle, Leo Lionni), artists (Norman Rockwell, Kagaya), sports/outdoor brands (Karrimor, Dunlop, Slazenger), and corporate trademarks (Kelloggs, Royal Doulton, SPAM, Corona Beer). Mr. Berman established ZenWorks in 2010 to deliver specialized license consulting, sales development and strategic support services to content creators and IP owners entering Japan and East Asian markets as well as facilitating international market expansion for Japanese companies. Consulting clients range from publicly-listed companies to one brand-focused small and medium enterprises. Roger may be contacted at rmb@zenworks.jp.

Lanning G. Bryer is a Partner in the New York office of Ladas & Parry LLP, Angela Lam is an associate in the New York office of Ladas & Parry LLP, and Lorena Mersan, is a recent L.L.M. graduate of Columbia University School of Law and Visiting Lawyer in the New York office of Ladas & Parry LLP.

Hubert Co is President of Empire Multimedia Corporation, one of the largest and most established licensing agencies in Asia. Based in the Philippines, Empire Multimedia also has several offices in Southeast Asia and Greater China. For more than 30 years, Empire has represented a diverse portfolio of intellectual properties from character, lifestyle to entertainment brands targeting all ages across all markets in Asia. Being in the licensing for three decades, Empire has achieved several firsts in the Philippines: first to license direct to retailer in the early '80s, first to license attraction walks multi-level marketing and wireless licensing. With Hubert's leadership and vast licensing experience, Empire Multimedia has become one of the most trusted licensing agents in Asia.

Marilu Corpus is President and Chief Executive Officer of Click! Licensing Asia, Inc. Founded in 1988, Click! Licensing has grown to be one of the leading brand management companies in Asia managing 9 countries in Greater China, Southeast Asia, with Korea as the latest addition, representing world class brands from pre-school brands as well as entertainment, fashion and lifestyle brands. CLICK's work begins from creating strategies to implementation of licensing programs for the long term benefit of the brands. Marilu started her career in Licensing in 1984 with United Media Licensing International Division in New York working on the PEANUTS and GARFIELD for 7 years and later as Vice President of MGM (Metro Goldwyn Mayer) as Vice President of International Licensing and Merchandising. Marilu is currently on the Board of Directors of the Licensing Industry Merchandisers' Association (LIMA).

Elias Fasja is Founding Partner and President at Tycoon Enterprises, one of the largest and most influential licensing and merchandising agencies in Latin America. Tycoon has consistently introduced to the market the hottest contemporary entertainment brands, as well as big "classics" and a careful selection of premium properties derived from the film, television, interactive, sports and lifestyle fields, including Angry Birds, Hello Kitty, The Simpsons, Plaza Sésamo, Real Madrid and Universal Pictures, among others. Tycoon has recently expanded its scope of services and geographical coverage, raising the bar for industry standards across Latin America, from Mexico to Brazil. Previously, Mr. Fasja was the President of PROMARCA from 2008 to 2012, and CEO at Grupo Carel S.A. de C.V. from 1977 to 1992.

Marici Ferreira is Director of Espaço Palavra Editora and Chairman of Brazilian Licensing Association (ABRAL). Ana Kasmanas is Director of Kasmanas Licensing and ABRAL. Glenn Migliaccio is Director of BR Licensing and ABRAL.

Hussein Ftouni is the Founder & CEO of Copyright Licensing Agency, Dubai, United Arab Emirates. Mr. Ftouni is an entrepreneur with over fifteen years of experience in the licensed consumer products industry, with expertise gained first in distributing licensed products for other licensees, then acquiring licensing rights, developing and manufacturing, marketing and distributing various ranges of licensed products, then into developing strategies for brand building, launching licensing programs for various international brands and properties.

Kelvyn Gardner is Managing Director at LIMA UK Ltd. Mr. Gardner can be reached at kgardner @licensing.org.

Elias Hofman is President of EXIM Licensing USA, Inc., a marketing organization which explores all opportunities involving licensing, promotions, merchandising, entertainment, TV and stage shows productions and which covers the entire Latin America region. As a regional player with 30 years of experience, the group has 15 offices across the region with + 300 local executives and employees with great knowledge and expertise in the different markets. Mr. Hofman can be reached at ehofman@eximlicensing.com.

Fuad Khan is a an accomplished licensing and marketing executive, running his own firm called Word of Web, a Sales & Brand Management Consultancy where he is helping brand owners as well as licensees find a solid revenue stream through brand extension and licensing. Prior to going independent, Fuad served as a Senior Sales Executive at Alicom Licensing, where he has done deals in the Nordic across all categories for more than six years for FOX Consumer Products, CBS Consumer Products, Paramount Licensing, Jim Henson Company and American Greetings. Mr. Khan holds a M.Sc. in International Business Administration from the LiU School of Management (Linköping University). He is fluent in 4 languages and lives happily married with two young children in Stockholm, Sweden.

Kyeongwon Kwak is the LIMA Representative for Korea. Kyeongwon can be reached at kkwak @licensing.org.

Sir Michael Ah-Yue Lou is President of V.I.P. Entertainment & Merchandising AG, Hamburg. Sir Michael, originally an investment banker who mainly advised governments in developing countries on loan syndication, became by coincidence the licensee for the DALLAS board game. As a result of the success of his first venture into licensing, in 1981 he founded V.I.P. Promotions, which soon became one of the leading licensing agents in the German speaking area and was converted in 1999 into the present stock corporation. Over the years, VIP has represented numerous proprietors of renowned brands, including IBM, Pepsi Cola, General Motors, Fabergé, Pierre Cardin; characters and celebrities including, Star Wars, Indiana Jones, James Bond, Tarzan, Terminator, James Dean, Elvis Presley, Marilyn Monroe, Michael Jackson, Madonna, Britney Spears and The Beatles; sport properties like the NFL National Football League, UCLA, NCAA, the International Tennis Federation; charities like the Princess Diana Memorial

Fund, the Vatican Library or Deutscher Tierschutzbund and other popular properties. Sir Michael (M.B.A.) is the author of numerous articles on licensing and merchandising and a frequent speaker at various seminars, business schools and universities. He was also the founding President of the European License Marketing & Merchandising Association (ELMA) and its CEO through 2008. www.vip-ag.com.

Gianfranco Mari is the co-founder and Chairman of DIC2, the first Italian independent licensing agency he founded with his brother Loris. The firm represents hundreds of licensors, including LCA, Twenty Century Fox, Larry Harmon, Carolco, CBS, Marvel Comics, Hanna & Barbera, MGM, Universal Studios, Edgar Rice Burroughs, Zorro Productions, Mattel, Les Editions Albert Rene, Minikim, Hallmark, Nintendo, LCI, The Pokémon Company, Viacom, NFL, General Motors, John Sands, Penthouse and many others.

Gaurav Marya is Chairman, Franchise India Holdings Limited and the LIMA Representative in India. Gaurav can be reached at gmarya@licensing.org

Luis Salazar is President of Compañía Panamericana de Licencias (CPL), one of the largest promotional and licensing agency in Latin America. The company has more than 30 years of experience working with the marketing departments of local and multinational companies to improve their marketing performances. This is achieved through promotions and/or the successful use of licensed characters, movies, artists, singers and other properties. The Peruvian-based company handles many popular properties from the entertainment industry. These include cartoons, animated series, movies, live TV series, artists, singers, etc, and representation covers most of South and Central America. Companies represented include Cartoon Network, Dreamworks, IMPS, Nerdcorps, Nike, Sony Pictures, Televisa, Twentieth Century Fox, Warner Bros. Consumer Products, 41 Entertainment among others. As a result of strategic commercial expansion, the company now has operations in Argentina, Brazil, Bolivia, Chile, Colombia, Ecuador, Mexico, Paraguay, Peru, Uruguay, Venezuela, Honduras, Panama, El Salvador, Guatemala, Costa Rica, and Dominican Republic. Compañia Panamericana de Licencias (CPL) handles licensing and promotions throughout Latin America, that range from local and pan-regional to those conducted globally. Visit CPL's web site at www.cpl.com.pe

Rohit Sobti is Vice President of Licensing & Merchandising at Yash Raj Films Pvt. Ltd, also known as Yash Raj Films Licensing ("YRFL"), which is a division of Yash Raj Films (YRF), and the leading player in the Indian film industry and India's premier studio conglomerate. Over the 18 years of his illustrious career in India's entertainment sector, Sobti has worked closely with a variety of music publishers, record labels, Film Theatre and Television channels both in India and Overseas. Sobti's broad knowledge of various entertainment disciplines has enabled him to play a key role in the development of YRFL, which has become a principle entity in the development of India's nascent licensing industry. YRFL has recently expanded its operation to include the licensing representation of third party properties for the Indian market, in addition to continuing to license those properties developed by YRF. rohit@Yashrajfilms.com.

Cyril Speijer is one of the co-founders of BN Licensing B.V., an independent and experienced licensing agency in the Benelux. Founded in 2011, BN Licensing represents a broad collection of some of the world's most well-known character properties, design properties, entertainment and sports brands. The company handles all sales and marketing-related business as well as the monitoring and protection of all brands represented. Before founding BN Licensing, Cyril was the founder of Wavery Productions B.V. in 1967 and has over 46 years of experience as a licensing agent. For 22 years, Cyril was director of NFL Properties B.V. and for NHL Enterprises B.V., which was the international office based in Holland for trademarks, licensing and overseeing the international agent network for these "Americana" brands. Cyril is an active participant in LIMA, where he served twice as a board member and in 1994 was awarded the "LIMA International Licensing Agent of The Year" award.

Hakan Tungaç is the Turkish representative of the International Licensing Industry Merchandisers' Association (LIMA) and is currently a doctorate student of History at Istanbul University. Mr. Tungaç is a Board Member and International Relations Director of the Turkish Press & Publishers Copyrights & Licensing Union. He is currently the managing director of Sentries Licensing Company. Besides his professional work career, he is an actor and has appeared on 3 TV series and a motion picture.

Tani Wong has over 16 years in licensing business and has gained extensive experience in the industry. She has in-depth knowledge about licensors, licensees, merchandising, publishing, marketing, promotions and events. To recognize her dedication and service to the licensing industry, she was awarded the "20 Most Outstanding Licensing Practioners" at The 8th China Beijing International Cultural & Creative Industry Expo in 2013. Apart from running her own consultancy, she is the Managing Director of LIMA China office since 2009. Tani served as Sales Director for Greater China, Southeast Asia & India at Warner Bros. She managed a wide portfolio from animation, movie to sports team and events with local agents in the region. Prior to that, Tani joined Disney Consumer Products where she cultivated her enthusiasm in licensing.

Christian Zeidler is Owner and Managing Director of 20too – The Premium Licensing Specialist. 20too – The Premium Licensing Specialist is a leading licensing company located in Dubai, United Arab Emirates. The company specializes in representing global entertainment brands and portfolios of IP owners such as Hasbro, Paws, IMPS, CreaCon and others. In his role as Managing Director, Christian Zeidler manages one of the leading licensing agencies in the region of the Middle East and North Africa. Together with his team they represent some of the world's most popular entertainment and character brands, such as Transformers, My Little Pony, The Smurfs, City of Friends, Garfield, Nerf or Monopoly. In addition, 20too also specializes in teens/adult brands and are currently managing the IP portfolio of India's leading film studio called Yash Raj Films. Besides this, Christian Zeidler has successfully introduced additional servicing components to his clients and 20too also offers excellent product design and premiums sourcing services to the local industry.

Preface

The licensing of brands, characters, sports team names, college logos and artwork, often called "merchandising," has become a huge business. While it may have begun as a fad, it has exploded into a $100+ billion industry at retail and generates more than $7 billion annually in royalty income for those property owners who are savvy enough to license their properties for use on a wide variety of consumer products.

While the roots of licensing can be traced back to the 1800's, the real growth of the licensing industry began in the 1970's with the explosion of such blockbuster motion pictures as STAR WARS and JAWS, which were highly merchandised for a wide variety of products.

Although the entertainment industry was the genesis of licensing, it has expanded rapidly to include many different types of properties: entertainment/character, corporate/brand, sports, fashion, collegiate, art, music, non-profit, and publishing. As a result, licensing has evolved from its humble beginnings to that of a regularly accepted marketing strategy for owners of intellectual property rights, and all around the world, many companies and corporate licensing divisions have been established solely for the purpose of representing marketable intellectual properties.

Some licensing programs are designed to take advantage of a current trend or fad sweeping the marketplace, and therefore have a relatively short lifespan, or appeal to a narrow segment of the public. Other licensing programs have the potential to remain relevant indefinitely, by virtue of their ability to attract interest from a wide and diverse range of consumers. Regardless of the type of licensing program or the industry that spawned it, merchandising has established itself as a viable and important form of marketing.

While licensing is attractive to property owners who see it as a way to help promote their underlying properties and generate licensing revenues in the process, it is similarly attractive to manufacturers as it permits them to leverage the value and popularity of a brand, character or sports entity to drive sales of their product. Under the right circumstances, licensing can be a win–win collaboration for all parties.

What has not kept pace with the growth of the licensing industry, in our collective opinion, is the availability of informative materials for persons who desire knowledge about the various practices of the licensing industry, individuals who are seeking information that will help them to hone their licensing skills, and those who want a worldwide perspective of the licensing industry.

We are of the opinion that the industry needs definitive guide books on various aspects of the licensing industry appropriate for anyone who is interested in capitalizing on this potentially lucrative market. In satisfying this need, we were not content merely to generate a single book that attempted to provide cursory coverage of the entire span of the licensing industry. Our objectives, thus, have always been two-fold: to develop a series of books, each focused on particular segments of the licensing industry, and to write them in a manner that would prove useful for those entering the licensing field and, by incorporating relevant and practical information, these books would prove useful to an experienced licensing professional. Our efforts have resulted in the development of the *BASICS OF LICENSING* series that LIMA has endorsed, received favorable reviews from readers, and enjoyed strong sales. The *BASICS OF LICENSING* now numbers three books, which are the following:

BASICS OF LICENSING: This book is primarily intended for those new to licensing, and those who are looking to improve the knowledge of the business. Written more from the point of view of the licensor, the book has proven useful to all segments of the licensing spectrum.

BASICS OF LICENSING: Licensee Edition: As its title implies, is a look at licensing from the perspective of the licensee. The book covers all aspects of licensing that every licensee should know before undertaking the costs and obligations associated with the acquisition of a license. Although written primarily for licensees, a significant number of licensors have found this book very useful in gaining a perspective of licensing from the licensee's point of view.

BASICS OF LICENSING: International Edition: The book which you holding, is the first of its kind; an effort to provide information on the key licensing markets around the world in addition to coverage of the basic practices of licensing employed around the world.

With the help of acknowledged licensing experts from key licensing markets worldwide, the primary focus of this book is to provide an understanding of how licensing operates in different regions of world. The book divides the world (excluding the U.S. and Canada) into five primary regions: Asia, Greater Europe, India, Latin America, and MENA.

The book begins with the obligatory "dictionary" of licensing terms, which is followed by a breakdown of the different market segments in the licensing industry. We also have provided a summary of what is happening in the licensing industry today.

We have also included a series of chapters that are intended to provide licensors with a roadmap for merchandising their properties on a worldwide basis. We have specifically provided a detailed discussion of how best to develop and administer a licensing program, a chapter on the all-important license agreement, and a segment on the role of licensing agents and consultants. Finally, we have concluded with an appendix containing a useful set of forms that can be used in your business to launch and manage an international licensing program.

The preparation of a book of this scope requires the input and efforts of many people, and a preface is the ideal place to give recognition to their contributions and express our appreciation and gratitude for their efforts. First and foremost is our former editor Rob Gessinger, and our current editor Michelle Houle, who have worked tirelessly on helping us pull this book together, interfacing with our international contributors, publisher and keeping us on track all along the way. Most importantly, Michelle helped us refine the work into something that can be readily understood by both the novice and experienced licensing professional.

The ability to compile authoritative information about the key markets throughout the world is only possible with the generous efforts and support of leading members of the international licensing community, and we are indebted to those persons who provided us with such material. On a separate page we have acknowledge who they are, as an acknowledgement and in appreciation of their contribution.

It is also important for us to note that this book has been developed with the endorsement of the International Licensing Industry Merchandisers' Association ("LIMA"), the central trade organization for this industry and who will participate financially from its sales. As such, the folks at LIMA deserve special mention, particularly an individual who we consider to be one of five nicest people in the entire world, LIMA's Vice-President of Member Relations and resident historian, Louise Caron. Her help in developing the chapter on the history of licensing is greatly appreciated.

And last, we want to express our very special thanks to Charles Riotto, LIMA's President. Charles, as he has from the very beginning, continues to provide us with great support and guidance at every step of the way.

We hope you find this book to be both an informative and useful guide to the world of international licensing. Enjoy the read,

Danny Simon & Greg Battersby

Table of Contents

Chapter 1: Defining the World of Licensing 1
  1.1 Definitions and Terminology 1
    1.1.1 Forms of Licensing 1
    1.1.2 Contractual Terms 3
  1.2 Types of Properties 6
    1.2.1 Art 6
    1.2.2 Celebrity 7
    1.2.3 Collegiate 9
    1.2.4 Corporate 10
    1.2.5 Entertainment 12
    1.2.6 Fashion 14
    1.2.7 Music 15
    1.2.8 Non-Profits 16
    1.2.9 Publishing 17
    1.2.10 Sports 18
  1.3 Types of Licensed Products 20
  1.4 Reasons for Its Popularity 21

Chapter 2: Glossary of Licensing Terms 23

Chapter 3: The Licensing Industry Today 27
  3.1 Size and Scope of the Industry 27
  3.2 International Scope of the Industry 33

Chapter 4: Protecting Trademarks and Copyrights Internationally 35
by Lanning G. Bryer, Angela Lam and Lorena Mersan
  4.1 Introduction 35
  4.2 International Protection of Trademarks, Copyrights and Related Rights 37
    4.2.1 Harmonization of IP Laws 37
    4.2.2 International Intellectual Property Treaties 38
  4.3 Trademarks 43
    4.3.1 Trademark Clearance and Adoption 44
    4.3.2 Basis of Registrability of Trademarks 45
    4.3.3 Reasons for Registering Your Trademark 47

4.3.4 Deciding Where to Register
Your Trademark 49
4.3.5 Maintaining Your Trademark Rights 54
4.4 Copyright and Related Rights 55
4.4.1 Copyrights 55
4.4.2 Related Rights 58
4.4.3 Collective Management of Copyrights
and Related Rights 60
4.5 International Enforcement of Trademarks,
Copyrights and Related Rights 61
4.5.1 Issues an International Enforcement
Program Should Address 61
4.5.2 When and Where to Set Up an
Enforcement Program 64
4.5.3 Resources for an Enforcement Program 67
4.6 Conclusion 72

INTERNATIONAL LICENSING MARKETS

Chapter 5: Greater Europe 77
5.1 Introduction to Greater Europe
by Francesca Ash 77
5.2 Benelux
by Cyril Speijer 80
   5.2.1 Introduction 80
   5.2.2 Demographics and Geography 80
   5.2.3 Languages 80
   5.2.4 Licensing in Benelux 82
   5.2.5 History 83
   5.2.6 Licensing Today 84
   5.2.7 Consumer Behavior 88
   5.2.8 Other Differences between the Dutch and
Belgian Markets 88
   5.29 Challenges 89
5.3 Germany
by Michael A. Lou 91
   5.3.1 Introduction to "GAS" 91
   5.3.2 Background 91
   5.3.3 The History of Licensing in GAS 93
   5.3.4 Beyond Entertainment Licensing 94

5.3.5 The TV Market 95
5.3.6 Recent Changes in Licensing 95
5.3.7 Licensing Today 97
5.3.8 Key Players in the Market 99
5.3.9 Unique Challenges 100
5.3.10 Roles of Agents and Consultants 101
5.3.11 Outlook, Projections and Conclusion 102
5.4 Italy
by Gianfranco Mari 105
5.4.1 Introduction 105
5.4.2 History of Licensing 105
5.4.3 Licensing Today 107
5.4.4 Changes and New Licensing Promotional Media 108
5.4.5 Brands-Characters-Events 109
5.4.6 How to Spot the Next Phenomenon 113
5.4.7 Proven Classics 114
5.5 Spain
by Eric Belloso 116
5.5.1 Introduction 116
5.5.2 History of Licensing 117
5.5.3 Licensing Today 118
5.5.4 Conclusion 123
5.6 The United Kingdom
by Kelvyn Gardner 124
5.6.1 Introduction 124
5.6.2 History of Licensing 124
5.6.3 Licensing Today 125
5.7 The Nordic Region
by Fuad Khan 131
5.7.1 Introduction 131
5.7.2 History of Licensing 133
5.7.3 Licensing Today 134
5.7.4 Outlook, Projections and Conclusion 136
5.8 Turkey
by Hakan Tungaç 138
5.8.1 Introduction 138
5.8.2 History of Licensing 139
5.8.3 Licensing Today 140
5.8.4 Turkish Properties 142

5.8.5 Conducting Business in Turkey 143
5.8.6 Outlook, Projections and Conclusion 146

Chapter 6:
Middle East and North Africa (MENA) 149
  6.1 Introduction to Licensing in MENA
  by Hussein Ftouni... 149
  6.2 MENA
  by Christian Zeidler... 153
    6.2.1 Introduction 153
    6.2.2 History of Licensing 154
    6.2.3 Licensing Today 156
    6.2.4 Outlook, Projections and Conclusion 160

Chapter 7: India... 163
  7.1 Introduction
  by Rohit Sobti 163
  7.2 India
  by Gaurav Marya 167
    7.2.1 Introduction 167
    7.2.2 History of Licensing 168
    7.2.3 Licensing Today 169
    7.2.4 Outlook and Conclusions 175

Chapter 8: Asia 177
  8.1 Introduction to Asia
  by Hubert Co 177
  8.2 Japan
  by Roger Berman 180
    8.2.1 Introduction 180
    8.2.2 Licensing Market Characteristics 181
    8.2.3 Retail Market Characteristics 184
    8.2.4 Licensing Trends at Retail............................... 186
    8.2.5 Media Environment 187
    8.2.6 Licensing Legal Nuts and Bolts 188
    8.2.7 Seven Licensing Pointers for the
    Japanese Market 188
  8.3 China
    by Tani Wong 191
    8.3.1 Introduction 191

xxvi

    8.3.2 History of Licensing 191
    8.3.3 Licensing Today 193
    8.3.4 Outlook, Projections and Conclusion 197
  8.4 Korea
    by Kyeongwon Kwak 199
    8.4.1 Introduction 199
    8.4.2 History of Licensing 199
    8.4.3 Licensing Today 201
    8.4.4 The Role of Agents in Korea 204
    8.4.5 Outlook, Projections and Conclusion 205
  8.5 Southeast Asia
    by Marilu Corpus 207
    8.5.1 Introduction 207
    8.5.2 History of Licensing 209
    8.5.3 Licensing Today 210
    8.5.4 Challenges of Doing Business in SEA 214
    8.5.5 Outlook, Projections and Conclusion 216

Chapter 9: Latin America 217
  9.1 Introduction to Latin America
    by Elias Hofman 217
    9.1.1 Media 218
    9.1.2 Television 219
    9.1.3 The Internet and Social Media 220
    9.1.4 The Retail Market 221
  9.2 Brazil
    by Marici Ferreira, Ana Kasmanas and
    Glenn Migliaccio 224
    9.2.1 Introduction 224
    9.2.2 The History of Licensing 225
    9.2.3 Licensing Today 226
    9.2.4 The Role of Local Agents, Consultants
    and Manufacturers 229
    9.2.5 Best Practices for Marketing, Advertising and
    Promoting Licensed Products 229
    9.2.6 Retail Sector 230
  9.3 Colombia, Chile, Ecuador, Peru, Venezuela and
    Central America
    by Luis Salazar 232
    9.3.1 Introduction 232

9.3.2 History of Licensing 234
9.3.3 Licensing Today 235
9.4 Mexico
    by Elias Fasja and Dalia Benbassat 238
9.4.1 Introduction 238
9.4.2 History of Licensing 241
9.4.3 Licensing Today 245
9.4.4 Codes of Conduct 248
9.4.5 Unique Challenges 249
9.4.6 Role of Local Agents 252
9.4.7 Marketing, Advertising and Promotion 255
9.4.8 Retail 257
9.4.9 Outlook, Projections and Conclusion 258

Chapter 10: The Licensor-Licensee Relationship 263
10.1 Introduction 263
10.2 The Deal 263
10.3 Establishing Payment Terms 264
    10.3.1 The Guarantee 265
    10.3.2 The Advance 266
    10.3.3 The Royalty Rate 266
10.4 Product Development 267
    10.4.1 Style Guide 267
    10.4.2 Legal Notices 268
    10.4.3 Forms 268
    10.4.4 Approvals 268
10.5 Approval Process 269
10.6 Royalty Payments and Statements 269
10.7 Product Liability Insurance 270
10.8 Terms and Extensions 271

Chapter 11: The License Agreement 273
11.1 Introduction 273
11.2 Negotiating the Terms of a License 273
11.3 Term Sheets/Deal Memos 280
11.4 The License Agreement 281
    11.4.1 Definitions 282
    11.4.2 Grant of Rights 282
    11.4.3 Term of the Agreement 286
    11.4.4 Compensation Provisions 287

11.4.5 Sub-Licensing.. 289
11.4.6 Accounting Provisions..................................... 290
11.4.7 Quality Control Provisions.............................. 293
11.4.8 Representations and Warranties 295
11.4.9 Indemnifications and Insurance....................... 296
11.4.10 Termination Provision................................... 298
11.4.11 Boilerplate Provisions 299

Chapter 12: Best Practices in Licensing Administration... 305
12.1 Introduction... 305
12.2 The Licensing Department................................. 306
   12.2.1 The Marketing Group 307
   12.2.2 The Sales Group 310
   12.2.3 The Contract Administration and Legal Group.. 315
   12.2.4 The Finance Group 319
   12.2.5 The Retail Group 319
   12.2.6 The Creative Group 321
12.3 International Licensing 323
12.4 International Agents 325
   12.4.1 Sub-Agent vs. Agent 325
   12.4.2 Role of the International Agent 326
   12.4.3 Selecting International Licensing Agents........ 327
   12.4.4 International Agent Compensation.................. 328
   12.4.5 International Agent Exclusivity and Territory.. 329
12.5 Ethics in Licensing... 330
12.6 Ensuring Compliance... 331

Appendix.. 335
Appendix A: Merchandising License Agreement............. 337
Appendix B: Sub Agent Agreement 354

Chapter 1

Defining the World of Licensing

1.1 Definitions and Terminology

Over the years, the licensing industry has developed a set of terms that need to be familiar if one is to understand how the industry works. In addition to the materials below, there is a glossary of licensing terms in the chapter that follows.

1.1.1 Forms of Licensing

> **Licensing:**
> *The contractual right to use protected materials owned or controlled by a third party, in return for consideration.*

The term "licensing" typically means any transaction in which the owner of a piece of intellectual property grants another party the right to use such intellectual property, typically in exchange for some form of consideration or payment. Absent the grant of such a right or license, the other party's use of the intellectual property would be considered infringing use. Thus, the license constitutes a defense to infringement.

"Intellectual property" can take many forms including, for example, musical works, literary works, artwork, drawings, inventions, discoveries, designs, patents, trademarks, names, logos, legends, industrial designs, trade dress, celebrity rights, etc. Regardless of the type of intellectual property, the one constant is that it must be protectable under some form of intellectual property protection, e.g., as a patent, trademark, copyright, right of publicity or trade secret. Intellectual property is frequently referred to simply as "IP."

> *Intellectual Property ("IP"):*
> *The intangible rights protecting the products of human intelligence and creation, which include copyrightable works, trademarks, patented inventions, and trade secrets.*

There are many types of licensing, virtually all of which will depend, in large measure, on the type of intellectual property involved. For example, when the intellectual property being licensed is technology or is covered by a patent, the licensing of such technology or patent is typically called "technology licensing" or "patent licensing." Similarly, when the property being licensed is computer software, the licensing of the software is normally called "software licensing." When a trademark is being licensed, it is typically referred to as "trademark licensing."

When a character from a book or motion picture is the property being licensed, such licensing is commonly called "character licensing." Similarly, when a corporate brand is the subject matter, it is typically called "brand licensing." When one licenses a highly recognizable brand or character for goods or services in categories different from the one where the brand or character had originally been popularized, such licensing is frequently called "ancillary product licensing," "merchandise licensing" or simply "merchandising."

This book will focus primarily on merchandise licensing, the primary focus of which is the use of copyrights and/or trademarks. In the licensing industry the terms merchandising and licensing often have the same meaning, and therefore may be used interchangeably throughout this book.

It should be appreciated that the term merchandising may have other meanings, particularly in the retail or marketing fields. In the retailing field, merchandising means something other than licensing, usually referring to some form of

Chapter 1: Defining the World of Licensing

"sales promotion as a comprehensive function, including market research, development of new products, coordination of manufacture and marketing, and effective advertising and selling."

1.1.2 Contractual Terms

The grant of a license to a manufacturer is typically done pursuant to a written contract, commonly referred to as a "license agreement" or "licensing agreement." While oral licenses can occur, the vast majority of licenses are granted under formal license agreements.

In the context of licensing, the owner of the IP that is granting the license is commonly called a "property owner" or "licensor" while the party receiving the license to use the intellectual property on their product is typically called a "licensee."

The intellectual property being licensed is normally called a "property" or, more accurately, "licensed property," while the products for which the license is being granted are typically called "licensed products or "licensed articles." If the intellectual property is being licensed for use in conjunction with a service, e.g., for advertising services, those services would be called "licensed services."

It is quite common to include "schedules" in a license agreement to more accurately and completely define both the licensed property and the licensed products or licensed services.

There are a number of different types of license grants. An "exclusive license" is one in which the licensee is the only party receiving the right to use the licensed property for the licensed products. There may be some instances, however, in an exclusive license where the licensor reserves the right to use the licensed property itself for such products, but that would have to be specifically stated.

A "non-exclusive license" is one in which the licensee is granted the right to use the licensed property for the licensed products on a non-exclusive basis so that the licensor may make similar grants to other parties.

Basics of Licensing: International Edition

Today, many licenses are granted as non-exclusive, even where the licensor may have no intention of granting a similar right to anyone else. This is done primarily to protect the licensor in the event that the licensee should declare bankruptcy. In such event, the licensor might be able to find others to step into the shoes of the bankrupt licensee.

Virtually all licenses are granted for a defined period of time, e.g., two (2) to three (3) years or for so long as the licensee continues to sell licensed products. The length of a license grant is typically called its "term." In many cases, a licensee is given an "option" to renew the term of the license upon meeting certain conditions. In such cases, the initial period may be called an "initial term" and the renewal period may be called a "renewal term."

Most licenses will restrict the licensee's use of the property to a particular geographical area, e.g., North America or the European Union, and this is typically called a "licensed territory."

Similarly, a licensor may want to restrict the licensee's sales of the licensed products to a specific market or channel of trade, e.g., "mass market" or "Internet." Such distribution limitations are commonly referred to as "channels of distribution."

Licensors may want to exclude certain rights from the license grant, either to give it the freedom to exploit those rights itself or to be able to grant such rights to others. Many licensors will exclude from a license grant the right to use the property as a "premium" or in conjunction with a "promotion." The reason for such an exclusion is that premiums and promotional products are not typically sold as merchandise through the normal channels of distribution but, instead, are given away to the public to promote the sale of another property, e.g., McDonald's BAKUGAN Happy Meal Program, in which BAKUGAN toys were given away by McDonald's to help promote the sales of its restaurant services.

The most common form of compensation in licensing is the payment of a "royalty" to the licensor, which is most often based on a percentage of the licensee's "net sales" of the licensed products. "Net sales" is almost always a defined term in any license agreement and will vary from license

Chapter 1: Defining the World of Licensing

agreement to license agreement. It is often defined as the licensee's gross sales of licensed products, less certain agreed upon deductions or credits, usually referred to as "discounts and allowances."

At the time a licensee enters into a license agreement, typically there is the requirement to pay the licensor an "advance" against future royalty obligations. In most instances, the advance is creditable or deductible against the licensee's future earned royalty obligations. Thus, if the licensee paid a $100,000 advance, it would normally not need to pay any additional royalties until its earned royalty obligation had exceeded $100,000.

In the licensing area, most licensors require that the licensee pay a "guaranteed minimum royalty," often referred to simply as a "minimum" or "guarantee." Guarantees are intended to protect the licensor in the event that the licensee's net sales prove to be lower than anticipated. As the name would imply, the licensee is actually guaranteeing that it will pay the licensor a certain minimum amount of royalties over a given period during the term of the license.

Although there are a number of ways to apply this guaranteed minimum royalty obligation, in most instances it only applies when the licensee's earned royalties fall below an agreed upon level for a particular period. In such case, the licensee is obligated to supplement its earned royalty payments to meet the guarantee for that period.

In addition to the payment of a royalty, many licensors require their licensees to also contribute to the licensed property's "marketing fund" which is to be used by the licensor to support and promote the property and the licensing program. These payments are often called a "marketing royalty" because they are frequently calculated as a percentage of the licensee's net sales of licensed products for a particular period in much the same manner that the royalty is calculated.

While most licensees are allowed to use third parties to manufacture the licensed products for them as "approved manufacturers," there is a difference between such practice and "sub-licensing," which is almost always prohibited. In sub-licensing, the licensee actually grants a third party the same rights that it had received from the original property

Basics of Licensing: International Edition

owner or licensor, not simply the right to manufacture products for it.

1.2 Types of Properties

There are a number of different types of properties that can be merchandised or licensed, although the vast majority of them constitute words, names, titles, symbols, designs, character or personality images or likenesses that have acquired a wide degree of public recognition through mass media exposure. Licensing properties typically fall into a number of different categories, including:

- Art
- Celebrity
- Collegiate
- Corporate
- Entertainment
- Fashion
- Music
- Non-Profit
- Publishing
- Sports

1.2.1 Art

Art properties can be virtually any image or other piece of artwork. In the case of prominent artists such as Thomas Kinkade, Warren Kimble or Mary Engelbreit, the artist's name can also be included as part of the licensed property.

It's been said that in art licensing, "it's all about the image." Consumers are purchasing the licensee's products primarily because of the artwork or image that appears on the products, and manufacturers are licensing the artwork for the same reason. Licensing the artwork of an outside artist lowers the licensee's development costs which makes it very attractive. While artwork is licensed for a host of different types of

Chapter 1: Defining the World of Licensing

licensed products, including apparel and printed matter, it is also extensively licensed for use in advertising and on packaging.

While publishers and manufacturers have been using other people's artwork and images for decades, the actual licensing of artwork has been a more recent trend. In the "early days," artwork was typically purchased by a manufacturer for nominal sums of money, rather than licensed on a royalty-bearing basis.

As the licensing business grew, however, artists (and their agents) recognized the shortfall of selling off all rights in the artwork to publishers and manufacturers who would then reap far greater profits from its use. Consequently, many artists started declining to sell their artwork outright and, instead, turned to licensing as a way to potentially share in the merchandising profits that the artwork generated.

As art licensing grew in popularity, so too did the sizes of the advances and guarantees that a publisher or manufacturer would be willing to pay for the right to use the artwork. In many instances, these advances and guarantees were significant and frequently were never earned off by the licensee.

As a result, the business model changed...again. While most artwork is still licensed rather than simply sold or assigned, the current trend is towards smaller advances and guarantees. Though the artist may still be able to ride the crest of a very successful licensed product, these smaller advances and guarantees protect the licensee if the licensed products do not sell up to the expectations of the parties when the agreement was negotiated. In short, business sanity has set in.

According to the current LIMA Survey of the Licensing Industry, the three largest categories of licensed products for art properties were gifts & novelties, housewares and home décor. The largest channel for the distribution of licensed artwork products was specialty retail.

1.2.2 Celebrity

Undeniably, we live in a world in which people are fascinated by the lives of celebrities. Magazines such as *People*

Basics of Licensing: International Edition

and *In Touch* have generated subscriber bases in the millions and huge web followings simply because people want to closely follow the lives of their favorite celebrity figures. It should not, therefore, come as any surprise that when a celebrity elects to put their name on a product or otherwise associate themselves with that product, more people will want to buy that product. The celebrity licensing category functions according to this basic premise.

In a nutshell, celebrity licensing is the licensing of a celebrity's name, image or likeness for use on a licensed product, or in association with the advertising or promotional material for that product, to enhance the sales of such product. The value of the license is tied directly to the popularity and standing of the celebrity which, unfortunately, can change over time or, in some cases, very abruptly.

In the early days, the celebrity might actually be required to act as a spokesperson for or even to endorse the licensed product, e.g., appearing in an infomercial on television or in print ads extolling the virtues or benefits of the licensed product and telling consumers why they should buy it. It has, however, evolved into one where the celebrity often simply licenses the right to use his or her name or image on the licensed product in a more classic licensing style.

In some instances, the celebrity might be required to make a promotional appearance or two with selected retailers, appear on the Home Shopping Network or to wear the licensed product on the "Red Carpet" before a Hollywood event, but the promotional support required is usually fairly minimal.

Ironically, the celebrity doesn't even have to be alive to be successful. The licensing of deceased celebrities has become big business, and as a result there are licensing agencies that specialize in this particular niche area. For example, it has been reported that the estates of such deceased celebrities as Elvis Presley and Michael Jackson continue to derive significant revenue from licensing their names and likeness despite their passing.

Chapter 1: Defining the World of Licensing

A manufacturer needs, however, to be careful when taking a celebrity license of a living celebrity since their fame and public image can be fleeting. If the celebrity's personal life doesn't go the way everyone expected, not only will the celebrity's career suffer, but so will the sales of their licensed products. For example, after evidence of Tiger Woods' marital infidelity hit the media, not only did his golf game suffer but so did the sales of TIGER WOODS licensed products.

1.2.3 Collegiate

Over the past two decades, collegiate licensing has become a very important part of the licensing industry, as colleges and universities now regularly license the right to use their names, logos or mascots for a host of different types of licensed products. The royalty income generated by such licensing programs is used by these schools to support a wide variety of their athletic, academic and other quality of life programs.

While sales of collegiate licensed products were initially confined to college bookstores and alumni catalogs, distribution channels for such products have greatly expanded as collegiate brands continue to grow in popularity. Today, a significant amount of collegiate licensed products are carried by major retailers on a national basis.

As one might expect, the success of a college licensing program is frequently tied to the success of its athletic teams. If a college wins a national football championship or makes an appearance in the NCAA's Final Four basketball tournament, the college will almost certainly enjoy a meteoric rise in the sale of its licensed merchandise with a corresponding jump in the royalty revenue that it receives—a double win.

An example of how athletic fame and fortune can translate into increased royalty revenue is BOISE STATE's experience. When it decided to change its logo and take its football program onto a national stage, the college experienced a ten-fold jump in its royalty revenues over a six year period. More significantly, the sale of its licensed products expanded from local stores to national retailers.

The viability of a college brand is not just limited to success on the athletic field. Schools such as Oxford, Harvard and Princeton have developed strong licensing programs on the strength of their academic reputations.

Interestingly, even colleges with unique or "catchy" names or from popular geographical regions have found success in the marketplace, e.g., SLIPPERY ROCK UNIVERSITY and UNIVERSITY OF HAWAII.

Not to be outdone by its member schools, the NCAA has even jumped into the licensing arena, developing licensing programs based on the names of its various tournaments, e.g., the FINAL FOUR. Similarly, the various football bowl games, e.g. the ROSE BOWL, have licensed such names for a variety of different products.

The collegiate licensing marketplace is an interesting one because almost half of the colleges and universities use the same agent, i.e., The Collegiate Licensing Company ("CLC"), which is now owned by IMG. Another significant portion of the schools use a second agent, the Licensing Resource Group ("LRG"), while the remaining schools are independent and conduct their own licensing programs.

According to the current LIMA Survey of the Licensing Industry, the three largest categories of collegiate licensed products were apparel (by a large margin), software and video games and accessories. The largest channel for the distribution of collegiate licensed products was specialty retail.

1.2.4 Corporate

In the early years of licensing, the corporate world watched with great interest as the entertainment industry jumped in and found it to be an excellent way of promoting their brand names and underlying products, while generating additional revenue at the same time.

It is, therefore, no surprise that corporations would eventually follow suit and use licensing as a means of both increasing their bottom lines and further enhancing their

Chapter 1: Defining the World of Licensing

brands' identities. Today, more and more major corporations with highly recognizable brands and trademarks have turned to licensing.

While the prospect of generating additional revenue is always important to most corporations, many have developed licensing programs for other reasons. For example, some have found it to be a cost-effective vehicle for diversifying their product lines and entering product categories that they had not previously explored.

For example, in the early 1980's Winnebago Industries was mired in a depressed recreational vehicle market. While sales of RV's were down dramatically due to the gas crisis, the WINNEBAGO mark was still a widely known and respected brand. Capitalizing on the public awareness of its name, Winnebago decided to diversify into the exploding camping market by licensing the WINNEBAGO mark for a line of sleeping bags, tents and other outdoor products. It was a classic example of how licensing can permit a company to leverage the power of its brand into other markets for little or no capital investment or risk.

Other corporations have entered the licensing arena to help strengthen their underlying trademark rights. For example, the Coca-Cola Company decided to pursue licensing opportunities at the suggestion of its trademark attorneys who were concerned about the company's ability to enforce their valuable trademark rights against individuals who were selling a variety of COKE products in categories and on goods that were totally unrelated to soft drinks. Coca-Cola proceeded by setting up what has become one of the largest corporate licensing programs in the world, with more than 300 different licensees manufacturing thousands of such diverse licensed COCA-COLA products as beach towels, boxer shorts, baby clothing, jewelry and even fishing lures. The company opened up a number of COCA-COLA stores around the world carrying a wide array of licensed products, many of which express a nostalgia theme based on early COKE advertising campaigns.

More significantly, the Coca-Cola licensing program has been financially successful beyond anyone's wildest imagination, and the revenue that it generates adds directly to the bottom line. At one point, it was reported that the program netted at least $70 million in annual profits or about 0.3% of its total net operating revenues—all while strengthening the company's trademarks in the process. It also does not hurt, of course, that the widespread sale and distribution of licensed COCA-COLA merchandise continues to help promote (and some may say advertise) the primary COKE soft drink products.

Some companies, particularly those in the alcohol and tobacco industries, have relied on licensing for promotional purposes since governmental regulations significantly restrict their ability to advertise through conventional media channels. Licensing permits these companies to still convey their marketing messages through the sale of licensed products which bear their marks, while also serving as a lucrative revenue producer.

According to the current LIMA Survey of the Licensing Industry, the three largest categories of licensed products for corporate brands were food & beverage, apparel and housewares. The largest channel for the distribution of corporate branded licensed products was mass market retail.

1.2.5 Entertainment

Entertainment and character properties are, of course, the most visible of all types of licensing properties and always produce the largest revenues in the industry.

Entertainment properties come from virtually all segments of the entertainment industry, although the largest source of such properties is Hollywood through its motion pictures and television shows. For example, the SPONGEBOB character featured in Nickelodeon's hit television show SpongeBob SquarePants, has become a major force in child-

Chapter 1: Defining the World of Licensing

ren's licensing, as well as the subject of dozens of promotional programs for virtually all of the major retailers and fast food chains.

Similarly, the Sesame Street characters, ELMO, BIG BIRD and OSCAR THE GROUCH, have become licensing legends due, in large measure, to the constant exposure that these properties receive every day on television. Such children's characters as MICKEY MOUSE, WINNIE THE POOH, BUGS BUNNY and PETER RABBIT found their origins in various media formats in the early 20th century, and remain popular today as a result of their continued media exposure.

Blockbuster Hollywood motion pictures have produced some of the most successful licensing programs in the industry, the best example being the STAR WARS films. In recent years there has been a string of motion pictures based on superheroes, e.g., SPIDERMAN, HULK, BATMAN, and SUPERMAN that have spawned successful licensing programs. The tremendous licensing success of such characters has resulted in the studios creating their own "Consumer Products Divisions", a/k/a licensing departments, responsible for the licensing of their properties.

Highly popular toys and video games have also been successful incubators for entertainment properties. BARBIE started out as a popular fashion doll for Mattel and, through licensing, has become a franchise. Similarly, the BRATZ line of dolls by MGA Entertainment and the GI JOE action figure by Hasbro have both been extensively merchandised for a wide array of products. MARIO was the featured character in an early Nintendo video game called Donkey Kong and was not only extensively licensed, but even became Nintendo's official "mascot."

Interestingly, this category has expanded with the growth of technology. Software, video games and mobile phones have made significant use of entertainment properties as the basis for games, wallpaper and even accessories such as game controllers or mobile phone cases.

Basics of Licensing: International Edition

According to the current LIMA Survey of the Licensing Industry, the three largest categories of licensed products for entertainment properties were toys & games, software and video games and apparel. The largest channel for the distribution of entertainment licensed products was mass market retail.

1.2.6 Fashion

Fashion or designer properties have been a staple of the licensing industry for years, due in large measure to the wide variety of different properties available and the vast number of products for which they are licensed. One need only walk through the clothing section of any department store or, for that matter, look at the different fashion brands in his or her own closet to see the impact that these properties have had. The reason for their success is very simple and one that retailers readily understand: the presence of a fashion brand on a product sells.

Consumers have come to expect seeing a fashion brand—any fashion brand—on an article of apparel since it conveys the impression that the underlying product is better designed and of a higher quality than the generic version. Irrespective of whether that proposition is true or not, in fashion licensing, perception becomes reality and, as a result, a vast number of clothing products and related accessories today carry some fashion brand—either that of a real designer or a "house" brand to convey the same impression.

Designers such as PIERRE CARDIN, ANNE KLEIN, BILL BLASS, OSCAR DE LA RENTA, and CALVIN KLEIN clearly started the trend and paved the way for the next generation of designers, including TOMMY HILFIGER, DONNA KARAN and VERA WANG. Spin-offs or extensions of these properties, such as TOMMY or POLO, have enjoyed enormous popularity in their own right.

Fashion brands don't always have to be a designer's name. They can, instead, convey a certain lifestyle image, e.g., NAUTICA, FUBU, TOMMY BAHAMA, GUESS? and

Chapter 1: Defining the World of Licensing

HANG TEN. Many retailers have developed their own fashion brands, e.g., the ROUTE 66 apparel line at K-Mart, or Wal-Mart's FADED GLORY brand.

The names of some of the famous design houses are also licensable, as demonstrated by the success of the CHANEL and LOUIS VUITTON lines of licensed products where good design prevails.

Some of the top catalogs have not only branded their own products, but licensed out their names for ancillary products such as the EDDIE BAUER line of SUV's by Ford. That said, some fashion designers are uncomfortable with the idea of licensing, since they would like the public to believe that all products bearing their brands are actually produced by their company, not by a third-party licensee.

At the end of the day, however, fashion licensing is all about design and quality. Fashion properties that feature good design and offer quality and value will ultimately prevail and bring the consumer back, year after year.

According to the LIMA Survey of the Licensing Industry, the three largest categories of licensed products for fashion properties were apparel, accessories and health and beauty products. The largest channel for the distribution of licensed fashion products was tie between specialty and mass market retail.

1.2.7 Music

The music industry rocks when it comes to producing hot licensing properties. Such bands and performers (alive or dead) as the BEATLES, ELVIS PRESLEY, MICHAEL JACKSON, BRUCE SPRINGSTEIN, BILLY JOEL, CHER, MADONNA, CELINE DION, the DOORS, KISS and OZZY OSBOURNE have not only sold a vast amount of merchandise at their concerts and while on tour (called "venue sales"), their licensed products have also found their way into traditional channels of retail distribution.

The JESSICA SIMPSON brand has proven to be enormously

Basics of Licensing: International Edition

successful at retail, most notably through the sale of licensed shoes, handbags and accessories, selling hundreds of millions of dollars in licensed products over its first five years. USHER has licensed his name (and persona) for a wide range of products, including cologne and aftershave lotion. Similarly, the total concert merchandise sales of BRITNEY SPEARS' licensed products have been in the tens of millions of dollars, the BRITNEY SPEARS' line of cosmetics for Elizabeth Arden and JENNIFER LOPEZ's line of toiletries have all sold well.

Rock bands have likewise come to recognize the power of their brand. At their height, the all-female British group ATOMIC KITTEN even created its own branded line of clothing called AK BRANDS. The use of music videos has proven to be an excellent way to sell branded merchandise for rock stars, as Australian pop star KYLIE MINOGUE proved when she appeared in a music video that successfully promoted her licensed line of lingerie for Agent Provocateur.

1.2.8 Non-Profits

Foundations, organizations, charities and associations regularly use licensing as a means to both convey their message to the public as well as a source of fundraising. Non-profit organizations, such as the American Society for the Prevention of Cruelty to Animals ("ASPCA"), have embraced licensing for these purposes. Revenue generated from the ASPCA's licensing program helps fund its national humane initiatives while promoting brand recognition in the minds of consumers.

Similarly, the World Wildlife Fund ("WWF") works closely with companies and individuals in marketing partnerships, where licensees are permitted to use its PANDA logo and WWF name. Again, such programs serve the important dual function of not only generating royalty income for the WWF but also of building awareness for its activities. In ad-

Chapter 1: Defining the World of Licensing

dition, the WWF engages in cause-related marketing promotions and sponsorship programs.

Some associations even set up their own related entities to directly engage in licensing. For example, the American Association of Retired People ("AARP") created AARP Financial Inc. to license and endorse credit cards, insurance products and financial services. The AARP name appears on mutual funds, IRAs, CD's, and a group that provides financial advice to its members. New York Life sells AARP Life Insurance policies and annuities; The Hartford sells AARP-branded auto and home insurance to AARP members; and other "partners" sell AARP motorcycle and mobile-home insurance. An AARP Visa credit card is offered by Chase Bank.

According to the current LIMA Survey the three largest product categories carrying Non-Profit Properties were apparel, publishing and gifts & novelties. The largest channel for the distribution of licensed non-profit merchandise was specialty retail.

1.2.9 Publishing

Many of the most popular entertainment properties trace their roots back to the publishing industry, particularly the children's book market.

There is, of course, a fine line between pure publishing properties and entertainment properties since many entertainment properties actually came from the publishing industry and vice-versa. For example, the PEANUTS and GARFIELD characters grew out of syndicated comic strips of the same name while the popular characters PETER RABBIT and WINNIE THE POOH first appeared in books. Many of the superhero characters that became enormously popular as a result of blockbuster motion pictures originated in comic books, including SUPERMAN, BATMAN, and SPIDER-MAN.

Basics of Licensing: International Edition

According to the current Survey of the Licensing Industry, the three largest categories of licensed products bearing publishing properties were publishing, accessories and stationery / back to school products. The largest channel for the distribution of licensed publishing goods was mass market retail.

1.2.10 Sports

For decades, sports properties have consistently been among the most popular licensing properties due, no doubt, to the worldwide passion for athletics. Sports licensing is a global business and, with few exceptions, appeals to a very wide group of potential consumers. While the popularity of certain sports such as soccer, basketball, cricket and hockey transcend geographical boundaries, others such as baseball and football are enormously popular mainly in the United States.

The major professional sports leagues in the United States, i.e., Major League Baseball, the National Football League, the National Basketball Association and the National Hockey League, all have strong licensing programs that are run by the "Properties" divisions of their respective league offices. These entities control the licensing rights for all of their team logos and properties. Thus, if a company wants to take a license to use, for example, the NEW YORK GIANTS logo, on its product, it would need to coordinate this through NFL Properties. The same is true for each of the other professional sports leagues.

Team names and logos are not the only type of licensable sports properties; certain individual players are themselves equally popular. Professional athletes, such as MICHAEL JORDAN, LEBRON JAMES, PEYTON MANNING and DEREK JETER, are all featured in very prominent and successful licensing programs.

In professional sports, the licensing rights for individual players are typically handled by the player or their agent,

Chapter 1: Defining the World of Licensing

while "group licensing rights" are typically handled through the respective players association for that sport, e.g., the NFL Players Association.

Since sports licensing will frequently involve the licensing of both teams and players, it can get complicated. For example, if someone wanted to run a promotion featuring all members of the Los Angeles Dodgers that also included the DODGERS mark, they would need to apply for a group license from the MLB Players Association for the names and likenesses of these players and to MLB Properties for the right to use the DODGERS mark.

Professional sports leagues and players are not the only sources of sports properties. The United States Olympic Committee ("USOC") has long relied on its licensing and sponsorship programs to generate revenue to help underwrite its costs. Licensees regularly pay royalties to the USOC to use the OLYMPICS LOGO, while sponsors pay sponsorship fees and provide goods and services for the right to be called an "Official Sponsor" of the program. Some of these fees are substantial because of the esteem that a sponsor gains through its ability to associate itself with one of the strongest and most recognized marks in the world.

The International Federation of Association Football ("FIFA"), which is the international governing body for soccer and who oversees the FIFA World Cup tournaments, also relies extensively on licensing to support its efforts.

Tennis and golf stars such as MARIA SHARAPOVA and TIGER WOODS, look to licensing as a major source of their income. Not to be outdone, the governing bodies for these sports, e.g., the PGA, LPGA, and USTA, all regularly license out the use of their names and logos to raise money and help to support the growth of their respective sports.

According to the current LIMA Survey of the Licensing Industry, the three largest categories of licensed products for sports properties were apparel, gifts & novelties and software and video games. The largest channel for the distribution of licensed professional sports merchandise was mass market retail.

1.3   Types of Licensed Products

In the early years of licensing, the majority of licensed products were low end products, typically called "buttons, badges, and posters." That has changed dramatically as the industry has grown and become more established. Today, licensing has expanded into almost every imaginable product and service category including those that feature high-end luxury goods and services.

If one simply reviewed the Classification List published by the United States Patent & Trademark Office, they would find that there is at least some licensing activity in more than 30 of the 42 different classes.

According to LiMA's Annual Survey of the Licensing Industry, the following categories of licensed products generate most of the licensing revenue in the industry:

Apparel: (Adult, Kids)
Accessories: (Head Wear, Jewelry & Watches, Other)
Consumer Electronics: (Headphones, Smartphones and Tablet Accessories, Children's Electronics)
Food/Beverage: (Beverage, Candy, Other)
Footwear: (Adult, Kids)
Home Decor: (Furniture, Home Furnishings)
Gifts/Novelties: (Collectibles, Gift, Other)
Health/Beauty: (Health, Cosmetics, Other)
Housewares: (Kitchenware, other housewares)
Music/Video
Infant Products
Publishing
Sporting Goods
Paper Products / School Supplies: (Art, Greeting Cards, School Supplies, Lunch Boxes, Bags/Totes, Other)
Toys/Games: (Dolls/Action Figures, Games, Pre-School, Other)
Software/Videogames: (Handheld, Software, Accessories, Other)

Chapter 1: Defining the World of Licensing

Of these possible categories, the three categories that recorded the most sales were apparel, toys & games and gift and novelty. The LIMA Survey also shows that the breakdown of retail distribution of licensed products was the following:

Mass Merchandisers (37.7%),
Specialty Retail (36.8%),
Department Stores (17.8%)
Direct Sales (7.5%)

While the industry has come to expect licensed toys and T-shirts, there have been some "non-traditional" licenses granted over the years that one prominent licensing agent categorized as, "What Were You Thinking???" Examples of these "non-traditional" licenses include NORMAN ROCKWELL boxer shorts, a WIZARD OF OZ Menorah, MICKEY MOUSE full-sized toilet seats, a PACMAN diamond bracelet and DALLAS barbecue grills. Time magazine recently published an article on the "Top Ten Oddball Celebrity Branded Products," which included: HULK HOGAN's Pastamania, SHAQUILLE O'NEAL's Shaq-Fu video game, STEVEN SEAGAL's Lightning Bolt energy drink and DANNY DEVITO's Limoncello.

1.4   Reasons for Its Popularity

What makes licensing so popular? The obvious answer to this question is that it sells products. From a property owner's perspective, there is little doubt that the opportunity to generate additional royalty income is the primary motivating factor behind setting up a licensing program. Furthermore, though, property owners have also come to realize that licensing provides a number of secondary benefits, including:

- Reducing the cost of product development;
- Providing additional exposure for the licensor's underlying products or services;
- Allowing the licensor to better leverage its advertising expenditures;

- Providing a hedge against the normal fluctuations of a licensor's basic business model;
- Allowing the licensor to achieve a high return on a minimal investment;
- Permitting the licensor to expand into new markets and test different new product areas;
- Allowing the licensor to further promote products of a type where there are governmental restrictions on what can be said; and
- Strengthening the licensor's underlying trademark rights by expanding the breadth of the goods or services on which the brand is used.

For the manufacturer, or licensee, the advantages that licensing provides include:

- Creating instant credibility through the use of a well-known, trusted brand or property;
- Providing a shortcut to the marketplace without the time and cost of building a brand from scratch;
- Allowing the manufacturer to create a product line that will have instant recognition and appeal to retail buyers; and
- Giving the manufacturer the ability to compete against larger, more established, companies.
- Providing an opportunity to expand distribution of its product line.
- Generating increased consumer recognition of its brand name.

Chapter 2:

Glossary of Licensing Terms

Advance: Often based on a percentage of the guarantee, the advance is a sum of money the licensee is required to pay to the licensor upon signing of the licensing agreement, and/or commencement of the licensing agreement. Most often the advance is creditable or deductible against the licensee's future royalty obligations.

Approved Manufacturer: An independent manufacturer, which has been approved by the licensor for the production of the licensed article(s), on behalf of the licensee.

Channels of Distribution: The specific market(s) or channel(s) of trade (e.g. mass market, specialty retail or Internet sales) in which the licensee is allowed to sell the licensed articles.

Contract: An written agreement, commonly referred to as the license agreement or licensing agreement, under which the rights to use intellectual property is granted, and contains the specific terms between two or more persons or entities in which there is a promise to do something in return for a valuable benefit known as consideration.

Discounts and Allowances: These terms applied to those specific deductions and/or credits that the licensee can use to calculate net sales revenue.

Exclusive Agreement: A licensing agreement in which the licensee is the only party receiving the right to use the licensed property for the licensed products.

Guarantee: Sometimes referred to as a Guaranteed Minimum Royalty or Minimum, the guarantee is the minimum amount of royalties the license is obligated to pay the licensor, regardless of sales, during the term, or within a specific period of time during the term, of the licensing agreement.

Initial Term: The first period of time that the licensee has the rights to use the property.

Intellectual Property: The intangible rights protecting the products of human intelligence and creation, such as copyrightable works, trademarks, patented inventions, and trade secrets, and is often referred to as the property.

Licensed Articles or **Licensed Products:** The products for which the license is being granted.

Licensee: The party receiving the licensing rights to use the intellectual property for development of specific goods or services defined in the licensing agreement.

Licensing: The contractual right to use protected materials owned or controlled by a third party, in return for consideration.

Licensor: The owner of the intellectual property, and is the party granting use of its intellectual property to another party. The licensor can also be referred to as the property owner.

Marketing Fund: Money collected by the licensor from licensees that is used to support and promote the property and/or its licensing program.

Marketing Royalty: Paid in addition to royalties due from sales of the licensed articles, these payments are made by the licensee to the licensor's marketing fund. Marketing Royalties are frequently calculated on the same basis as royalty payments, but often cannot be recouped from advances paid and/or used to offset guarantee obligations.

Chapter 2: Glossary of Licensing Terms

Net Sales: The licensee's total gross revenue from the sales of the licensed article(s), less any agreed upon deductions or credits. The definition of net sales is a defined term in any license agreement and can vary between license agreements, based on the parties agreeing to the specific deductions or credits that can be applied to the gross sales.

Non-Exclusive Agreement: A licensing agreement in which the licensee is not granted the sole right to use the licensed property for the licensed products, and the licensor retains the right to grant other parties the same or similar rights.

Premium: Product that is either sold at a reduced price or given away in conjunction with the sale of an additional product.

Product Approvals: The right of the licensor to approve the licensed articles(s), corresponding packaging and all materials related to the marketing of such product.

Promotion: A marketing event during which time product(s) may be available for sale at a reduced price or given away, and which may or may not require purchaser to meet certain terms and/or conditions.

Renewal Term: Each and any period of time, after the first term, under which the licensee has the rights to use the property.

Royalty: The amount of money paid by the licensee to the licensor under a licensing agreement, which is based on either a percentage of the income received by the licensee from sales of the licensed articles, or is a fixed sum of money that the licensee pays the licensor from the sale of each licensed article.

Schedule: Attachments to a licensing agreement that contain information that relates to a specific element or section of the licensing agreement.

Sub-licensing: The licensee's right to grant a third party the same rights that it received from the property owner or licensor.

Term: The period or length of time which the licensee is granted the rights to use the intellectual property.

Territory or **Licensed Territory:** The specific geographical area in which the licensed articles can be sold and/or distributed.

Chapter 3
The Licensing Industry Today

3.1 Size and Scope of the Industry

It's unlikely that any of the exhibitors and attendees who gathered in the basement of a New York City hotel for the first Licensing Show in 1981 would have ever imagined that they were witnessing the birth of an industry. That first show, which was produced by Expocon Management Associates and its president, Fred Favata, had a couple of dozen tabletop exhibits and less than a thousand attendees. Thirty years later, that same show would morph into a Las Vegas extravaganza with over 20,000 people from all segments of the industry in attendance.

It is also unlikely that any of the attendees in 1981 would have ever believed that it would spawn almost a dozen licensing shows outside the United States, many of which are significantly larger than the original New York Show. Brand Licensing Europe, held every fall in London, is perhaps the largest of these international shows and drew more than 280 exhibitors displaying more than 2200 brands in 2013.

Other international licensing shows include the Brand Licensing India, Shanghai Brand Licensing Hall, LIMA's Licensing Mart and the Day of Licensing in Germany, Bologna Licensing Trade Fair, the Dubai International Brand Licensing Fair, the Hong Kong International Licensing Fair, Licensing World Russia, Expo Licensing Brazil and Licensing Japan.

In addition there are licensing events or pavilions taking place at other industry-specific trade shows such as MIPCOM in France, as well as a number of other trade shows that feature licensed products such as the MAGIC, Sports Licensing & Tailgate Show, Kidscreen Summit, and the Consumer Electronics Show.

Likewise, few of the attendees at that first licensing show could have envisioned that the licensing industry would grow to a size that supports more than half a dozen trade publications devoted exclusively to licensing, including *The Licensing Letter, Total Licensing, License! Global, The Licensing Book, Royalties* and *The Licensing Journal* as well as publications in Spain (*Licencias Actualidad*, based in Barcelona), Germany (the *Licensing Press*, based in Rodermark), France (*Kazachok*, based in Paris) and India (*License India*, based in New Delhi). In addition, licensing topics are regularly covered in industry-specific publications, including Kid-Screen, *Brand Week, Billboard, Variety* and *Women's Wear Daily*.

Similarly, it is difficult to imagine that those who attended the Licensing Show in 1981 would ever believe that the "licensing industry" could actually support a trade association with more than 1,000 corporate members—the International Licensing Industry Merchandisers Association "("LIMA"). LIMA was formed in 1985 through the merger of two separate organizations: the Licensing Industry Association ("LIA"), which had only licensor members, and the Licensed Merchandisers Association ("LMA"), whose members were primarily licensees. The "licensing industry" also supports another trade association directed exclusively to collegiate licensing, the International Collegiate Licensing Association, which has almost 500 members.

Since 2000, LIMA has sponsored and published an annual Licensing Survey conducted by a professor in the business school at Yale University that reports on licensing revenues received by licensors through the sale of licensed products in North America. The Survey breaks down the revenues by property type and product category. These Licensing Surveys not only report on the industry for the present year, but also compare the results with prior years to identify trends.

For every year since the inception of the Survey in 2000, these Licensing Surveys show that licensors received more than $5 billion in licensing revenues from their licensees as a result of the sale of licensed products in North America. Total licensing revenues actually reached a peak of more than $6 billion in 2006, but this figure has decreased in subsequent

Chapter 3: The Licensing Industry Today

years due largely to a slowing of the worldwide economy and, of course, the recession that began in 2008. According to LIMA's 2013 Survey, licensors received $5.454 billion in licensing revenue in 2012 from the sale of licensed products in North America by their licensees. This was 2.5 percent higher than they had received in 2011, which augurs well for the upcoming year.

Attempting to translate total licensing revenue to actual retail sales of licensed products is challenging because retail markups and discounts vary. Nevertheless, the study estimated that such licensing revenue would have corresponded to retail sales of approximately $112.1 million in licensed products for 2012.

Past Surveys are available at no cost to LIMA members and are accessible through the LIMA website at www.licensing.org. The results of the 2013 LIMA Survey for all of North America were as follows:

HISTORICAL RETAIL SALES OF LICENSED PRODUCTS BY PROPERTY TYPE (2003-2013)

Estimated Retail Sales (in million dollars)

Property Type	2003	2004	2005	2006	2007	2008	2009	2010	2011	2012	2013	% of Total Sales	% Change from 2012
Art	$4,896	$4,986	$5,133	$5,338	$5,133	$4,517	$3,980	$3,754	$3,872	$3,930	$3,989	3.45%	1.5%
Entt./Char.	$48,389	$49,607	$50,787	$51,831	$52,411	$50,381	$46,416	$45,952	$47,963	$49,317	$51,444	44.44%	4.3%
Collegiate	$3,766	$3,729	$3,766	$3,766	$3,729	$3,858	$3,710	$3,636	$3,766	$3,821	$3,877	3.35%	1.5%
Fashion	$18,580	$17,835	$18,010	$18,185	$17,747	$16,980	$15,447	$15,118	$15,994	$16,542	$16,871	14.57%	2.0%
Music	$2,505	$2,705	$2,838	$2,926	$2,771	$2,594	$2,439	$2,550	$2,660	$2,705	$2,683	2.32%	(0.8%)
Non-Profit	$866	$888	$931	$974	$931	$844	$758	$736	$758	$779	$779	0.67%	0.0%
Sports	$14,825	$14,604	$14,880	$15,155	$14,972	$13,594	$12,124	$11,849	$12,308	$12,583	$12,822	11.08%	1.9%
Corp./Brand	$24,709	$25,198	$25,315	$25,408	$24,709	$22,727	$20,513	$19,697	$21,212	$21,632	$22,494	19.43%	4.0%
Publishing	$899	$857	$857	$857	$857	$773	$711	$690	$752	$732	$732	0.63%	0.0%
Others	$465	$317	$381	$254	$190	$127	$106	$63	$63	$63	$63	0.05%	0.0%
Total	$119,900	$120,725	$122,896	$124,695	$123,449	$116,396	$106,211	$104,044	$109,349	$112,105	$115,754	100%	3.25%

Chapter 3: The Licensing Industry Today

The chart below illustrates total sales of licensed products by property type. Clearly, the licensing of entertainment and character properties dominates the industry, producing more than $51.4 billion in sales (or about 44% of the total North American licensing revenues for 2013). The sale of licensed products bearing corporate or brand properties was second, generating about $22.4 billion (or about 19.4% of all retail sales). The sale of fashion properties represented about $16.9 billion in sales which amounts to about 14.5% of the total for the year. From this, the study projected retail sales of licensed products for each of these property types in 2013 as follows:

Property Type	Retail Sales of Licensed Product
Art	$3.99 billion
Entertainment/Character	$51.4 billion
Collegiate	$3.9 billion
Fashion	$16.9 billion
Music	$2.7. billion
Non-Profit	$779 million
Sports	$12.8 billion
Corporate/Brand	$22.4 billion
Other	$63 million

The 2014 LIMA Survey reported yearly licensing revenues broken down by each product category, as follows:

Estimated Licensing Revenues
by Property Type (2013)
(Figure 1)

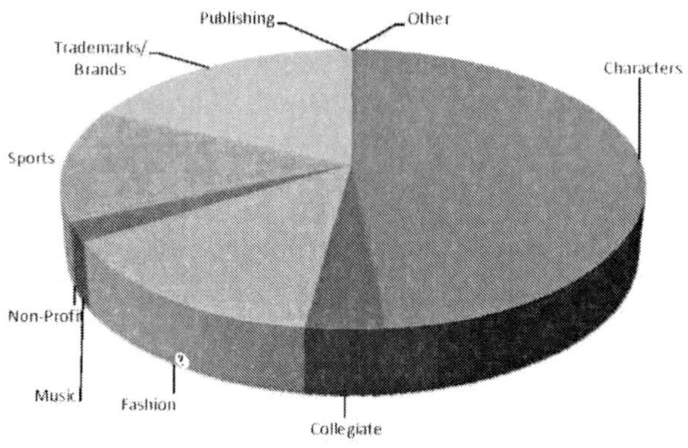
Publishing
Other
Trademarks/
Brands
Characters
Sports
Non-Prof
Music
Fashion
Collegiate

The Survey also addresses and considers which channels of distribution, e.g., specialty markets, mass merchandisers, department stores and direct sales, produce the most licensing revenues. The 2014 Survey found that licensed products bearing entertainment, corporate, fashion, sports and publishing properties were more likely to be sold through mass merchandisers, while licensed products bearing art, collegiate and non-profit properties were more likely to be sold through specialty channels. Estimated licensing revenues by distribution channel for 2013 were reported in as follows:

Chapter 3: The Licensing Industry Today

ESTIMATED LICENSING REVENUES BY DISTRIBUTION CHANNEL (2013)

	Specialty	Mass Merchandisers	Department Stores	Direct
Art	55%	25%	15%	5%
Characters/Celebrity	30%	50%	10%	10%
Collegiate	60%	15%	15%	10%
Fashion	35%	35%	25%	5%
Non-Profit	55%	20%	10%	15%
Sports	25%	45%	15%	15%
Trademarks/Brands	25%	50%	15%	10%
Publishing	23%	55%	15%	7%

Mass Merchandisers: Includes mass merchandising, supermarket and drug stores
Select Outlets: Includes college stores and specialty chains
Department Stores: Includes premium and mid-tier stores
Direct: Includes websites, telephone and catalog marketing

3.2 International Scope of the Industry

While merchandising may have started out as an American phenomenon, it has since become truly international in scope. Properties are being developed and promoted in virtually every country in the world and products bearing those properties are similarly being sold worldwide. The global reach of merchandising is reflected in the makeup and structure of LIMA, which now has offices in the United Kingdom, Germany, China, Hong Kong and Tokyo as well as regional groups in Italy, Spain and Portugal, New Europe, India, Dubai, Brazil and Australia.

LIMA's membership is further reflective of the international scope of the industry, with approximately half of its membership coming from countries outside the United States. Most significantly, it is readily apparent to anyone working in this industry that future growth of licensing activity will occur primarily in emerging markets and on a global scale.

Chapter 4

Protecting Trademarks and Copyrights Internationally

by Lanning G. Bryer, Angela Lam and Lorena Mersan

4.1 Introduction

Intellectual property ("IP") refers to the creations of the mind such as inventions, literary and artistic works, designs, symbols and names[1]. The protection of rights in these creations ("IPR's") is important because of the value they represent to their owners in terms of generating significant commercial benefits.

The licensing of IPR's is a growing business in international trade. According to a survey issued by the International Licensing Industry Merchandisers' Association (LIMA), trademark owners generated $5.454 billion in royalties in the year 2012[2]. Licensing can help a company enhance its business. It can act as a consistent revenue stream for licensors and licensees such as in the case of the copyrighted song "Happy Birthday to You which brings its owner an estimated $2 million dollars annually in royalties. Licensing also provides new market opportunities. Well executed licensing can help a company expand its geographic markets and product lines. Licensing in high technology industries helps fill new product pipelines and minimizes the risks associated with manufacturing and distribution. IBM Corporation generates an estimated $1 billion a year [3] by actively licensing its

---

[1] http://www.wipo.int/about-ip/en/index.html
[2] http://www.licensing.org/news/updates/licensing-industry-revenue-rises-for-second-consecutive-year/
[3] http://bits.blogs.nytimes.com/2013/01/10/the-2012-patent-rankings-ibm-on-top-again-google-and-apple-surging/?_r=0

Basics of Licensing: International Edition

40,000 patents to companies that manufacture products based on IBM IP, without incurring additional expenditures or risks[4].

Considering the profits that licensing of IPR's can produce, IP owners are wise to invest the time and resources needed to implementing appropriate protection strategies and enforcement programs. IPR's must be enforced to retain their value. IP owners should take action to address misuse and infringement of their rights by third parties to reduce the risk of confusion and prevent others from defending their unauthorized use IP owners should implement plans to police and enforce their rights by preventing unauthorized used. A well rounded international business plan should include a strategy for enforcing IPR's.

Globalization and the easy access of companies to international markets have change the manner and scope of protecting IPR's. Protecting IPR's internationally and of guaranteeing IP owners a "greater sense of security, control and certainty"[5] led to the harmonization of IP laws. Through the harmonization of IP law, countries from different legal systems converged to create common principles and standards of intellectual property rights. The continuous efforts in the harmonization of intellectual property laws through international and multilateral treaties and agreements have helped to simplify the process of protecting IP internationally. Nevertheless, there are still areas of IP where harmonization and unified protection mechanisms have not yet been achieved. In those circumstances, companies and individuals must still rely on national IP laws of the countries in which they do business.

This chapter will discuss two main subjects relevant to IP which can be the subject of license arrangements, namely, (1) the adoption and protection of trademarks, copyrights and related rights throughout the world, and (2) the enforcement and anti-counterfeiting processes relating to trademarks and copyrights.

---

[4]https://www.experience.com/alumnus/article?channel_id=engineering&source_page=Additional_Articles&article_id=article_1216819655187.
[5] http://www.ladas.com/Trademarks/IntTMProtection/IntlTM02.html

4.2 International Protection of Trademarks, Copyrights and Related Rights

This section is a broad overview of the international protection of IPR's with particular emphasis on trademarks and copyrights. First, we will discuss the rights granted to IP owners by international treaties. Second, we will look at the factors that should be considered when protecting trademarks internationally, its benefits, as well as the risks of not implementing an adequate protection program. Finally, we will explain the differences between the protection of trademarks and copyrights and the strategies that IP owners should implement to reduce the risk of infringement of their rights.

4.2.1 Harmonization of IP Laws

The increasing globalization of business led to the need for the harmonization of intellectual property laws and policy. IP owners doing business worldwide should be aware of the scope of their IP rights as they consider their enforcement. The ultimate goal of harmonization is to obtain consistency in the operation and application of IP laws internationally. Harmonization is desirable in that it provides a reliable framework within which IP owners can plan their international marketing strategies and be reasonably certain that their IP rights will be protected from country to country, and under multilateral treaties in large blocks of countries.

Attempts of harmonization began bilaterally or regionally, but later evolved into the accession to multinational treaties when nations wanted to ensure that its nationals would not be greatly disadvantaged by the laws or practices of other nations. The World Intellectual Property Organization ("WIPO")[6] played a significant role in the harmonization of intellectual property laws by sponsoring numerous multinational treaties and offering cost-effective mechanisms for protecting trademarks, patents and designs in multiple countries by filing a single international application. WIPO also pro-

---

[6] WIPO is a specialized agency of the United Nations, which objective is to promote the protection of intellectual property throughout the world (Article 3 of WIPO Convention).

vides facilities for alternative dispute resolution such as arbitration and mediation on IP matters, as well as for domain name disputes[7].

4.2.2 International Intellectual Property Treaties

Paris Convention. The harmonization of intellectual property rights began with the Paris Convention of 1883. The Convention applies to patents, trademark, industrial designs, utility models, trade names, geographical indications and unfair competition. 175 countries are currently members of the Paris Convention.

The Paris Convention created a multinational regime governing intellectually property rights. It established minimum standards for the protection and enforcement for IPR's. It recognized the national treatment standard, were by each Member State should afford the same protection it grants to its own nationals to nationals of other Member States.

In relation to trademarks, the Convention established common rules to be incorporated into the national laws of parties to the Convention Among these rules are: (1) a six month priority right for filing trademark applications worldwide, (2) the grounds for refusing registration and (3) the compulsory use of a mark. It did not regulate the conditions for filing and registration of marks, which were left to treaty members to determine and regulate through their domestic law.

Berne Convention for the Protection of Literary and Artistic Works. The Berne Convention protects "every production in the literary, scientific and artistic domain, whatever may be the mode or form of its expression". It sets the basics principles for copyrights, such as the automatic protection from the date of creation of the work without the need of any formality, the principle of national treatment[8] and of the

---

[7] For more information about WIPO Arbitration and Mediation Center, see http://www.wipo.int/amc/en/

[8] Works originating in one of the contracting States (that is, works the author of which is a national of such a State or works which were first published in such a State) must be given the same protection in each of the

Protecting Trademarks and Copyrights Internationally

"independence" of protection[9]. The treaty also established minimum standards of protection and the duration of copyrights which was of 50 years after the author's death[10].

TRIPS - Agreement on Trade Related Aspects of Intellectual Property Rights, Including Trade in Counterfeit Goods. During the Uruguay Round negotiations to revise the General Agreement on Tariffs and Trade (GATT) a new framework was established to operate under the World Trade Organization (WTO). The general provisions of GATT's Agreement on Trade Related Intellectual Property Issues (TRIPS) recognized that treaty members must not discriminate in favor of their own citizens against the IPR's of foreigners who are citizens of other GATT member countries, nor favor the rights of citizens of one country over the rights of citizens of another. In addition, the framework included a "most-favored-nation clause", under which any advantage a party gives to the nationals of another country must be extended immediately and unconditionally to the nationals of all other parties, even if such treatment is more favorable than that which it gives to its own nationals.

The principal provisions of GATT as they relate to trademarks are:
1. Any visually perceptible sign that is capable of distinguishing goods or services of one party from goods of another is capable of functioning as a trademark and registerable as such. Treaty adherents are however; free to refuse registration of signs that lack inherent distinctiveness, unless those signs have acquired distinctiveness through use.

---

other contracting States as the latter grants to the works of its own nationals.

[9] Such protection is independent of the existence of protection in the country of origin of the work (principle of the "independence" of protection). If, however, a contracting State provides for a longer term than the minimum prescribed by the Convention and the work ceases to be protected in the country of origin, protection may be denied once protection in the country of origin ceases.

[10] For more information see http://www.wipo.int/treaties/en/ip/berne/.

Basics of Licensing: International Edition

2. Registration may be conditioned on the mark being used. However, actual use must not be a prerequisite for filing an application for registration. Nor shall an application be refused simply because an intended use has not commenced within three years of the application date.
3. Countries that provide for cancellation of registrations on the ground of non-use must allow a period of non-use of at least 3 years before such provisions may be invoked;
4. Although member countries may impose conditions on the terms under which trademarks may be licensed, compulsory licensing of trademarks is banned as are prohibitions on the right of a trademark owner to assign a trademark without transfer of the business to which the mark belongs;

The major provisions of GATT in regard copyright protection include the following:

1. An obligation to comply with the provisions of the Berne Convention;
2. A requirement to treat computer programs as literary works for copyright protection purposes;
3. A requirement to give to authors of computer programs and cinematographic works and producers of phonograms the rights in certain circumstances to control commercial rental of the originals or copies of their works;
4. Fair use provisions and similar limitations on the exercise of copyright shall be limited to "certain special cases which do not conflict with normal exploitation of a work and do not unreasonably prejudice the legitimate interests of the right holder;" and
5. Obligations to afford certain minimum rights for the protection of performers, producers of phonogram, and broadcasting organizations.

The treaty also requires member states to provide procedures and remedies under their domestic law to ensure that IPR's are effectively enforced by foreign right holders as well as by their own nationals, The treaty included the availability of provisional remedies. Judicial authorities must have the authority to act promptly to prevent infringement and in appropriate circumstances to act "ex parte". Damages awarded for infringement of IPR's must be "adequate to compensate for the injury". In addition to the civil remedies, countries are also required to provide for criminal procedures and penalties for "at least" willful trademark infringement and copyright piracy on a commercial scale. Treaty member are also required to establish procedures to facilitate interception of counterfeits as pirated copyrighted goods by customs authorities at national boundaries[11].

Madrid System[12] A major success in the harmonization of trademarks was achieved through the Madrid System. This system is governed by two treaties: the Madrid Agreement Concerning the International Registration of Marks (1891), and the Protocol Relating to the Madrid Agreement (1995). The Madrid System creates a centralized system for the filing, registration and maintenance of trademark rights in multiple jurisdictions. Trademark applicants may file a single trademark application and have that application serve as a basis for an International Registration which may be extended for the same goods/services to other member states designated by the applicant. The protection enjoyed by an owner of an International Registration is identical to the protection that would result from a national registration with the trademark office of a contracting country. The resulting registration is known as an "International Registration", essentially a bundle of national rights in a single registration which can be renew or assigned.

Under the Madrid Agreement, owners of registered trademarks may extend the protection of their trademark to all other signatory countries of Madrid Agreement. The difference with the Madrid Protocol entitles owners of a pending application in the country of origin to extend their rights to

---

[11] To see which countries are signatories of the TRIPs Agreement, visit http://www.wipo.int/wipolex/en/other_treaties/parties.jsp?treaty_id=231&group_id=22.
[12] For more information see http://www.wipo.int/madrid/en/

Protocol countries. As from September 1, 2008, International trademark registrations are governed by the Madrid Protocol only in all member countries which are a party to the Protocol and also in those which are party to both the Protocol and the Agreement[13]. Both the Madrid Agreement and Madrid Protocol are administered by WIPO[14].

Other Treaties: Other treaties that have helped to harmonize intellectual property laws and facilitate the international protection of IPR's are the Nice Agreement on International Classification of Goods and Services (1957) which established a classification system for the registration of trademarks. The Nice Classification comprises a list of 45 Classes, 34 classes for goods and 11 classes for services as is followed in most countries pf the world having replaced local classification systems. The Vienna Agreement (1973) serves the same purpose as the Nice Agreement, but it applies to the classification of figurative elements of trademarks such as designs, pictures, drawing and logos.

Other treaties are intended to harmonize procedural and administrative aspects of the trademark registration process, such as the Trademark Law Treaty (1994) which removes the requirement of notarization and legalizations of signature and Singapore Treaty on the Law of Trademarks (2006), which provides a modern framework for the administrative procedures of the registration of trademarks.

In the copyright area there is the Universal Copyright Convention (1952)[15], International Convention for the Protection of Performers, Producers of Phonograms and Broadcasting Organization (1961, also known as the Rome Convention)[16], the Convention for the Protection of Producers of Phonograms Against Unauthorized Duplication of Their Pho-

---

[13] http://www.inta.org/TrademarkBasics/FactSheets/Pages/InternationalTrademarkRightsFactSheet.aspx

[14] To see which countries are signatories of the TRIPs Agreement, visit http://www.wipo.int/export/sites/www/treaties/en/documents/pdf/madrid_marks.pdf

[15] For more information, see http://www.wipo.int/wipolex/en/other_treaties/details.jsp?treaty_id=208

[16] For more information, see http://www.wipo.int/treaties/en/ip/rome/

nograms (1971, also known as the Phonograms Convention)[17] and the Convention Relating to the Distribution of Programme-Carrying Signals by Satellite (1974, known as the Satellites Convention)[18].

The rapid advancement of technology, particularly the Internet, has affected the way in which works can be created, used and disseminated. In order to clarify and adapt the existing copyright norms to the new digital era, WIPO has adopted the WIPO Copyright Treaty (WCT)[19] and the WIPO Performances and Phonograms Treaty (WPPT)[20].

4.3 Trademarks

The most efficient way of protecting brand identity in the marketplace is through the registration of trademarks. A trademark can be a word, a logo, a number, a letter, a slogan, a sound, a color, or a smell. Trademarks are a distinctive signs that identify the source of goods and/or services with which the trademark is used. When a trademark used in connection with services, is referred to as a "service mark".

IPR's can also be protected via trade dress, although distinctions between trademarks and trade dress have largely disappeared because many types of designations protectable as trade dress are also registerable as trademarks.[21] Trade dress is the overall appearance of a product/or service, such as the size, shape, color, color combinations, labeling, packaging, decorative elements. Examples of trade dress are the appearance and décor of the restaurant such as McDonalds, the cover of a book or magazine, the appearance of a teddy bear toy, the "G" shape of the frame of a GUCCI watch, the COCA-COLA bottle, the FERRARI car, Hermes handbag,

---

[17] For more information, see http://www.wipo.int/treaties/en/ip/phonograms/
[18] For more information, see http://www.wipo.int/treaties/en/ip/brussels/
[19] For more information, see http://www.wipo.int/treaties/en/ip/wct/
[20] For more information, see http://www.wipo.int/treaties/en/ip/wppt/trtdocs_wo034.html
[21] J.Thomas McCarthy, Trademarks and Unfair Competition § 8:1 (4th ed. 2010)

Basics of Licensing: International Edition

and Tiffany's packaging[22]. In most countries, trade dress is protected by trademark law; however, in others such as the United States, there are specific requirements applicable only to trade dress. Trade dress is usually protectable when they satisfy the same standards as a trademark (i.e. when they are distinctive). Trade dress is protected in order to prevent consumer confusion with other products that have a similar appearance. Generally, a trade dress must be both non-functional and distinctive to be protected[23]. If a company offers products and/or services that encompass a particular appearance, they should verify whether the country of interest has specific standards which have to be met for protecting their trade dress or if they can be registered through the trademark system.

4.3.1 Trademark Clearance and Adoption

Companies that want to expand their horizons beyond their national borders by offering products or services in foreign markets must consider the selection of their trademarks very carefully[24]. One of the first steps in selecting a new trademark is conducting a trademark clearance in the countries where the proposed mark will likely be used. This step is crucial in order to verify if the proposed mark does not violate any third party rights or any domestic trademark laws. Once the relevant markets have been identified, a trademark search has to be performed to determine whether there are identical or similar trademarks that could impede registration and use of the proposed mark. Obviously, if you have chosen an identical trademark or one that is a confusingly similar trademark to one that is already used or registered by a third party for similar goods or services, a new trademark should

---

[22] J.Thomas McCarthy, Trademarks and Unfair Competition § 8:4.50 (4th ed. 2010) (citing cases).

[23] Wal-Mart Stores, Inc., v. Samara Brothers, Inc., 529 U.S. 205, 54 USPQ2d 1065 (2000); Two Pesos, Inc. v. Taco Cabana, Inc., 505 U.S. 763, 23 USPQ2d 1081 (1992).

[24] MELVIN SIMENSKY, LANNING BRYER & NEIL J. WILKOF, INTELLECTUAL PROPERTY IN THE GLOBAL MARKETPLACE 12.2-4 (John Wiley & Sons, Inc., 2d ed. 1999)

be selected. Otherwise, unnecessary time and expense could be expended, including a possible adverse judgment for damages.

When two trademarks are similar, a legal analysis shall be performed to determine if upon a combination of factors (e.g. the similarity in the trademarks, the similarity in the goods and services, the channels of trade in which the goods or services are marketed, and the distinctiveness of the trademarks) the proposed mark is suitable or not for use and registration.

When you start thinking about selecting a trademark, do not limit yourself to a single selection. Rather, have several possible selections in mind. If your first selection proves to be unavailable, perhaps you will have better luck with your second or third choices. If the trademark availability search indicates that the trademark you selected is available, you should seek to register the trademark in the countries of interest as soon as possible while the search results are still relevant.

4.3.2 Basis of Registrability of Trademarks

The harmonization of IP laws helps unify international standards for the registration of trademarks. Nevertheless, there are still some particularities of registration systems that vary from country to country. Sometimes trademarks in the domestic market may not be received favorably by foreign consumers and trademark offices[25]. Therefore, it is necessary to understand the basic registrability standards that have worldwide application.

The distinctiveness of a mark is a basic requirement for registration of a trademark in many countries. A trademark is distinctive if it is "capable of performing the function of identifying and distinguishing the goods [and services] that bear the symbol[26]". However, some countries may even permit

---

[25] MELVIN SIMENSKY, LANNING BRYER & NEIL J. WILKOF, INTELLECTUAL PROPERTY IN THE GLOBAL MARKETPLACE 12.2-4 (John Wiley & Sons, Inc., 2d ed. 1999)

[26] J.Thomas McCarthy, Trademarks and Unfair Competition § 3:2 (4th ed. 2010)

registration of a mark which, albeit not currently distinctive or distinctive per se, may become distinctive when used over a number of years so as to create a sufficient reputation and recognition by consumers. Marks that are only capable of distinguishing are usually more difficult and more costly to register. Some countries that follow British law even create a separate register for marks that are considered only capable of distinguishing[27]. In United States, there is a Supplemental Register for marks that may eventually acquire distinctiveness.

Trademarks may not be either generic or merely descriptive of the goods or services to which they pertain. As such, the word "vegetable" cannot be registered as a service mark of a supermarket, since it is certainly descriptive of items which a supermarket sells. Likewise, it cannot be registered as a trademark for carrots, since it is a generic term for carrots. On the other hand, the word "vegetable" might well serve as a trademark for bicycles since it has little or nothing to do with bicycles.

The name of a company, individual, or firm may be registerable, although some countries may require the name to be protected through special procedures. It its very important knowing the special procedures that applies especially when a company's name and primary trademark are the same (e.g. Kodak, Apple, Sony), in which case the mark is referred to as "house mark".

Invented or arbitrary words constitute the best kind of trademarks because they are prima facie distinctive and imitations can be prevented easily. Mere combinations of words or slight variations in spelling or letter order may not be sufficient to qualify as inventions if the same idea would be conveyed to the consumer by the words in their ordinary form.

A geographical name may not qualify for registration of a mark. "Paris" cannot serve as a trademark for perfume in many countries. However, if the goods have some connection with that particular place it could be registerable. If the only

---

[27] MELVIN SIMENSKY, LANNING BRYER & NEIL J. WILKOF, INTELLECTUAL PROPERTY IN THE GLOBAL MARKETPLACE 12.2-4 (John Wiley & Sons, Inc., 2d ed. 1999)

Protecting Trademarks and Copyrights Internationally

significance of a word is a geographical one, the word is considered to be a geographical name in its ordinary significance, therefore non-protectable.

A surname may also be excluded from registration. However, if the mark is both a rare surname and an ordinary word with a specific meaning that is much more commonly known, the mark may be allowed registration.

Words that are clearly laudatory or descriptive do not qualify for registration. Pictorial or device marks and graphic designs may constitute distinctive marks if the representation has no reference to the character or quality of the goods they identify. (e.g., the NIKE check symbol). A device must contain some striking feature that will fix itself in the mind of consumers so as to enable them to remember the device and identify the goods bearing the mark. Device marks are particularly useful, in countries with a low literacy where consumers may recognize a device more easily than a mere word mark.

In many countries, trademarks that comprise mere letters and/or numbers (i.e. the proposed trademark cannot be pronounced as a word or words or just has too few letters) are considered to be non-distinctive.

In addition, marks must not be offensive to morality. A mark could be considered offensive in a particular country but not in another. Finally, a mark must not contain a negative connotation within a particular jurisdiction.

4.3.3 Reasons for Registering Your Trademark

The most important reason to register your trademark internationally is to preserve your rights in this valuable asset and obtain a tool by which enforcement is possible. In the case of a trademark licenses, it necessary for the licensor to ensure that the trademark is available and protected and for the licensee to ensure that it has proper legal authority to make use of the mark. Registering your trademark provides an exclusive right to use the mark and an exclusive basis for infringement claims of unfair competition. Relying only on trademark use as a way of protecting rights is generally expensive and time consuming, not to mention that it may be

Basics of Licensing: International Edition

unsuccessful if the usage is not sufficiently notorious or extensive enough in use and scope. Thus, a trademark registration is a valuable tool for use in asserting trademark rights against other parties and possibly obtaining statutory damages, which in many countries require registration. Finally, since a trademark registration is viewed as a definable and scheduled asset, it can be used to collateralize a loan, sold or licensed to a third party.

Trademarks can be misappropriated innocently or intentionally, by competitors, distributors, or professional trademark pirates. Trademark pirates which knowledge of newly adopted mark may seek to register these trademarks in strategic foreign countries. They hope to sell these trademarks back to their rightful owner. By registering a mark first, it frustrates the intentional act of a trademark pirate and, it also makes it easier for more honest parties to determine that the trademark is already protected when they do a trademark search on a new trademark that they are considering using and adopting.

Another important reason to register trademarks is to prevent what is known as "dilution". Dilution occurs when a number of companies use similar trademarks on similar goods. Potential purchasers are then exposed to numerous trademarks that have certain similarities as to these related goods, and this minimizes the legal and practical value of a trademark as a source identifier. Other companies are much less likely to adopt a trademark which is similar to or identical to your trademark if the necessary steps to register it have taken place. It is much more difficult for other parties to become aware of your interest in the trademark if it is not registered.

Another danger is the loss of goodwill which can arise by an infringing product or service of poor quality. This can happen when someone else enters the marketplace and commences the sale of goods or services with the same or a similar mark. If those goods or services are of poor quality, purchasers may well associate the poor quality item with the company, resulting in loss of brand goodwill and sales. However, this is less likely to occur if trademarks are register, since many companies take steps to avoid infringing a third party's trademark of which they become aware.

Trademarks can also be registered in nearly all countries in the world as a defensive measure. In those countries, a company or individual need not use of its trademark prior to obtaining a registration. Therefore, even in potential markets, you can prevent a third party from registering or using a trademark if you are the first party to obtain a registration. By obtaining a registration in advance of your use, you can be virtually assured of the unfettered ability to exclusively use your trademark in that country provided you begin use before the registration is subject to cancellation for non-use as most countries have statutory requirements to make commercial use of the mark to maintain these rights.

Finally, it is of vital importance to register trademarks because of the monetary value they enhance. Besides being a property right which can be sold or collateralized, a trademark can be licensed. Companies enjoy substantial revenue in royalties from licensing their trademarks. If a trademark is licensed, however, it is very important, not only to register the trademark, but also to record the license agreements, where possible. License agreements must be carefully drafted to assure quality control of the licensed products and/or services by the trademark owner. Many countries require that a licensed trademark be registered before they will register the trademark license agreement at the national trademark office.

4.3.4 Deciding Where to Register your Trademark

Differences between Common Law vs. Civil Law Countries. One of the goals of harmonization is to minimize the distinctions between the common law and civil law legal systems. Trademark owners should be aware of the type of legal system that applies to the jurisdictions in which they intend to market their products and services. For example, common law jurisdictions generally do not require registration of a trademark for a user of that mark to claim a proprietary right in the mark. In this case, rights will be created through mere commercial use. Conversely, civil law jurisdictions, generally grant rights in a trademark only upon registration. The party who registers first, that is "wins the race to the Register" obtains priority of the registration in the mark, although exceptions are made in cases of "well-known" marks or in obvious cases of bad faith. Nevertheless under both legal systems, registration is imperative for securing a monopoly to use a particular mark, as well as the right to license, assign, or create a security interest in the mark[28].

Planning Your Protection Strategy. You protect a trademark initially by registering the trademark. Historically, the registration process begins with the filing of a trademark application at the Trademark Office in each country where you desire the protection afforded by a registered trademark. More recently, the filing of trademark applications on an international basis has been simplified by European Community Trademarks (28 current member states) and the Madrid System.

Deciding where to register your trademark is a complex issue. If no adequate plans are implemented for protecting your rights overseas, companies may encounter many problems. Companies need to determine the countries in which they will be doing business, their expansion strategy, as well need to be aware of the timeframe it takes to obtain a trademark registration in different jurisdictions. For example, a pharmaceutical company that currently operates in the United States market but plans to export its product to Brazil in 2 years needs to understand that obtaining a trademark registration takes approximately 3 years. So if they wait until the last minute to register their mark, they may be forced to postpone their sale of products to Brazil.

Registering a trademark in every possible country is very expensive. Consequently, companies shall plan strategically in the way of protecting their trademarks internationally. If the mark is not a house mark, but rather a mark for a particular product or service or of more limited economic importance it might not be necessary to register the mark in all

---

[28] MELVIN SIMENSKY, LANNING BRYER & NEIL J. WILKOF, INTELLECTUAL PROPERTY IN THE GLOBAL MARKETPLACE 12.1 (John Wiley & Sons, Inc., 2d ed. 1999)

countries. Instead, if it is house mark, it might be necessary. Also, it is important to consider the market for a particular product or service. If the market is a small one and modest sales are anticipated, it may not justify seeking protection there. Therefore, planning in advance is advisable to avoid surprise and reduce costs.

By applying for a registration in advance of your use, you help assure unfettered use of your trademark. However, in countries where you can obtain a registration in advance of the use of your trademark, you must begin use of the trademark within some time period, typically two to five years after registration, otherwise your registration may lapse or be subject to attack for non-use. Additionally, the fact that trademarks can be registered before they are used also presents you with certain risks. The biggest risk is that another party will register that which you regard as your trademark. And since they often do not need to make use of the trademark for a two to five year period after registration, you may find yourself in a position where it is either very difficult or even impossible to take legal action against them. Thus, they are certainly in a position to cause you considerable difficulties once you decide to start exploiting the trademark in the relevant country. While using a Trademark Watch service can help alert you to possible third party conflicting rights, you still need to register your trademark(s) where you plan (or hope) to do business, either directly or via distributors or agents. If you do not take action to protect your trademarks by registering them, someone else may do so.

Once you decide to proceed with the registration process in the countries of interest, certain forms must be completed and official fees paid. The trademark application identifies the goods and/or services for which you are seeking trademark protection. The application is then reviewed by a government official, who is typically called a Trademark Examiner. The Examiner may refuse or object to registration of your trademark for a number of reasons. This process typically takes between one and three years (and in some countries considerably longer), and generally culminates with the publication of your trademark in a government periodical, published for the purpose of allowing third parties to contest the

Basics of Licensing: International Edition

registration of your trademark by filing either an opposition or a cancellation action. If no third party contests your application or after an opposition is successfully resolved, your trademark will then be registered, thereby providing you with the unfettered right to use that trademark (and similar trademarks) in that country with respect to the goods and/or services designated in the registration (including closely related goods and/or services).

International Registration — The Madrid System. The international protection of trademarks has been significantly simplified with the implementation of the Madrid System. In order to take advantage of the Madrid Agreement and Protocol, a company or individual must be from a Madrid member country. The company or individual can seek an International Trademark registration. However, an International Trademark registration does not immediately result in a trademark registration that is enforceable everywhere. Rather, individual countries must be designated in the resulting International Registration with an additional cost being incurred for each country designated. Also, a number of the individual countries can (and do) issue official actions, and/or allow objections to be filed by third parties, to which responses must be filed by a local trademark agent or attorney. Thus, while there can be a substantial cost benefit to using the Madrid Agreement and Protocol filing mechanism, that cost benefit can be illusory if objections are encountered in many of the designated countries. As a result, the cost of protecting a trademark internationally can still be substantial under the Madrid Agreement and Protocol. The Madrid System eliminates the filing costs associate with filing separate national application in each foreign country. Also, it reduces the cost for renewals, recordals of changes of name or address, and assignments because they are filled at WIPO directly instead of recording them separately in each designated country.

One of the major disadvantages of the Madrid System is that the rights granted by an International Registration can be extinguished if its home application does not mature to registration or if is home registration is cancelled during its first five years.

Multilateral Agreements Protection.

Community Trade Mark – CTM. Trademarks in Europe can be registered on a supra-national basis by seeking to register a trademark with the European Community Trademarks Office at the Office for Harmonization of the Internal Market ("OHIM"). There are a number of advantages in using OHIM to register marks throughout the European Union (EU), not the least of which is that it is far less expensive to use OMIH than it is to file trademark applications through each of a number of different national trademark offices.

In contrast to the Madrid Agreement and Protocol, the filing of a single trademark application for a Community Trademark can result in a single trademark registration enforceable throughout the EU. The cost advantage of filing for (and renewing) a Community Trademark is substantial compared to filing for (and renewing) trademark registrations in the individual countries making up the EU. Also, the use of a registered trademark in one EU country will satisfy the use requirements in all EU countries in the case of Community Trademarks. A bona fide use on a reasonable scale in a single Member State is normally sufficient to maintain the validity of the CTM registration throughout the EU and prevent it from being vulnerable to cancellation through non-use over any five-year period after registration. It is also increasingly fast to obtain a CTM registration; it takes 6 -9 months from filing to registration.

The Community Trade Mark (CTM) offers the opportunity to protect a trademark in all Member States of the European Union (EU) by filing a single application[29]. As new Member States join the EU, existing CTMs automatically expand, without any action or payment on the part of CTM owners. The initial registration period is ten years from the date of filing the application.

---

[29] The jurisdictions covered by the CTM are Austria, Benelux (Belgium, the Netherlands and Luxembourg), Bulgaria, Cyprus, the Czech Republic, Denmark, Estonia, Finland, France, Germany, Greece, Hungary, Ireland, Italy, Latvia, Lithuania, Malta, Poland, Portugal, Romania, Slovakia, Slovenia, Spain, Sweden and the United Kingdom.

Basics of Licensing: International Edition

Besides the traditional "absolute" grounds for refusal of a trademark application (such as the mark lacking distinctiveness), there are also certain rules governing the registration of shape marks. In terms of "relative" grounds for refusal, prior CTM and/or national marks that are similar or identical may preclude the registration of a CTM application, as may non-registered trademarks or other signs used in the course of trade, where the owner of such a mark successfully lodges opposition.

The main disadvantage is that an earlier registration in one Member State alone may defeat a CTM application in its entirety, even if the CTM owner has no interest in or intention to use the mark in that Member State. Also, if applications are met with several oppositions, the costs of dealing with those oppositions may be high and registration may still not be ultimately forthcoming.

Regional Agreements. Other ways trademark owners can seek international trademark protection is through regional procedures that facilitates multilateral filings such as the African Intellectual Property Organization (OAPI)[30], African Regional Industrial Property Organization (ARIPO)[31] and Benelux Office for Intellectual Property (BOIP), which covers Belgium, Luxembourg and the Netherlands.

4.3.5 Maintaining your Trademark Rights

Trademarks require care and attention. Once the rights are obtained, companies should also develop strategies to maintain those trademark rights. Trademark registrations can extend in perpetuity but need to be renewed periodically by

---

[30] OAPI is headquartered in Yaoundé (Cameroon). Organization centralizes all the procedures for issuing industrial property rights such as patents and trademarks in all 16 member countries. The member countries are: Benin, Burkina Faso, Cameroun, Centrafrique, Congo, Côte d'Ivoire, Gabon, Guinée, Guinée Bissau, Guinée équatoriale, Mali, Mauritanie, Niger, Sénégal, Tchad, Togo and Union des Comores

[31] OAPI established a regional office for filing trademark applications and covers Botswana, the Gambia, Ghana, Kenya, Lesotho, Malawi, Mozambique, Namibia, Sierra Leone, Liberia, Rwanda, Somalia, Sudan, Swaziland, Tanzania, Uganda, Zambia and Zimbabwe.

the filing of trademark renewal applications. Generally, the duration of each trademark registration (and each subsequent renewal) is ten years. However, most countries require that trademarks be used in order to be maintained. In addition, in many countries third parties can seek cancellation of registrations for trademarks which have not been used for a certain period of time (often after two to five years of non-use). When applications to renew trademark registrations are filed, some countries require that you submit evidence that the mark is in use. Also, some countries require that evidence of use be submitted at other times as well.

In most foreign countries, registrations may be successfully challenged after several years of registration if the mark has not been used in that country since the registration issued. For example, the UK Intellectual Property Office has recently cancelled GUCCI's GG logo, registered in 1984, on the grounds of non-use[32]. The trademark laws of foreign countries vary considerably, and care should be taken to verify that you are suitably protecting and enforcing your rights throughout the world. For further discussion of developing an enforcement program to help maintain trademark rights, see Section 4.5.

4.4 Copyright and Related Rights

4.4.1 Copyrights

Copyright protects the original works of authorships ("works"). Works covered by copyright include, but are not limited to: novels, books, poems, plays, reference works, newspapers and computer programs; databases, films, musical compositions, cinematographic work and choreography; artistic works such as paintings, drawings, photographs and sculpture; architecture; advertisements, maps technical drawings and computer programs [33]. Copyright only provide protection to expressions, not to ideas, processes, methods or

---

[32] http://www.worldipreview.com/news/gucci-loses-gg-trademark-in-the-uk
[33] http://www.wipo.int/copyright/en/#copyright

Basics of Licensing: International Edition

procedures. Therefore, in order to obtain copyright protection, the works have to be fixed in some material form[34].

Copyright is largely dependent upon the nation of origin of the author and where the work was created and first published. There is no single "international law of copyright" because each country sets its own substantive and procedural rules with respect to the protections and use of works in their respective jurisdiction. Nevertheless, several international copyright treaties exist which were adopted to harmonize copyright laws and provide for reciprocal protection. The Berne Convention is perhaps the most well-known international copyright treaty because it established core copyright rights such as the right to reproduction, to be enjoyed by authors regardless of nationality. More importantly, it grants an "automatic protection" of copyright, without the need for formal national registration systems. This means that the author's copyright is born from the moment the work is fixed in a tangible medium of expression. Consequently, neither registration nor publication is required to secure a copyright. While it is not mandatory to register a work in order to secure copyright, in many countries such as in the United States, it is necessary to file a copyright registration in order to proceed with a copyright infringement action. Interestingly, authors of foreign works need not obtain registration as a precondition to suit, while U.S. nationals must do so. Further, there are many advantages to obtain a registration. For example in the U.S. registration provides a presumption of validity, recognition of the statutory damages and right to claim attorney's fees. Therefore, in countries where you think your copyright might be infringed, it may be advisable to seek registration of the work.

Copyrights are limited in duration. The Berne Convention provides works to be protected for a minimum of life of the author plus 50 years. The duration of copyright varies from country to country and depending on the type of work (e.g. artistic works at least 25 years from creation, books at least 50 years from author's death), but the common term in most countries is the life of the author plus 70 years. In addi-

---

[34] Article 2 of the Berne Convention

tion, the Berne Convention establishes the rule of the shorter term. This rule provides that the term of protection granted in the country where the work was published first should be applied. This means that member countries are not required to provide a longer term of protection than the one received in the country where the work was first published. Knowing the duration of the copyright in a particular jurisdiction is important for licensee and licensors because once the work enters into public domain, the work is available to use.

The Berne Convention also grants moral and economic rights to authors. Moral rights (or "droit moral") include the right to claim authorship of the work, right of the author to object to any distortion, mutilation or other modification of the work that might be prejudicial to his honor or reputation[35]. Countries with Anglo-American tradition such of United States, Canada, Australia and New Zealand minimize the existence of moral rights and focus more on the economic rights[36]. Licensors should be aware if the domestic law recognizes moral rights because in some countries moral rights cannot be assigned by the creator to a third party. In comparison, economic rights are always assignable and they include the rights to use or to prohibit its use, reproduction, distribution, broadcasting, public performance, translation or adaptation of a work.

Another well-known treaty is the Universal Copyright Convention ("UCC"). This Convention was adopted under the auspices of the United Nations Educational, Scientific and Cultural Organization ("UNESCO"). Like Berne, it established the principle of national treatment, but reduces the minimum term of protection to the life of the author plus 25 years[37]. The Convention required that all copyrighted work should include the symbol © accompanied by the name of Copyright proprietor and the year of 1st publication[38].

---

[35] Article 6bis of Berne Convention
[36] http://www.rightsdirect.com/content/rd/en/toolbar/copyright_education/Inte rnational_Copyright_Basics.html
[37] To see which countries are signatories of the UCC, visit http://www.wipo.int/wipolex/en/other_treaties/parties.jsp?treaty_id=208&group_id=22
[38] Article 3 of UCC

Basics of Licensing: International Edition

Most copyrighted works have to be licensed by the owner in order to be used. However, there are exceptions and limitations that permit the use of works without authorization and without payment of compensation. These exceptions and limitations are established in national copyright laws and vary substantially from jurisdiction to jurisdiction. They are often expressed in concepts such as "fair use" or "fair utilization". The common fair uses are for educational purposes, for reporting current events, ephemeral recordings for broadcasting purposes and reproduction in certain special cases. Nevertheless, the limitation usually never covers the normal commercial exploitation of the work made by companies that could unreasonable prejudice the legitimate interest of the author[39]. Although, there are many countries that allow compulsory licenses, meaning that authorization from the copyright holder is not required to use the work, but compensation for its use has to be paid.

4.4.2 Related Rights

Related rights are also known as "neighboring rights" to copyright because they concern other categories of owners' rights. They are the rights that performers, producers of phonograms and broadcasting organization hold in relation to their performances, phonograms and broadcasts, respectively[40].

Related rights are linked with copyright because the three categories of related rights are auxiliaries or intermediaries in the production, recoding or diffusion of author's work. "A musician performs a musical work written by a composer; an actor performs a role in a play written by a playwright; producers of phonograms -- or more commonly "the record industry" -- record and produce songs and music written by authors and composers, played by musicians or sung by performers; broadcasting organizations broadcast works and phonograms on their stations[41]". For example, Bono composes the lyrics for all the U2's songs; therefore this means that

---

[39] Article 9(a) of Berne Convention
[40] http://www.wipo.int/about-ip/en/about_collective_mngt.html
[41] Id.

Protecting Trademarks and Copyrights Internationally

Bono holds copyright for the composition of the songs and rights to his performance. RCA Records produce the music recording of many popular artists such as Shakira, Britney Spears, Alicia Keys, Justin Timberlake, Miley Cyrus among others. A record company usually handles the production, manufacture, distribution, marketing and promotion of the music recordings and music videos that they publish and sometimes even the enforcement of the copyright.

The Rome Convention established the related rights. Similar to the Berne Convention, the Rome Convention determines the minimum standards of protection that Contracting States should grant to performers, producers of phonograms and broadcasting organizations. Likewise, it established the principle of national treatment, were the contracting states should grant foreigners the same rights it grants to their nationals[42].

According to the Rome Convention, performers are granted the "possibility of preventing" certain acts without their consent[43]. These acts include the prevention of broadcasting or communication to the public of a live performance; recording an unfixed performance; and reproducing a fixation of the performance[44]. Producers of phonograms have the right to authorize or prohibit the direct or indirect reproduction of their phonograms[45]. Broadcasting organizations have the right to authorize or prohibit (a) the rebroadcasting of their broadcasts; (b) the fixation of their broadcasts; (c) the reproduction of fixation of their broadcasts and (d) the communication to the public of their television broadcasts when they accessible to public against payment[46]. Under the Rome Convention, the minimum term of protection is 25 years from the end of the year in which the fixation was made or when the performance or broadcast took place[47]. Like in copyright, there are limita-

---

[42] http://www.wipo.int/export/sites/www/copyright/en/activities/pdf/international_protection.pdf
[43] Article 7 of Rome Convention
[44] http://www.wipo.int/export/sites/www/copyright/en/activities/pdf/international_protection.pdf
[45] Article 10 of Rome Convention
[46] Article 13 of Rome Convention
[47] http://www.wipo.int/export/sites/www/copyright/en/activities/pdf/international_protection.pdf

tions that allow the private use of the related rights. Each country regulates the limitations through their domestic law.

4.4.3 Collective Management of Copyrights and Related Rights

In today's world, the individual management of rights is virtually impossible. An author is incapable of monitoring all the uses of his work. An author cannot, for instance, contact every single radio or television station to negotiate licenses and remuneration for the use of his works. Equally, it is impossible for broadcasting organizations to seek specific permission from every author for the use of every copyrighted work. Considering the impracticability of managing these activities individually, collective management organizations were created in order to act in the interest of the owners of copyrights. Collective management organizations are an important link between creators and users of copyrighted works because they ensure that users pay creators the adequate remuneration for the use of their works.

There are many kinds of collective management organizations, depending on the category of works involved (e.g. music, books, multimedia, production, etc.)[48]. Creators join them so that the organization can manage their copyrights and related rights. As a result of such membership, the collective management organization negotiates the rates and term of use with users, issue licenses authorizing uses, and collect and distribute royalties back to the creators[49].

Some examples of well-known international collective management organizations include:
- International Confederation of Societies of Authors and Composers (CISAC)
- International Federation of Reproduction Rights Organizations (IFRRO)
- Association of European Performers Organization (AEPO)
- International Federation of Actors (FIA)
- International Federation of Musicians (FIM)

---

[48] Id.
[49] Id.

- International Federation of the Phonographic Industry (IFPI)

4.5 International Enforcement of Trademarks, Copyrights, and Related Rights

Whether a licensor is in the final stages of executing a license agreement or a licensee is in the process of registering its license as required by its country's trademark laws, it is never too early for the parties to consider how the subject intellectual property rights will be protected in light of the new business arrangement. This protection may come in the form of extending its preexisting enforcement program or creating a new program to incorporate its licensees. Without a broad enforcement program, there may be uncontrolled and unauthorized activities, which can ultimately harm the licensor/rights holder's or licensee's overall image or economic value. Strong brand value can drive improved business performance and further a company's longevity.[50] Top companies are successful and maintain valuable brands because their products are intuitive and are seamlessly deployed into our lives. Therefore, interruption in the association between consumer and product caused by inconsistent or unauthorized use of trademarks or copyrighted works can have a detrimental effect on the brand. A well designed enforcement program can help ensure that the licensed intellectual property rights are adequately policed and protected.

4.5.1 Issues an International Enforcement Program Should Address

The more business a licensor develops in the international arena, the more likely its brand will gain notoriety and strength. However, business growth may not be readily apparent. For a licensor, growth can be attributed to the creation of new intellectual property that must then be licensed to its existing international licensees. There may also be growth when a licensor wishes to enter into a new country's market-

---

[50] Smith, Gordon V. and Parr, Russell L. Intellectual Property: Licensing and Joint Venture Profit Strategies. (John Wiley & Sons, Inc. 1993).

Basics of Licensing: International Edition

place and engage in a new overseas licensor/licensee relationship. From an international intellectual property perspective, the two main issues to address in an enforcement program is (1) alleviating the misuse of authorized rights caused by a burgeoning and undermanaged intellectual property portfolio, and (2) controlling unauthorized use of a licensor's rights by third parties whom are exploiting or trading off the company's success.

Misuse. Misuse of a trademark can occur both within a company and outside of a company. A licensee who is misusing the licensor's trademark or copyrighted work may end up doing so without intent or knowledge. It is up to the licensor to ensure that the nature of the licensee's use is proper.

First, it is important for a licensor to understand whether the licensee is using its intellectual property at all. In most countries there is a statutory requirement to make use of a trademark. Nonuse of a trademark for an uninterrupted and extended period of time (in many countries anywhere from 2 to 5 years) can leave the mark vulnerable to cancellation by third parties. Licensors may not realize that its licensees have been placed on notice of a cancellation proceeding against their intellectual property.

Next, a licensor should become familiar with the field and form of the licensee's use. Under the European Community, a trademark licensor may be held liable for product defects if the licensee presents the licensor to be the manufacturer, supplier or importer. A licensor may wish to consider requiring the licensee to place a disclaimer on the goods that the trademark has been licensed and the product was manufactured by the licensee or its agent, therefore absolving the licensor from liability. On the other hand, a licensor may determine that there is a business interest in only labeling its goods with its own brand and not with the name of third party manufacturers. Whatever the interests, the licensor will want to include language in its license agreement to address the burden of such liability.

A permutation of misuse is the concept known as "naked" licensing in the United States[51]. When a valid license is created in the United States and the licensor does not demonstrate control over the licensee's quality or use of its trademark rights, the trademark may be considered abandoned.

In addition to proper use of the mark, a licensor should also ensure that its international registrations are properly marked. Product labeling of copyrighted material should include relevant copyright notices, where possible, for design marks, packaging, usage manuals, instructions and all other copyrightable matter used in connection with the sale of the product. This can come in the form of an attribution statement and © symbol, for example: "All Licorice characters and the distinctive likeness(es) thereof are Copyright © 1900–2013 Candy, Inc. ALL RIGHTS RESERVED." Some countries require the use of a © symbol on copyrighted material.

Within most countries, the marking of the ® symbol following a trademark is an optional requirement. However, there are still a handful of countries that have specialized requirements regarding markings. For example, in Mexico, products made under license must bear the name and domicile of licensee and the owner with indication that the use is made under license. In Canada, if the mark is licensed then the products should indicate the same and bear the name of the mark owner (also requirement of English and French). In Indonesia, registration number of a trademark must be indicated on the packaging of its goods. If the goods are not packaged, then the registration number must appear on the catalogues or instruction manuals of the respective goods and services. Whereas in Egypt all imported products from abroad should bear the Arabic name and country of manufacturer. In China, "Registered Trademark" or Chinese equivalent of the ® symbol is a requirement.

---

[51] Wildman, Edwards, "Losing a trademark under naked licensing law" World Trademark Review June/July 2013, accessible at: http://www.worldtrademarkreview.com/issues/Article.ashx?g=ac00f9fd-fd49-4d33-b349-5f8b13d036aa

Unauthorized Use. The increase in popularity of a licensor's trademarks or copyrighted work inevitably invites infringement on a national or international scale. In many cases, infringers willfully engage in unlawful conduct. However, there are also occasions where an infringer is unaware that its activities are illegal or may even be unaware of existing intellectual property rights. Licensors should consider the impact that unauthorized use may have on its business and on its relationship with its licensees. Licensees may become unhappy that it has offered due consideration for the rights to the intellectual property, only to see that the licensor has done little to manage or prevent the unauthorized use of the rights by third parties. On the other hand, licensees who are responsible for, but neglect, implementing enforcement initiatives may provide cause to their licensors to terminate their license relationship.

Allowing a few uninvited participants may result in a flooding of the market with rampant and uncontrollable counterfeiting, infringement and piracy. This may further result in the loss of consumer confidence in the product or service embodied by the copyright or trademark. The counterfeiting of products is frequently not a victimless crime. The sale of counterfeits often fund further criminal activity. Moreover, the manufacturing of counterfeited products, such as baby formula, pharmaceuticals or airplane parts, is unregulated and can impose many hazardous and dangerous risks to consumers. An active enforcement program can promote public awareness of intellectual property rights and place lurking potential infringers on notice of the aggressive policing of the intellectual property rights by its licensor. Ultimately, all licensors, licensees, consumers and the marketplace will benefit from a robust enforcement program.

4.5.2 When and Where to Set Up an Enforcement Program

New Rights. When a new license agreement is contemplated, the licensor may wish to require provisions within its agreement that would adequately address the responsibilities of the licensee as to its proper use of the licensed intellectual property rights. These provisions can serve as a roadmap for the licensee in discerning the type of responsibilities that it could face when using its licensed rights. A licensor and licensee should consider questions such as, "can you record a trademark or copyright license in country X?", "is recording the license mandatory or optional?", or "will a licensee have standing to enforce its rights in the country or does it need to come from the licensor?"[52]

It is important for protections within the licensing agreement to guarantee that the licensee will effectively adhere to certain standards of quality control.[53] Quality control ensures that the value of the intellectual property is not negatively impacted. The standard is not necessarily one of degree (high quality vs. low quality), but always one of consistency. Take for example, a licensee that has been granted a license in Brazil to sell t-shirts displaying the children's cartoon character, MINNIE MOUSE. However, after a period of time, the licensee decides that the shirts will be more profitable if the character was altered to engage in activities such as smoking a cigarette and wielding a gun. However, this would tarnish the wholesome image of MINNIE MOUSE which is mainly targets at a younger audience. While a provision in the license agreement may prohibit this and similar types of misuse, the licensor who is based in another country may not be aware of the activity for an extended amount of time and therefore unable to act quickly. Instead, a licensor may wish to include within the agreement and as part of its enforcement program a provision to allow a representative of the licensor to conduct quality checks of licensee's factories. Or, perhaps a local representative would evaluate the licensee's retail locations to ensure that the use of the copyrighted work is considered proper under the licensor's standards. The quality of one product can have a ripple effect upon other licensees and their goods. By maintaining consistent quality, the consumer will readily trust the trademark or copyrighted work.

---

[52] See http://www.sabaip.com/NewsArtDetails.aspx?ID=372 which provides license recordal information for a few Middle East jurisdictions.
[53] See generally 3 J.Thomas McCarthy, McCarthy on Trademarks and Unfair Competition §18 (4th ed. 2010).

A license agreement should also contemplate a provision that authorizes termination of the license agreement if the licensee were to use the trademark or copyright in an inappropriate or disparaging manner that would tarnish the brand. The termination provision should also address the return of remaining materials or supply to goods in order to prevent the products from being released into the counterfeit or secondary market.

There are a number of provisions that a licensor and licensee can incorporate into their agreement in order to help identity the rights and responsibilities regarding protection and enforcement. Additional clauses to consider in a license agreement are the following:

- *Discretion on prosecution and enforcement* – A clause that specifies whether a licensor or licensee has particular jurisdiction over prosecution and enforcement of specific matters can help alleviate confusion later.
- *Duty to inform of infringement* – A licensor may wish to rely on the licensee to raise a red flag when there is notice of infringement. A licensee may become aware of unauthorized activities that may impair its own right to use the trademark or copyrighted material.
- *Standing to bring a legal claim* – A licensor may prefer that its licensee control its own localized enforcement program and authorize the licensee to file lawsuits where necessary.
- *Costs/awards* – In order to avoid future disputes between licensor and licensee over the costs associated with enforcement and the benefit of monetary awards from settlements or lawsuits, a provision addressing both is encouraged.

Existing Rights. If license agreements are already in place, the preliminary step to establishing an enforcement program is for the licensor or licensee to undergo an assessment of its IP portfolio in order to determine within which countries it should or must proceed to enforce its IP rights. Given that trademark rights are territorial, it would be in the

Protecting Trademarks and Copyrights Internationally

licensor's best interest to consult with its in-house counsel or an intellectual property law firm to consider the laws of each respective territory where rights may exist. Licensors and licensees may also wish to receive comments from its marketing or loss prevention teams in order to have a broader understanding of where vulnerability to its intellectual property may exist. For example, a member from the marketing team may be aware of the launch of new advertisement campaigns for an existing product which will certainly bolster demand, and likely peak interest in potential infringers.

In addition to considering the provisions of the license agreement, a few key questions that a licensor may wish to consider are the following:

- What efforts are in place to regulate quality control?
- Is there a licensee representative who is or can be called upon to handle localized infringement issues?
- In what countries are there licensees? Are there certain countries that the business is considering entering into?
- Which international markets pose the most risk of loss?
- What products are entering the market or already on the market? How are they valued?
- Are there adequate resources and an appropriate budget available?
- Is there a designated brand protection manager, administrator or counsel for the licensor that will manage the enforcement program?

If the agreement does not have the provisions as discussed further above, an enforcement program can serve as a way to safeguard the intellectual property of the licensor and licensee. The licensor and licensee will risk losing great value if its intellectual property rights that are not properly enforced.

4.5.3   Resources for an Enforcement Program

A global company will require a global enforcement program. The most effective type of enforcement program for a particular licensor may depend on the nature of its relationship with its licensees. For example, a licensor may wish to ask its international licensees to engage with their local counsel to help format a localized program that would take into consideration national trademark law and practices. Or, a licensor may wish to coordinate with an intellectual property firm that has experience with enforcing rights in multiple jurisdictions and thus maintain more control over the centralized program. Another way that a licensor may wish to tailor its program is by prioritizing the goods or services or copyrighted works that it wishes to protect. A licensor may find that its copyrighted work that is about to fall into the public domain will not be worth investing in or protecting. Alternatively, a licensor may determine that its newly acquired trademark is vulnerable to cancellation in multiple jurisdictions that have use requirements and thus may wish to tailor its enforcement program to aggressively enforce those rights.

This section will discuss the different stakeholders that an enforcement program should consider involving in the process. The degree of involvement of each will depend on the considerations from Section 4.2.

In-House Counsel/Outside IP Firms. A licensor or licensee may wish to have its in-house counsel spearhead the brand protection efforts so as to timely implement the program in order to coincide when those intellectual property rights are obtained or transferred. If no steps are taken, a licensor's rights may become vulnerable or forfeited. In-house counsel or their outside law firms are often the people that intimately understand the rights of its licensor and licensee and can practically advise when rights are being infringed.

Enforcement should take the form of administrative practices and designed procedures with respect to accountability and quality control. When those safeguards have failed and infringement has been identified, the licensor may wish to pursue civil action or criminal action (where permitted) against the infringer. By having a point person such as in-house counsel, various key stakeholders will know who to turn to when its intellectual property is threatened. For example, a customer service representative for a licensor may receive a phone call from a customer indicating that a flea market is overrun with the licensor's counterfeit sneakers or pirated DVDs. The licensor will want to ensure that little time is wasted for action to be taken.

Licensees. Licensors should disseminate information about any new ventures including mergers or acquisitions to their licensees. Having a licensor and licensee regularly engage in dialogue regarding the licensed IP rights helps build a cohesive understanding of the importance of brand integrity and ensure proper use and markings on goods and services. Moreover, it allows multiple licensees to establish the same understanding of or commitment to the intellectual property and therefore create uniformity across the brand empire. Licensees are an asset to an enforcement program because they are able to witness the frequency and depth of infringement in their respective jurisdiction as well as possibly knowing the most effective methods of combating the illegal activity. Requiring licensees to spearhead an enforcement program in its own country can help the licensor conserve time and money as long as a licensor does not totally abdicate discretion and control as the brand owner.

Investigators/Law Enforcement/Customs. Sometimes civil action brought on by the licensor or licensee will not deter recidivist activity from infringers. Law enforcement can be an asset in providing a stronger message to infringers or potential infringers that the licensor and licensee have a vested interest in maintaining its rights. Coordinating with law enforcement to raid a location identified to house counterfeit product can result in effectively seizing the products and preserving the evidence for a possible criminal action.[54] It is also helpful to provide training to law enforcement officials so that they can be educated in identifying infringing or coun-

---

[54] Lewin, Harley I. "One Perspective On Anti-Counterfeiting: From T-shirts in the Basement to Global Trade" The Trademark Reporter, 100th Anniversary Edition, January-February 2011, Vol. 101, No. 1.

Basics of Licensing: International Edition

terfeit goods over authentic products. The more stakeholders that are on the lookout for unauthorized goods, the more successful the enforcement program can be.

In many countries, counterfeits and infringing goods will have to enter or exit local borders. A licensor and its licensees should consider recording its trademarks and copyrights with local customs offices as an additional protective measure. Some jurisdictions, such as the U.S.[55] and China[56], will allow for customs recordal of a rights-holder's trademark or copyright registrations. In doing so, customs may be authorized to seize infringing or counterfeit goods. Otherwise, without recordal, customs may be authorized to release the goods to their final destination.[57]

The Internet. The Internet is a hotbed for infringing copyright and trademark material. Licensors and licensees should consider reviewing country specific laws that addresses notice and takedown of copyrighted works.[58] A licensor may wish to include adequate provisions in its agreement with its licensee regarding use of its intellectual property on the Internet. For example, a copyright holder may license the performance rights to a copyrighted work without any mention of broadcasting rights. When the performance of the copyright work appears on the Internet, it will be more costly and time consuming to try and remove the infringing broadcast than if the limitations were negotiated upfront. At that point, the licensor may wish to have the licensee incur the costs of policing the infringing use of the copyrighted work.

When determining enforcement efforts on the Internet, the question of establishing proper jurisdiction often arises. Licensors may wish to have its licensees address infringers on

---

[55] See U.S. Customs and Border Protection website accessible at: https://apps.cbp.gov/e-recordations

[56] See http://www.chinaipr.gov.cn/direrdcusarticle/directions/rdcustoms/rdcpdirections/200612/238960_1.html

[57] See: http://www.cbp.gov/linkhandler/cgov/trade/legal/informed_compliance_pubs/enforce_ipr.ctt/enforce_ipr.pdf and
http://www.chinalawblog.com/2012/05/using-customs-to-protect-your-brand-from-china-counterfeits.html

[58] See http://theipexporter.com/2013/03/25/enforcing-online-copyright-protections-abroad-understanding-foreign-takedown-notice-requirements/

Protecting Trademarks and Copyrights Internationally

the Internet that trace back to the licensee's territory. This is especially helpful in addressing websites that may not be in the licensor's native language. However, oftentimes it can be difficult to discern where an anonymous infringer present on the Internet actually resides. Licensors and licensees may wish to consider tools available from service providers in order to address infringement on the Internet. For example, eBay.com implemented the Verified Rights Owner (VeRO) Program which allows rights holders to report infringement and eventually suspend repeat infringers on its website.[59] While infringement on the Internet can pose difficulties to enforcement, it cannot be avoided.[60]

Trademark and Domain Name Watch Services. A licensor may find that neither it nor its licensees have the in-house resources or knowledge to police the marketplace for potential infringement of its marks and copyrights. It is important to assess your resources and where you may wish to engage in outside vendor services to help supplement the company's program. Some companies may find that they do not have enough resources to commit to an in-house program. Subscribing to a trademark watch service can provide timely information customized to your company's particular needs.[61] With trademarks, timing can be everything. If your company waits too long to take action, you may have missed your opportunity to effectively act.

Through watch services, trademark owners can be alerted to potentially conflicting trademark applications and

---

[59] See http://pages.ebay.com/help/tp/vero-rights-owner.html
[60] For further discussion of effect policing on the Internet consider the following resources:
http://www.inta.org/Advocacy/Documents/INTA%20Best%20Practices%20for%20Addressing%20the%20Sale%20of%20Counterfeits%20on%20the%20Internet.pdf;
http://cyber.law.harvard.edu/property99/domain/Betsy.html;
http://www.fas.org/sgp/crs/misc/R41927.pdf;
http://www.kaspersky.com/images/conflict_of_laws_in_cyberspace_a_need_to_overhaul_legal_regime.pdf
[61] There are many vendors that provide trademark watch services covering a wide range of jurisdictions, including Corsearch, Thomson CompuMark, TMDS, CSC and Ladas and Parry LLP.

registrations. Companies may also wish to monitor their competitors or third parties to ensure that they are not using confusingly similar trademarks that can affect the licensor or licensee's trademark rights.

Joint Efforts. In order to conserve financial and manpower resources, a licensor or licensee may also consider engaging in enforcement efforts with other companies that are encountering counterfeit or infringement by third parties in mutually problematic countries. For example, a group of technology companies that have copyrighted software may be finding that a particular warehouse in Hong Kong is mass producing pirated versions of the software. It may be practical for the companies to coordinate with local police to shut down the warehouse rather than rely only on sending in law enforcement or investigators to address its own software.

Organizations. There are many international organizations or databases that provide forums, conferences and access to resources and best practices for enforcement programs. A few examples include the following:

- International Trademark Association (INTA)[62]
- International Anti-Counterfeiting Coalition (IACC)[63]
- International Quality & Productivity Center (IQPC)[64]
- The Chilling Effects Clearinghouse[65]

4.6 Conclusion

Ideally, both licensor and licensee should engage in efforts to establish intellectual property rights and maintain those rights through effective enforcement. Without due consideration for such efforts, a company's brand can be negatively impacted leaving both licensor and licensee with little or diminished value. As discussed herein there can be many

---

[62] More information is accessible at: http://www.inta.org
[63] http://www.iacc.org
[64] http://www.iqpc.com
[65] http://chillingeffects.org

Protecting Trademarks and Copyrights Internationally

challenges when dealing with complex licensing matters. Accordingly, it is important to engage in a discussion with your licensing agent or in-house counsel to determine the necessary efforts that best fit the needs of your business or licensing venture and the subject intellectual property rights being used or licensed.

International Licensing Markets

Chapter 5

Greater Europe

5.1 Introduction to Greater Europe

by Francesca Ash

With over 40 different countries of varying sizes and a population now in the region of 740 million, Europe is probably one of the most complicated and diverse regions of the world. The European Union, with 28 country members plus the additional four of the European Free Trade Association, may be classified as a single body but, in reality, the cultural and economic differences between the member states are significant.

Europe has suffered, of course, over recent years, from a significant economic downturn which has impacted on the licensing industry as retail undergoes major changes. Countries such as Spain, Italy, Portugal and Ireland, all of whom are tied to the troubled Euro currency, have had particular problems. Retail sales in Italy last year suffered their worst ever drop, and while there have been some signs of recovery in Spain, consumer spending is still weak.

E-Commerce is the fastest growing retail market in Europe with sales in the UK, Germany, France, Sweden, The Netherlands, Italy, Poland and Spain in particular showing significant growth. In 2013, whilst traditional retail continued to suffer, online retail in Europe grew by around 21%, dominated by the UK, Germany and France who together are responsible for more than 80% of European online sales.

Quite apart from the economic situation, which has to a greater or lesser extent impacted all European countries, and which, in countries such as Germany, the UK and, to some extent France is showing shoots of recovery, the main point of difference in Europe is that while the territory is classified as one, in terms of consumer preferences and, consequently licensing activity, European countries are very much individual territories with individual tastes.

At this point, it is worth looking at some of the key drivers in the leading European markets.

Germany, of course, is the European powerhouse. From a licensing perspective the children's market is more driven by educational values than most other countries, and parents are less inclined to support some of the action properties that do so well in other European countries. As a result, the German market has some homegrown properties that are hugely successful at home but have yet to travel beyond German borders. Retail, too, in Germany is very different from other countries being decentralized and, in many ways, fragmented. In addition, the market moves slowly and it takes longer than most countries for a property to finally work.

France is more open to new licenses but this market can be difficult, particularly in terms of licensed apparel which, although a key product sector in most countries, is very much less so in France. Homegrown properties continue to be popular, such as Babar or Asterix, with properties from neighboring Belgium, such as Tintin and The Smurfs, continuing to occupy a strong position. However, France also has the global brands and properties that are present in so many territories with US-originated properties leading the way together with a number of Japanese brands. In terms of retail, France is home to some of the world's largest chains — Carrefour and Auchan — and these continue to be very important in terms of the retailing of licensed products.

Moving further north, the Nordic region (Sweden, Denmark, Finland, Sweden and Iceland) has traditionally favored non-violent properties which has, over the years, meant a number of brands that have been popular around the world have failed to have any traction in this region. However, this region has carved its own niche in terms of internet and app-based brands. Angry Birds from Rovio in Finland has been immensely popular around the world, and following this success, other Nordic tech companies are now entering the market.

Chapter 5: Greater Europe

And so onto the UK which, following a period of recession is now finally showing growth. Licensors, licensees and retailers are showing greater confidence in the market. However, the UK in terms of licensing is a mature market, and the number of properties, particularly in the preschool sector, outweighs demand. With regard to preferences, the UK still very much follows the lead of the US, probably more than mainland Europe, although the country has a long and proud history of producing properties that subsequently become popular around the world. It is worth remembering that the first true licensed product — the Peter Rabbit doll in 1904 came from the UK, and Winnie the Pooh was originally created by a AA Milne, a British author. More recently, the country has given the world The Teletubbies and Peppa Pig, both of which have enjoyed tremendous success on a global basis, as have personalities such as David Beckham and sports clubs such as Manchester United.

The retail situation in the UK is one of mixed messages. The key supermarket groups such as Tesco, Sainsburys, Morrisons and Asda (Walmart) are increasingly discounting and slugging it out for market share, a battle that has taken on new significance since deep German discounters Aldi and Lidl have recently become major players, whilst smaller chains are finding it increasingly difficult to compete, particularly when you add the explosive growth of online retailing into the mix. While consumers demand quality, they also demand low prices and while this benefits the end user, it also means the demise of retail stores and chains that have been part of the UK landscape for many years.

In summary, whilst Europe is often lumped together as one large trading bloc, doing business in the region successfully really does require an appreciation and understanding that each and every country within Europe operates very differently and has unique cultural, historic and other factors that make it unique.

5.2 Benelux

by Cyril Speijer

5.2.1 Introduction

Benelux is an economic union in Europe comprising the three neighboring countries of Belgium, the Netherlands and Luxembourg. These countries are located in northwestern Europe between France and Germany. Nowadays, it is mostly used in a generic way to refer to the cultural, economic, and geographic grouping. Even though Benelux covers three separate countries, the size and population of the region is rather small. Benelux is 1/7th the size of France. Benelux has one-third as many citizens as Germany. Nevertheless, Benelux is an important group of countries in Europe. With a very attractive financial climate in the Netherlands, many key market companies locate themselves in Holland.

5.2.2 Demographics and Geography

Entity	Capital	Population	Area	Population Density
Netherlands	Amsterdam	16.847.007	41.543 km²	403.7/km²
Belgium	Brussels	11.007.020	30.528 km²	354.7/km²
Luxembourg	Luxembourg	511.840	2.586 km²	194.1/km²
Benelux		28.365.937	74.640 km²	380/km²

5.2.3 Languages

In these three countries, four official languages are spoken; Dutch, French, German and Luxembourgian.

Chapter 5: Greater Europe

- 82% of the population lives in an area in which Dutch is the official language. In total, there are approximately 23 million people: 16.8 million Dutch citizens and 6.3 million Flemish Belgian citizens.
- 14% of the population lives in an area in which French is the official language. In total, there are approximately 4 million people: 3.5 million Walloon Belgians and 0.5 million Luxembourg citizens.
- 4% of the population lives in a bilingual area (Dutch, French), a total of approximately 1.1 million citizens.

Netherlands. Dutch is the official and foremost language of the Kingdom of The Netherlands. The nation consists out of 16.8 million inhabitants, of which 96 percent speak Dutch as their mother tongue. Within the Netherlands, there are many different dialects; however, these are often overruled by "Standard Dutch".

Belgium. Belgium, the neighboring nation of the Dutch, has a population of 11 million. Belgium has three official languages: Dutch (sometimes referred to as Flemish), French and German. Approximately 59% of all Belgians speak Dutch as their first language, although French is the mother tongue for over 40%. Dutch is the official language of the Flemish region (northern Belgium). In this region, Dutch is the mother tongue for 97% of the population. Belgian Dutch (Flemish), is the national variety of the Dutch language as spoken in Belgium (with dialect). It is used by default within schools, by the government, by the media and during informal occasions. Nevertheless, the use of the word "Flemish", as to refer to the official language in Flanders, is misleading. The only official language in Flanders is Dutch. In the region of Wallonia (South Belgium), French is considered the mother tongue and finally in a small part of Belgium, German is the official language.

Luxembourg. Three languages are officially recognized in Luxembourg: French, German and Luxembourgian. Each of these three languages is used as the primary language on certain occasions. Luxembourgian is the language that Luxembourgers generally use to speak amongst each other; however, it is not often used in writing. Most official (written) business communication is carried out in French. Usually German is the first language taught in school and is the most used language by the media and by the church. In addition to the three official languages, English is taught in compulsory school and most people in Luxembourg master English as a language, at least in Luxembourg City.

5.2.4 Licensing in Benelux

Until the formation of the European Economic Community (EEC) in 1958, product sales to consumers were easy to check and to monitor. This changed when new international players entered the market. In the field of apparel a couple of examples of those players are Zara, H&M, among others. In the field of supermarkets Carrefour and Lidl left their origination country. On the other hand, retailers such as Blokker, Zeeman and supermarkets like Albert Heijn and Makro relocated to foreign countries.

The Netherlands has its origins in export. In the 17th century it all started with the VOC, discovering other trade areas, and possible countries for production. With Rotterdam still being one of the world largest ports, the export position remains strong to this day. On the other hand, we did lose the status of being a country for production. Companies such as Philips, C&A, and many others mainly from the apparel industry, had to move their production towards low-wage countries, primarily to stay ahead of the competition price-wise.

In 1948, Benelux (Belgium, the Netherlands, Luxembourg) was formed, 9 years before the EEC was formed. The main goal for its formation was creating an open market between the three countries, and stimulating each other's import and export. From then on, licensing contracts were always concluded for the entire Benelux area. Belgium was a sole exception, since this area is divided in two parts, 50% is

Chapter 5: Greater Europe

French-speaking (Wallonia), and 50% is Dutch-speaking (the Flanders area). For publishing, the French rights are usually granted to French-speaking publishers. Almost all producers have representation in the whole Benelux area. Luxembourg produces few in the country, but still is included in the contract because it is part of Benelux.

The formation of the EEC changed many aspects of the licensing industry. The open market is now valid for the entire area, meaning each product now has free access across the EEC. The product is only legal, though, when it is officially entered into the EEC, or is produced in one of the EEC countries. Fortunately, there are EEC rules that apply for protecting licensing contracts per area. Non-exclusive contracts can only be concluded for one or more parts of the EEC. When concluding a licensing contract for the entire EEC, we talk about an exclusive contract. Adding a restriction in every contract by specifying the language of the licensing area helps to protect against exporting the product into other areas. But that requires that the parties define in the licensing contract that the product cannot be adjusted or changed after approval.

A grey area remains the issue of actively offering products to areas other than the specified area. This is a difficult case, because it is hard to determine whether the sale has taken place outside of the contractual area because of the open market.

5.2.5 History

Licensing in Benelux really began in the 1960s. In those days it was all about syndication. Benelux publishers were the first to license. In Belgium, examples of such publishers included Lombard and Dupuis, and in the Netherlands, Oberon and Strengholt were key players. The reason they started using licenses was to syndicate their comics into other publications. Opera Mundi, located in Brussels, at that time represented King Features among others, who was the only one who offered material of third parties.

Disney was the first American organization and was represented by an agent, André Vanneste. The first Dutchman working with rights was Mark Spits. Having worked in advertising, he observed licensing practices in the US, and brought them to the Netherlands. His first rights were Calimero and Little Bear Colico. A few years later, he ceased licensing activities, because business wasn't as expected. Besides the use for syndication, licensing rights were being used for promotional campaigns. In 1967, Cyril Speijer founded Wavery Productions B.V., the first company completely focused on licensing in Europe. As was the case with most licensing agents, Cyril started working on promotional campaigns, and as a result came into contact with licensors.

At that time television was still in its infancy. In the Netherlands, NPS had only one channel broadcasting between 8 PM and 10 PM, and on Saturday children's programs aired between 5 PM and 5.30 PM. In the Flemish area of Belgium, VRT was active and in Wallonia, the BRTF aired programming, but both had little broadcasting time. The climate began to change when airtime grew on a couple of channels. The biggest transformation came in 1989 when commercial channels came into being. More broadcasting time was offered, and the merchandising boom started.

5.2.6 Licensing Today

In some instances Belgium and the Netherlands are very similar markets, while in others the two are very different, which is quite interesting considering they share a language and almost seem to have no borders between them. Even so, very distinct differences do exist. When looking at the major properties within Benelux, we can determine that Disney, Sanrio's Hello Kitty and Studio 100 are top of mind at retailers, followed by Nickelodeon's Dora the Explorer, which unlike the others, can be found in virtually every store.

Unique properties from Benelux include those produced by Studio 100 and originating in Belgium, including properties such as: a.o., Bumba, K3, House of Anubis, Maya the Bee, Wickie the Viking as well as other properties and series focused on kids' entertainment from infant to preschool and all the way up to teens. In only a few years, Studio 100 produced over 10 properties within Benelux and has experienced

Chapter 5: Greater Europe

great local success with properties such as K3, Bumba, House of Anubis and more recently with Hotel 13, which is a co-production. While Studio 100 used to reign mainly within the Benelux and German borders, they have begun to co-produce some series with companies such as the BBC on an international level. Currently, they are expanding their territories due to the Maya the Bee brand. Studio 100 will be rolling out an extensive licensing program to support this children's property, which is centered around a show based on the popular '70s character. Studio 100 has already sold the Maya the Bee series in over 130 countries.

From the Netherlands, Mercis is the strongest and most well-known property, and Nijntje Pluis (Miffy) is a very successful international licensor these days, bringing Miffy to multiple territories and working with international partners such as KLM. The simplicity of Nijntje and the series of books has ruled Dutch bookstores for years. Originally a book character drawn by Dick Bruna, Miffy has grown into a worldwide children's property. Miffy is a familiar face at Licensing shows over the past few years, and is expected to keep growing and expanding in multiple territories.

Also from the Netherlands is Dromenjager and their property Woezel & Pip, two little dogs that go out on daily adventures. This property was reated by Guusje Nederhorst, a young Dutch woman who sadly past away, but whose legacy to her children was carried on by her husband and shared with children all over Benelux. The property has taken Benelux by storm in only a few years' time and created a broad and steady licensing program, which counts as its partners the most prominent infant and preschool brands and the largest Infant food company, Nutricia. Dromenjager conducts most business within Benelux, but are expanding steadily into other territories. Products can be found in almost every store, from pacifiers to complete bedrooms, publishing (where the property originated from) and toys, with most categories covered on a national level, making them one of the big favorites, next to Miffy.

Finally from the Netherlands is Lief! Lifestyle, a Dutch lifestyle brand that has grown internationally. With Benelux and Europe as their base markets, they are now expanding

Basics of Licensing: International Edition

into the Far East and even into the US. Lief! Lifestyle originally started out with a children's collection in apparel and accessories and now has numerous licensees in many other categories, such as stationery, health and beauty, and home decoration, The brand has even teamed up with a bike company, creating a special edition Lief! Lifestyle typical Dutch bike. The simplicity and brightness of the brand have a great appeal, together with their chosen ambassadors who are Dutch TV personalities and their kids. Lief! Lifestyle is known in almost any household within the Netherlands and is rapidly spreading throughout the rest of the world. Within the Netherlands they partner with mainly high end and some mid segment licensees to produce products for the home with bright colors and innovative design. Other very successful lifestyle brands are Blond Amsterdam & Studio Pip, which are also rapidly increasing licenses on an international level.

Although being a relatively small market, Benelux also proudly possesses some major licensees. For example, Bioworld, which has a prominent position within the top 20 licensees worldwide according to a License Global article published in May 2013. Bioworld has a strong apparel partner to focus on fashion and accessories, and has worldwide distribution carrying a variety of licenses.

Companies such as Leomil (apparel and footwear), BIP (candy), Cartamundi (card games), Sanoma (publishing) and several others are also located within Benelux and do very well in the international arena. It is interesting to see that, even though the apparel industry is suffering within the region, some of these players are still part of the international market and growing. On top of that, another interesting development is that some smaller companies are managing, in these harder times, to build out their companies by creating smart business strategies with regard to retail, but also by producing/ inventing very innovative new products (app-related, etc).

Retailers are struggling in this region, as in others, creating some obvious changes with respect to the shopping patterns of the consumer. A shift of ranks has taken place, where companies that used to be considered hard discount, no longer have that image, but are slowly growing into mid- (mass)

Chapter 5: Greater Europe

segment retailers, such as A.S. Watson's Kruidvat in the Netherlands and Belgium. Kruidvat is one of the largest retailers in Benelux with 19 formulas under their flag such as Kruidvat, Trekpleister, Ice Paris and Savers. Kruidvat welcomes over 3 million visitors in store and receives over 650,000 unique hits to their website on a weekly basis. When looking at the total population of the Netherlands, that is a massive amount of consumers. Employing over 12,000 people throughout the Netherlands and Belgium, Kruidvat has clearly taken over a larger part of business within this region. Being a drugstore by origin, they now carry all kinds of products in beauty and health, apparel, candy, and home decoration, while also becoming the number three player in toys. Kruidvat is still known for its bargains, but is no longer seen as a hard discounter and therefore a fully recognized player within Benelux when it comes to licenses.

In the Netherlands Kruidvat is joined by other major retailers such as the Blokker Group (Bart Smit, Blokker, Marskramer etc.), which are all household and toy-related retailers. In addition, there are supermarket chains such as Albert Heijn, C1000 and the Emte group (Jumbo & Sligro). In Belgium, retail channels differ quite a bit; within this region it is the larger supermarket chains that attract most consumers. Chains such as Colruyt, Carrefour and Delhaize offer complete ranges to meet the consumers' needs. Together they are account for 70% of the Belgian market when it comes to food, but being total suppliers they all offer a broad range of products reaching far beyond food. Colruyt, also containing Spar & Alvo stores, is the largest of the three, with around 600 stores; with 225 Colruyt-stores, 80 OKay-stores, 7 Bio-Planets, and 46 stores in the nonfood stores of DreamLand and DreamBaby. They also have several wholsesale outlets and various smaller outlets, making Colruyt good for a share of 27.7% (2012) of the Belgian market. Carrefour does have more outlets; 700 Carrefour-stores; 45 Carrefour planet stores and Carrefour-hypermarkets, 438 Carrefour market/GB-supermarkets and 222 Carrefour express neighborhood stores. They make up a smaller part of the total market in shares, at 22.6% (2012).Carrefour is followed very closely by Delhaize, who makes up a share of 22.5% (2012) within the Belgian market.

5.2.7 Consumer Behavior

Dutch people visit supermarkets, mainly for daily needs such as food, beauty and health and some dry goods. Next to that, daily shopping also takes place in drugstore chains, smaller privately owned and/ or specialized stores, toy chains, and smaller privately owned toy stores. Consumers shop in various outlets. Business consumers use wholesale outlets more frequently in comparison to the individual consumer. Whereas Belgians do often visit the larger supermarket chains for most of their needs (one stop), the wholesale business in Belgium is larger in comparison to the Dutch market for individual consumers as well. This also goes for the toy store chains (Dreamland & Fun BE), which are often situated next to these supermarkets and rule over smaller stores.

5.2.8 Other Differences between the Dutch and Belgian Markets

In the Netherlands, lifestyle brands are increasing their share within the licensing business and are rapidly expanding current programs in various categories. Mostly used in higher segments of retail or as special editions, companies such as The Royal Dutch Airline KLM, and brands such as Blond Amsterdam, Studio Pip and Lief! Lifestyle are very popular and can be found in many households. The Dutch designers and the fresh and bright patterns seem to appeal to the consumer. These brands distinguish themselves from the worldwide properties by blending into households in a more subtle way. Although Belgium has an eye and sense for haute cuisine, style and design, brands such as these are not yet catching on with regard to licensed products, or at least not on a big scale.

In Belgium, there is still a very strong market for superheroes like Spiderman, Batman and the Power Rangers, properties which are a very hard sell elsewhere within the Netherlands.

Chapter 5: Greater Europe

A similarity between the two main territories that seems to be a current trend in all of the Benelux's countries is educational collectivity programs. Both Belgium and the Netherlands have been very successful in this area. Driven by several supermarket chains, both territories had similar promotions where for 10 or 15 euros, the customer receives a collection of Animal Kingdom cards to collect and, in the Netherlands, archive in a custom-made collection album, containing information and background on these animals in small pockets the card is placed. In Belgium, they gave away a collection of cards with every 10 or 15 euros spent and for a small cost the consumer could buy a small device that would play the actual sound of the animal in question, by swiping it through the device. Both of these promotions were hugely successful, one of the major reasons being that these were not only accepted on the school playground, but they were used to in classrooms. Special trading events were even created around these collections. Following this success, several similar programs have been initiated, seemingly to prove that if the collectivity program is educationally accepted, you have a hit, as schools embrace them and word spreads like never before.

5.2.9 Challenges

The overall licensing business within Benelux appears to be decreasing at the present time. Many licensees struggle to keep their head above water and are taking fewer risks. The apparel business especially is suffering with many companies forced to close shop. Buyers are on a very tight budget in every category, due to the hard times, and simply go for the lowest prices and best deals. They expect much more form their suppliers, which in turn makes the suppliers' job more expensive.

Unfortunately many (potential) licensees are first cutting out the license expenses, which does not necessarily fix their problems. Without a license, it will cost a few cents less on the dollar per product to produce, but leaves the manufacturer with a little less volume in return. Selling into retail and keeping prices low are a challenge for (potential) licensees, with materials and fabrics getting more expensive and margins rapidly decreasing every day. Therefore, it has become the licensing agent's responsibility to be more of an advisor in the licensing process. A licensing agent must provide advice on properties, design and even the approach at retail, in order to make the difference and prove, in the longer run, that adding a property still is very valuable to sales of products.

People recognize characters, designs, sport brands and/or celebrities and relate to them. When the design is appealing and conforms to contemporary trends, the additional appeal of this property will make a difference. So, it most definitely has gotten tougher to sell licenses, but it is a challenge that can be overcome. On the other hand, in some cases, producers do turn to licenses, and are looking for something new, something fresh, something appealing. In some categories there is a slight increase in licensing, like newly-invented products like apps and game-related categories. High-end products that would like to distinguish themselves have also seen a slight increase. It seems there is a shift, and everybody is looking for that new way of earning money. If agents and (potential) licensees put their heads together, many more happy years of licensing will be created. However, creativity and teamwork are essential ingredients to make that work. Within Benelux we see this already, licensees and agents working together. We are also seeing more innovative designs, which are created by studios both for concept as well as presentations.

I would conclude with one last challenge to present-day licensing in Benelux. Due to EU regulations the borders have faded away, causing confusion and creating, so called, easy cuts to extra income. Discussions on this and keeping the markets clean is becoming harder and harder especially for the smaller companies, who have come to work under great restraints. It is an ongoing issue, which all agents are trying to minimize for the sake of their licensees. This is a very contemporary issue, costing a lot of time, efforts and business.

5.3 Germany

by Michael A. Lou

5.3.1 Introduction to "GAS"

The "German speaking markets" are often referred to as "GAS" for Germany, Austria and Switzerland, because in earlier times owners of intellectual property rights (IPR's) usually granted licenses by language areas. As a result, they included the two significantly smaller countries of Austria and the German-speaking part of Switzerland (at that time about 2 million Swiss citizens) within licenses granted for Germany.

At one time, almost all packaging, instruction booklets and care labels in these markets were in German only, so the 1957 Treaty of Rome, which facilitated the "free flow of goods within the European Union," had almost no impact. The purpose of the treaty was that once you licensed a company in/for one EU-member country, it can freely sell to buyers from other EU countries, provided they do no "active soliciting", e.g. do not display/market the products outside the licensed territory). Nowadays, almost all packaging and instructions for products in Europe (or at least the 28 member countries of the EU) are in at least the ten most common EU-languages, because most of them aim for an EU-wide distribution.

5.3.2 Background

Since its re-unification with the German Democratic Republic ("East Germany"), Germany has some 81.8 million people in about 24 million households (of which about 40% are single households). Austria has roughly 8.5 million citizen in 3.65 million households and Switzerland counts for almost another 9 million of which some 5.67 million have German as their native tongue (though many more speak German in this tri-lingual country).

GAS is not only the largest single language market in the 503 million people European Union (EU) but also houses the most wealthy citizens. Germany has a GNP of US $44.260,

Basics of Licensing: International Edition

Austria is $47.660 and "banking"-Switzerland is $89.970 (on Purchase Power Parity basis), according to the World Bank. (USA: $51.749). However, the other key markets in the EU are not far behind. In all 28 member countries of the EU, the average GNP per person is still US $30.494. The average wealth of Germans totals to about 195.200 Euros (France 229.300; Spain 285.300, despite the crises you can read about at this time).

This demonstrates the great potential the EU markets have and Germany and Austria in particular, having traditionally acted as the gateways for business with Eastern Europe. Many companies already have distribution subsidiaries or co-operations in the key markets in Eastern Europe (Poland, Hungary, Russia) which are now upgraded by local production facilities.

While the average income in the ten German states that formed part of "Western Germany" is relatively equally spread, the approximately 12.5 million people living in the six former Eastern German states reach only about 80% of the income of their western neighbours, with wages are still somewhat behind.

In Austria, of course, people in urban areas gain relatively more money than in rural areas, but the living standards and infrastructure allows countrywide distribution at even levels. And in Switzerland, wealth seems to part of the lifestyle.

Of course, there are also bad facts: A UNICEF study released in April 2013 reveals that one in seven German children between 11 and 14 years is "unhappy with his or her situation. And only about 30% of the children who are born today into a certain social group have a chance to change into a higher one compared to 37% of those born in 1950 as reported by the Scientific Centre for Social Research in Berlin.

Despite the EU economic problems that are reported on almost daily, GAS is indeed a stronghold within the European markets. GAS can be a productive market for licensing if licensors use common sense and do not expect that every licensing program that succeeded overseas will automatically also do well (or even better) in GAS. In fact, the opposing situation is also true: a property that was not successful in other countries may have a chance to succeed in the German speaking markets. That is because, according to market research organization Nielsen, 56% of Germans are open to trying new brands, when they asked over than 29,000 internet users.

5.3.3 The History of Licensing in GAS

It is difficult to estimate licensing numbers before World War II, because there was no tracking of significant brand or entertainment licensing activities in the German speaking markets before then. In 1950, right after World War II ended, the German producer of the popular "Hummel" figurines, Franz Goebel, acquired from Walt Disney the rights to produce Mickey Mouse, Bambi and other Disney characters.

Licensing according to today's standards began only with the TV market expanding. Leo Kirch, a young and emerging TV program and film dealer was one of the first people to realize the potential of the ancillary rights. (Berlusconi was not even in the business yet and Murdoch & Co. still thought print products were the media of the future.) Kirch's group initially bought the distribution rights from leading US studios like Warner, Paramount and MGM including the merchandising rights. Later Kirch started to produce its own programming like Pippi Longstocking, Heidi, Bee Maja, etc., that was also suited for licensing.

Guenther Vetter, who was General Manager of Kirch's licensing arm Merchandising Muenchen GmbH from 1972 through 1981, was the a real pioneer of licensing at that time and later said he needed "comprehensive negotiation and convincing skills" to sensitize companies in German-speaking markets for this new business opportunity called merchandising.

Some of these early pioneer licensing properties are still in the market today and are nowadays referred to as "classics." When I started in this business in 1980 (as licensee for the DALLAS TV series) there was almost no one to get expert advice from other than Guenther Vetter and Brigitte Gosda, who marketed at that time MGM, United Artists and Warner Bros. properties before doing most of the business for Sesame Street and later developed the properties of Bibi Blocksberg and Benjamin Bluemchen into the local kids classics they are today.

5.3.4 Beyond Entertainment Licensing

Brand licensing actually started, like in most other places, as brand extension (after the owners of core brands had exploited line extensions). Manufacturers of brand name products tried to extend their product lines away from their core products and, if possible, into other distribution channels. The main reason for extending their products, apart from making money, was to reach the consumer in "competitive-free" environments, i.e., where there was no product of their competitors for the core products. These companies hoped to strengthen their brand awareness, and hence their brand value, by being known to a larger consumer group.

Naturally, some brand companies were not set-up for such "brand extension" and soon consultants (later called licensing agents) appeared that helped the brand companies find the right licensees. Early cases of successful brand licensing strategies were the Olympic Games and the FIFA Soccer Championships (through Adidas subsidiary ISL International Sports Licensing). It is somewhat odd that the professional soccer leagues (Bundesliga), which are now so popular, did not begin to license in GAS until they saw what I was ablt to do with the NFL in the late 1980's, even though

Chapter 5: Greater Europe

American football was not very popular at all in the German speaking markets.

Quite certainly, Kirch´s TV and film licensing developed the entertainment licensing in German markets; Adidas, Puma and fashion brands like BOSS, Jil Sander and Wolfgang Joop, along with some local heroes (like HARIBO) and international corporations from abroad (Playskool was one of the first) developed the brand side of it; and soccer teams (Bayern Muenchen and Co.), FIFA and the Olympic Games were the properties that developed sports licensing.

5.3.5 The TV Market

With respect to television entertainment licensing, one must know that the TV scene in GAS was far behind all other larger European countries. Until 1962 there was only one (!) TV channel ("Deutsches Fernsehen", nationwide and operated by the government). Then a second governmental channel (ZDF Zweites Deutsches Fernsehen) commenced its nationwide broadcasting and each of the 10 Federal States started to launch its own regional channel (that at early times only broadcasted until the evening and was then joined with "Deutsches Fernsehen", today known as "Das Erste"). Consequently, the programming was limited in variety, and the bulk of foreign TV-series, which were better suited for licensing, started only when private TV stations commenced their business in 1984. So television licensing, which historically has generated a vast majority of the licensing business in other markets, started pretty late compared to GAS. I believe that this is why there are many more licensed products in the English, Italian, French or Spanish markets compared to GAS, though GAS represents a very strong licensing market and has probably the best merits with respect to its future development.

5.3.6 Recent Changes in Licensing

In recent years, the channels of distribution of licensed product have undergone significant changes, but so too have the ways licenses are marketed and sold, having refined and captured new ground. With respect to licensing itself, the tar-

Basics of Licensing: International Edition

get groups and/or potential licensees have widened. There are more direct-to-retail licenses being granted, which leaves the retail chains more freedom with respect to sourcing. And cross-licensing with other properties (Star Wars with Lego or and Angry Birds, Hello Kitty and Elvis) has become very popular.

As far as distribution, changes and developments were more significant in the past two decades, but channels continue to grow and diversify. For example, Tilmann Schneider, who in the mid-1980's headed licensing for the private TV-Giant RTL, "discovered" gasoline stations as new POS for his plush replicas of "Kommissar REX," the shepherd detective in a popular TV series, and selling them in greater numbers than the other traditional channels combined. Another example of the expanding distribution channels is the sale of animal health insurance using the licensed image of a popular dog character and distributed through pharmacies/drugstores.

While entertainment and sports licensing were well-established, it was not until the late 80's that brand licensing really became serious business. The German Railway Company used it to support the launch of its new high speed trains (ICE); Unilever, after they bought Fabergé in the US and went back to Europe to start an upscale brand licensing program, to re-launch its mass market body care line Fabergé (Brut de Fabergé); Pepsi Cola to leverage its tiny market share of 8% (vs. Coke with over 50%); followed by numerous fashion brands.

Celebrity licensing was strong in the 80's and 90's with legends like Humphrey Bogart, James Dean, Elvis Presley, Bruce Lee and Marilyn Monroe. Growth in the area continued into the late 90's with contemporary stars like Michael Jackson, Tina Turner, The Beatles, Rolling Stones and others that were popular through their respective music, just like in many other countries.

In the 21st century there were very few property categories introduced apart from charity licensing. The shift went more toward alternative or additional distribution channels and mainly to direct-to-retail licensing (DTR).

Chapter 5: Greater Europe

5.3.7 Licensing Today

Major Properties. Most certainly, among the top five most successful properties licensed for kids in GAS are SpongeBob, Mickey Mouse, Hello Kitty, Star Wars and the German classic Benjamin Bluemchen, a friendly elephant walking on two legs and primarily aimed at pre-schoolers. There has been little change during recent years with respect to the popularity of these properties. Depending on seasonal promotions, a new film release or TV broadcast, Barbie, The Smurfs, Cars and Spiderman are also very popular. A good source for tracking popularity and success of kid properties is www.iconkids.com.

The spectacular, ongoing success of Lego's Star Wars products is significant because it shows that two properties that at first glance do not fit can be a surprising success. The same goes for Elvis and Hello Kitty, which became another surprise hit, even if not the size of Lego. When I was the agent for Lucasfilm back in the 80's I could never have thought of offering Lego a Star Wars license, simply because Lego's bricks where square and old-fashioned, and Luke Skywalker & Co. were the state of the art in youth entertainment. So you see how easily you can be wrong in judging the market potential of your license. Nevertheless, the message left behind this example is: You never have a chance of getting your property noticed if you do not examine EVERY option.

Sports. In sports licensing there is very little apart from soccer. Soccer is the major sport in Western Europe and as such also of the Germans, Austrians and Swiss. Some fans will buy any merchandise featuring the logos of their favorite clubs, and the world's top leagues generate the bulk of the business, in addition to seasonal merchandise from the UEFA European championships or FIFA World Cup. Even though handball and basketball enjoy an increasing fanbase and greater TV coverage, there is hardly any significant licensing for these sports. Other than soccer, Formula 1 car racing has had some success and, quite surprisingly because of its limited media exposure, cycling is popular as well.

Brand. The brand licensing sector is dominated by the fashion licensors. Esprit is one of the main players thanks to its dynamic (and even aggressive) licensing program (that in my opinion tends to over-license the brand), followed by more or less local brands like S.Oliver, Tom Tailor, Bruno Banani, Bugatti, Mephisto (a shoe brand), and Scout (the brand of the leading school bag). Of course, you can also see the international luxury brands on some licensed products, including eyewear, watches and fragrance, most notably. Some "on air" brands are doing well, like the TV show Heidi Klum's Germany's Next Top Model, or DSDS Germany searching for the Super Star. These brands which appeal to the masses are well-equipped for successful licensing programs. On the other hand, there are no guarantees either. Some TV stations acquire licensing rights along with the show but do not really follow-up on it (for instance because they simply have too many of them). A good recent example is the popular show "Dance with the Stars", where the stations (RTL) licensing arm only signed two or three deals over three years. Even cooking shows with famous chefs became a good source for licensing, even in the food business, which seems still underdeveloped in GAS.

An emerging licensing segment is the cause-related licensing for charities like WWF, UNICEF, Greenpeace, Whatever It Takes, Ein Herz fuer Kinder (A Heart for Children) by the Axel Springer publishing company or Deutscher Tierschutzbund (Europe's oldest charity for the protection on animals and nature).

Mobile content licensing is, as everywhere, rather new and works to my knowledge in GAS as in most other key markets as it is still too early to make certain specializations.

Local Heroes. Almost all local properties that command notable sales originate from media exposure, mainly TV. From the same source of the elephant Benjamin Bluemchen comes another local character from Kiddinx GmbH: Bibi Blocksberg, a young witch that has been attracting a young audience for about 20 years now. Then there is "Die Sendung mit der Maus", Germany's answer to Sesame Street; Wendy,

Chapter 5: Greater Europe

a young girl with her horse known from year-long comic books and now from its TV series, and the Sandmaennchen, known by small children for 50 years from its little bed time story on TV. Of course, we also have numerous characters that come and go depending on their TV presence, just like in most other countries, but I cannot see anyone on the horizon with enough potential for a lasting licensing success. There is simply too much competition that looks confusingly similar.

On the brand side, we have the Adidas and PUMA brands as leading licensors, RED BULL and Swarovski from Austria, Bally from Switzerland, HARIBO (known for its fruit gummy bears), Thomas Sabo (a brand that solely emerged from fashion jewellery for young girls) and the various fashion brands mentioned before. A very unique property is the Deutscher Tierschutzbund, an animal charity with 800,000 members. In late 2012, it began to license its logo to endorse meat and poultry from animals that have been brought up in strict conformity with the highest legal standards, so becoming a seal of quality. Now, they are also starting a licensing program for products and services that foster the well being of animals.

5.3.8   Key Players in the Market

GAS is dominated mainly by licensors and agencies located in Germany, which houses four times as many consumers than Austria and Switzerland together. Most of the leading property owners who license their properties use agents, but of course we also have several companies who have their in-house licensing teams like Adidas, PUMA, Red Bull, Swatch, Hugo Boss, to name but a few.

From the international side we also have the Walt Disney Company, now located in Muenich; FremantleMedia in Potsdam (near Berlin); Nickelodeon/Viacom right in Berlin; subsidiarieis of The Licensing Company and CPLG Copyright Promotions Licensing Group, both in Muenich but with headquarters in the U.K.; and Warner Bros. Consumer Products with offices in Hamburg.

Basics of Licensing: International Edition

Today, almost all of the TV stations have created their own licensing arms, including:

- RTL Interactice (www.RTLinteractive.de)
- WDR MediaGroup (www.wdr-mediagroup.com)
- ZDF Enterprises (www.zdf-enterprises.de)
- ProSiebenSat1 Licensing (www.ProSiebenSat1Licensing.com)
- RTL Disney Fernsehen (www.Superrtl.de)
- RTL 2 Fernsehen GmbH (www.rtl2.com)

Among the various independent agencies are Bavaria Sonor, headed by Dr. Rolf Moser (www.bavaria-sonor.de); Euro-Lizenzen headed by Guenter Vetter (www.eurolizenzen.net), Team Licensing, headed by Katharina Dietrich (www.teamlicensing.de) and my own V.I.P. Entertainment & Merchandising AG (www.vip-ag.com). These are probably the most experienced ones, while there are several other agencies that were mostly founded by former employees of the other ones. A good source for information is the local licensing magazine at www.licensing-online.com.

5.3.9 Unique Challenges

Successful licensing in GAS begins with the understanding of what I stressed before: even if a licensing program is successful elsewhere, that does not mean that it can be carried over to the GAS markets in exactly the same way. There are a few cases where this works, mostly thanks to heavy media exposure like TV, but in most cases, products that can be licensed in GAS need to make advertising and promotion adjustments to account for local preferences and trade exposure, which has to meet the individual Point-of-Sale situations. Clearly, the property has to be protected by trademark rights in all relevant classes, and you should have a lawyer on the spot that has ample experience with local copyright and trademark law to defend the rights you want to license.

Chapter 5: Greater Europe

5.3.10 Role of Agents and Consultants

There is always the question of the hen and the egg. Should you first get legal advice on how to best protect your property in GAS to make it fit for licensing or find an agent to evaluate the market potential to see if licensing in GAS could generate more money than needed to cover the legal and administrative expenses? I recommend looking first for the right agent for your property. The biggest agent might not always be the best choice at a given moment and the TV station that airs your programming may have too many other properties to look after and may not give the property the desired attention. Of course, in most cases the TV station will try to insist on getting the licensing rights when buying the airing rights, but you always have to bear in mind the question what property TV station pushes most: Their own shows/properties or yours?

When George Lucas came to me with the Star Wars II property back in 1981, I was still relatively new in the business with a short track record. He asked me how much I would generate for Star Wars and how much of it would I possibly guarantee him in minimum royalties. Luckily, I had done my homework and could present him some evaluation on what I believed we could produce, but we signed no guarantee at all.

All licensors want to have such projections from their potential agents before granting the agency the rights, and all promise not to "bind" the agent to his projections. But if an agent has not lived up to projections, the licensor will remember. And if there is no viable reason as to why the agent could not meet expectations (change of exposure, economic crises, unexpected competition etc.), and this happens two or three times, good licensors will not want that agent to represent their properties. So the most valuable asset an agent has is credibility, in addition to ample market experience, objective judgement and innovative creativity as to the market approach for your property.

5.3.11 Outlook, Projections and Conclusion

Despite the negative news reported over the past year on the economic and financial problems in the EU that have also affected Germany and Austria, these markets are still strong with a positive outlook. But licensing in GAS has also changed dramatically over the past few years. What was formerly the "bread and butter" business in the region (T-shirts, toys, stationery, bags, etc.) does not generate as many sales for many properties. The market has become more fragmented, both on the property side and on the consumer side.

GAS has experienced an oversaturation of TV programming, all trying to make money at licensing; hence each of the properties has a smaller share of the market.

Moreover, the children's market has changed, with kids maturing earlier and attracted to properties aimed at older audiences. This is heavily influenced by the various new social media tools readily available at all age groups. It is not uncommon to see babies in strollers with computer games in front of them while at the same time parents are talking on their cell phones. Another example of licensees trying to catch up with this trend is the new PC game "Lego City Undercover", which shows obvious parallels to the "Grand Theft Auto" game. The near future of licensing in GAS is certainly influenced by Age — the following chart is of interest because it demonstrates to an alarming extent the shift of age group in Germany. Very soon the largest portion of consumers will be over 50 years old.

Chapter 5: Greater Europe

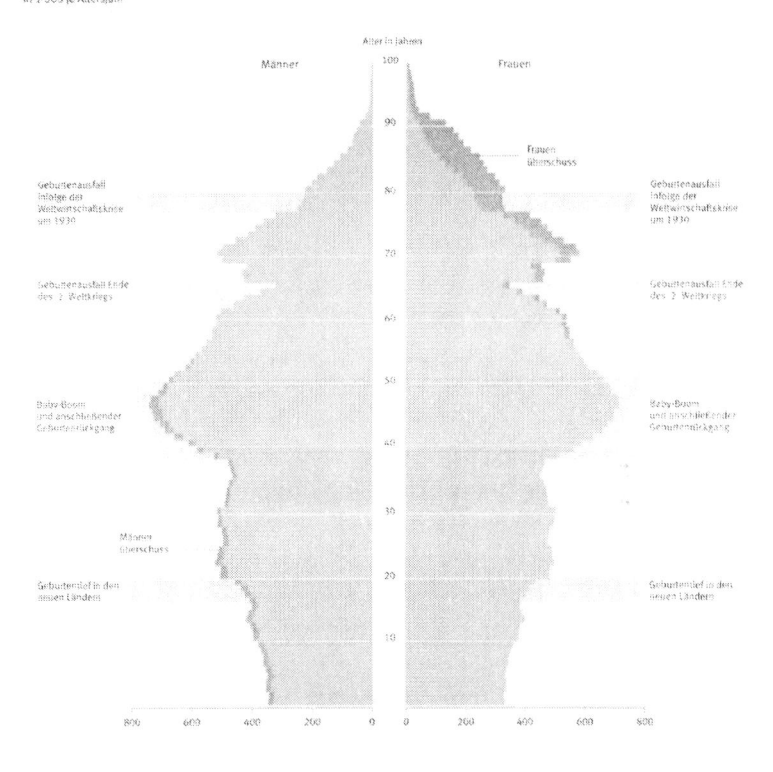

As a conclusion I can say GAS is probably the most fertile ground for licensing in Europe because it is –at least with respect to many categories of licensed products- still far behind France, Italy, Spain and the U.K. If you are not of the mind to "take the money and run" but are seriously interested in building a successful licensing program with longevity and willing to invest adequate funds, you have all that is needed for an attractive ROI.

Brand licensing, in my opinion, has a very promising future. There is a much wider target group and the core product is known as a result of years of advertising and promotion, hence these properties have an established pre-sold popularity and established positioning/image. Charity (cause-related) licensing is equally promising, yet with smaller target groups as the consumer has to decide what charity they favor most.

The new media being offered to consumers brings unpredictability. Licensing involving cell phone technology has not taken hold in this region, while the computer gaming industry has begun to make strides. These games usually have a longer market presence than theatrical releases and hopefully will provide an entry for cell phone games and other properties deriving from the new media scene. Even licensing virtual properties for PC game players and collectors has already reached a significant market size and seems to still grow, because of the increasing number of people who play on their Smartphones or tablets.

In conclusion, I can say that the German-speaking markets are similar in many ways to other key markets in industrialized countries, but offer greater opportunity because of its leading position within the EU and its position as gateway to the Eastern European markets.

We do not try to reinvent the wheel over here, but instead try to constantly smooth the ball-bearings. So, welcome to the "old world"!

Chapter 5: Greater Europe

5.4 Italy

by Gianfranco Mari

5.4.1 Introduction

It is a somewhat difficult exercise to talk about the forty-year history of licensing in Italy in a few short pages. Born in the second half of 1973—to the best of my knowledge—the licensing industry in Italy is complex and varied. As my company is the oldest independent licensing agency in this industry, I thought I would link my own story to that of licensing in Italy. In the second half of 1973, "Dan Junior Production" was founded, the first independent licensing agency in Italy, which after a few years became known as "DIC2 srl" (acronym for "Distribution International Characters"). Before that time, the only company granting licenses for the use of "characters" or "trademarks" was Disney, basically solicited by some advertising and marketing agencies that wanted to exploit the launch of new animated films for promotional activities supporting some of their customers' products. As a "merchandising" agency (this is how this new discipline was called at that time before it was more appropriately called "licensing"), we began to seek companies interested in acquiring licenses to characterize their products with the characters we represented or to exploit characters from television programs and animated movies.

5.4.2 History of Licensing

In the first years, talking about "licensing" or "merchandising" was like talking about quantum physics to babies. Customers neither wanted to pay nor calculate royalties for the proposed use of the characters and properties we represented, because no one had, up to this point, felt the need for the characterization of their products. We are extremely grateful to the first licensees, who faced a difficult task given the poor dissemination of audiovisual media at the time (one of Disney's animated movie was distributed every 3-4 years and a couple of TV channels were on air, one of which broadcast children's programs for an hour a day). However, due to the originality of their products and the wide audience that every movie or television series had, many licensees experienced initial success, and the merchandising activity that we were promoting quickly became an important new marketing tool.

Gradually, the licensing business gained more and more acceptance, and many companies began to take an interest in the various characters, well-known brands, editorial and artistic works, sporting marques and events that we represented. Companies saw a valuable strategy that could be used to characterize their products so as to differentiate them from their competitors' or to take advantage of the interest these properties generated among consumers. These early licensees saw the potential in transferring the character/brand awareness to their products which often resulted in considerable savings on marketing investments which many companies would not have been able to afford. Those were the days in which a character that was on television could be counted on to generate several hundreds of licenses and thousands of products with that character on the market. Easy identification of the right character reduced the risks of manufacturing unsuccessful products that would end up unsold on storeroom and inventory shelves.

Then in the mid-eighties, a boost to the licensing industry occurred with the emergence of major "private" television networks in Italy. These private networks were born from the merger of several local television channels which eventually became strong enough to compete with RAI, the public television network, for the purchase of important TV series. The TV programs, mainly aimed at children, teenagers and young people, were broadcast in prime time slots, which led to an exponentially increased number of potential interested licensees. At the same time, the number of specialists proposing licenses also increased. Besides the independent agencies, new representative offices of the major studios, such as Warner, Hanna-Barbera etc., and licensing offices of television networks such as SACIS (RAI) Mediaset etc., were opened in Italy.

Chapter 5: Greater Europe

What resulted was an excessive number of properties being offered with varied success. After years of introducing the same products and services to consumers, licensing began to experience a slowdown. Now, apart from a few strong properties which collect many of the opportunities, the others gather the crumbs. Today in Italy, there are two other factors that further hinder the licensing market: first, a severe economic crisis that has slashed the budgets of consumers who do not have enough money to spend on products which are not essential and, second, a strong reduction of companies that survived the economic crisis and tax oppression by the Italian government. The companies who were successful in important licensing areas such as games and toys, back-to-school, clothing and accessories, home products, food, promotions and traditional publishing, at one time numbered in the thousands. But today, it is difficult to determine how many survived the economic downturn and remained in business.

Are we pessimists? I think it is important to be realistic, and to be able, through the creativity that has always characterized the Italian people, to find new opportunities and new properties that will revitalize the licensing business and give back the successes of the past.

5.4.3 Licensing Today

It is clearly impossible to talk about the Italian licensing industry today without first analyzing the economic and financial situation in Italy, in the European Union and above all, in new emerging economies around the world. Historically, licensing has had the greatest impact in countries with capitalist economies, where fast-moving consumer goods and even luxury items have found in characters and trademark licensing a useful tool to characterize and impose various products on the market. In these countries, the increase in the price of the licensed products, because of royalties, in comparison to the "unbranded" ones, was not an obstacle, especially in a period when economies were thriving and those captivating products particularly attracted consumers. Besides the United States, the strongest growth in licensing has been

Basics of Licensing: International Edition

in Western Europe and in Japan. Today, because of the crisis (which we will highlight below), the new territories which major licensors are looking at are the Far East, with China leading the way as the second largest economy in the world, Russia and the Eastern European countries.

The reasons that led to the establishment of the EU are manifold. We will take into consideration only the economic and distribution aspects that most affect licensing. The EU was formed to ensure the free circulation of goods, more opportunities and financial certainty. Exchanges between the various countries should have become easier thanks to extensive trade networks in all countries. Borders have been opened, and export tax issues have been eliminated, which in theory should have improved economies. Unfortunately, 10 countries out of 28 have not adopted the Euro currency, and 8 have not adhered to certain Community rules. Each country operates independently with regard to VAT rates, taxation, and wages. The rules on the manufacture of goods, services and trade have caused a huge migration of capital, industry and workforces. All the above has led the individual economies to experience a tremendous collapse and created an insecure and unstable climate. Italy along with Greece, Spain, France and several Eastern European countries are facing a serious economic recession. The effect of recession has been a greater attention to spending by consumers, and consequently, a strong decrease in licenses and royalties generated.

5.4.4 Changes and New Licensing Promotional Media

In Italy, the first and most important change that has occurred with respect to licensing in 2013 is, as said before, the collapse of the licenses and, as a result, the collapse of the revenue due to the economic crisis. In 2013, a large number of licenses – which had been kept alive by licensees because they were somehow able to cover the minimum guarantees, although they didn't generate big revenues – has been abandoned to limit expenditures and investments and refocus resources on more performing properties. A wide proliferation of new thematic channels dedicated to children and teens has

Chapter 5: Greater Europe

occurred following the consolidation of the new digital TV technology. Unfortunately, this has caused the collapse of the audience of individual programs and a great disaffection of young viewers to the characters proposed and consequently the collapse of the licensees' interest for those properties.

The traditional media outlets of television, film, books and publishing, and console video games, which gave birth to characters and trademarks generating important licensing programs, today are being replaced by computers, iPods, iPads, tablets, phones and smartphones, Internet, Facebook, Twitter etc.. At the beginning, the Apps developing companies were used to acquire licenses of renowned characters: Superheroes, cartoons characters, sporting events brands, etc.., but soon the Apps themselves generated new characters like Angry Birds, Cut the Rope, etc., turning licensees into licensors.

These new tools are bringing teens back to licensing after they had abandoned the products supported by certain licenses, which were considered "for children". However, a significant share of their financial resources – previously addressed to important areas of licensing such as comics, gadgets, books – are now diverted towards the services offered by phone service providers, dedicated Apps and social networks.

5.4.5 Brands – Characters – Events

In the past, licensing was a tool used to differentiate from competitors, but the product was the essential part that had to generate the sales (therefore, the main features were: quality, price, warranty, need and service). Today, brands and characters are used as the main sale instrument, the "must have". Brands and characters are no longer chosen for their meanings or because they create a perfect synergy with the product, but only because they are coveted by consumers. There is an explosion of "phenomenon" brands and characters that are purchased because they sell! Generally they are able to exclude any competitor, even if more synergistic with the product.

The explosion of a licensing "phenomenon" often happens very quickly. In order to reduce risk, companies usually await the "explosion" before deciding to acquire a license without realizing that this is often the most dangerous moment to initiate a license, because as soon as they are ready to place the product on the market, the "phenomenon" could be over. As a result, the risk for the licensee is very high. The quantities manufactured are often very high, as well as the investments. When the "must have" effect ceases, there is an instantaneous death of the product, and everything that remains unsold can only be destroyed.

Today, licensing is mostly used to sell. Licensees chase the characters or brands that are sought-after by consumers in that particular moment. We will list a few as an example of what has been or are at moment a "phenomenon". They are not to be taken as current opportunities, because even the most important ones have an expiration date and certainly will not be topical when this book will be published. As with food products, licenses of this kind should bear a "Best before ..." date.

I'll try to give some guidance on how to identify in advance licenses which should give significant results. Take them with care because the identification of a "phenomenon" is something very difficult, particularly for an "old dinosaur" with 40 years of this work on his shoulders.

To better understand what we refer to, the following is a list of the characters and brands that we now call "Phenomenon":

- "The Smurfs" - Even if their first release is as comics in the early sixties, the phenomenon explodes in 1982 with the appearance of the cartoons on the Fininvest TV network. We don't know how many millions of tiny little blue characters have been sold but, thanks to them, someone bought a real castle. Besides being a great "phenomenon", The Smurfs may also be defined as a "classic" thanks to everything that has come after then.
- "The Ninja Turtles"- The famous turtles that have rocked the world of licensing in the years 1988-1990. They could also be listed as classic characters since lately they have been relaunched with various films

Chapter 5: Greater Europe

even though the extraordinary success of the late eighties has never been equaled.
- "The Simpsons" - A satiric parody on the American lifestyle. Canale 5 began airing the cartoon in the evenings at the end of 1991, and the outbreak of the Simpsons mania attracted the teen market, a target that until this point was not impressed by products featuring cartoons characters. The success of The Simpsons merchandise still continues thanks to the large amount of TV episodes released (over 500).
- "Beverly Hills 90210" - The first live action series dealing with sensitive issues related to the world of teens, such as drugs, AIDS, homosexuality, alcohol, etc. The series originally aired in 1992 in Italy and became an incredible success following the wave born in the USA and immediately exported throughout Europe and the world. 90201 was a great licensing success in our country that lasted for a few years with hundreds of different products in each category.
- "Sailor Moon" – Arrived in 1993/1994 on the Mediaset TV, it was a cartoon starring a middle school girl who turns into a warrior with powers that help her fight and save the earth. Four other girls with transforming power will join her to form the team "Sailor Warriors." Great is the success of this series that was supposed to have inspired the creators of The Winx and The W.I.T.C.H.
- "Pokemon" – The series arrived in Italy in 2000 and the licensing success was amazing; we could hazard a guess that it was the most important success in the past and present history. Thanks to Pokemon, some companies have tripled their value on the stock market, and we think that it could become a classic with a constant level of sales of licensed products. Inexplicably, in 2005-2006 the Pokemon Company decided to stop all licenses with the exception of trading cards, Nintendo Video Games and a few other products.
- "South Park" – The first satirical series which dealt with issues such as politics, religion, sex, etc., trying

Basics of Licensing: International Edition

to bust the taboo. The first episodes were broadcast on Mediaset in 2000, but thanks to the rumor of great success in the U.S., a large number of products is already in our market. The licensing success is big enough to compete with Pokémon despite its more restricted and adult target.

- The "Bratz"- launched worldwide around 2002-2004, and unlike most of the other licensing phenomena that have been developed from audiovisual programs (as a result of publishing successes), the Bratz were born as a toy product. In a short time, the Bratz dolls, which are 'caricatures' of the girls at that time, have achieved such success as to exceed sales of the undisputed queen of the industry, the BARBIE doll.
- "The Winx" - a group of "flying fairies" (who seem to have been inspired by the predecessor "Sailor Moon"), were born in 2004-2005 from a successful television series created by the Italian producer Rainbow to contrast the phenomenon Bratz and especially the classic female character par excellence, Barbie. The Winx success has exploded in Italy and is expanding throughout the world bringing Italian creativity to the highest levels of success in licensing.

Presently, here are some phenomena that are exploding in Italy and have attracted consumers of licensing products.

- From Disney come the characters from the animated feature film *Cars,* followed by *Cars 2* and the telenovela, *Violetta,* that is driving all girls from South America, Europe and Africa crazy.
- "Peppa Pig" - Although the cartoon series was born in the early 2000s in Italy, the great licensing success exploded at the end of 2012 and reached its highest peak in 2013. It is the first time that a "pre-school" character has become a great licensing phenomenon in our country. The success of "Peppa" prevails over the target and involves a good deal of the male and older target.

Chapter 5: Greater Europe

5.4.6 How to Spot the Next Phenomenon

With regard to the topical brands, it is important, and I am probably stating the obvious, to follow the consumer's taste who is targeted with the product. Usually, this is influenced by major advertising campaigns carried by well-known companies (Fiat 500), or there are companies that set a trend (fashion brand names as Guru, A-Style, Fix Design). Young people are very susceptible to "Testimonials", where actresses/actors /music bands star in TV shows (Amici, Zelig, Belen, One Direction).

It is more difficult to understand what will become a phenomenon when talking about characters generated from the entertainment industry. It is important to remember the following.

- Constantly monitor foreign markets such as the United States, United Kingdom, Japan, France, and Spain. Analyze the acquisition of a property by leaders in different categories with established history of licensees. In the future, we must certainly keep an eye on China and Russia since their production of entertainment programs and licenses is continuously growing.

- Attend trade fairs (Bologna Licensing Trade Fair, Las Vegas Licensing Expoand Brand Licensing Europe). They are all important sources in finding opportunities. Please note that not all that glitters...

- Attend all presentations of licensors and their agents, especially the most serious, to stay informed about licenses granted, properties' diffusion, promotions, co-marketing activities, style guides and relational difficulties of licensors.

- Try to know the properties that have been acquired by the traditional and most important master licensees both nationally and internationally.

- Keep up with national or international licenses of products related to new technologies and media (Internet, Apps, Social networks)

5.4.7 Proven Classics

In contrast to the phenomena category, characters and brands that have generated and continue to generate excellent revenues for licensees who acquire a license are definitely categorized as "classics". Long-lasting, they keep their value over time with features and performance that are completely different from those of the phenomena characters and brands. Because of their longevity you can acquire their license any time, they are properties that I think will be topical even when you will have the opportunity to read this publication. Clearly, if at a particular time, the property enjoys some particular event such as new television show or movie release of particular importance, anniversary or significant new license, which refreshes its relevance, it would be an important opportunity for the licensee, and a chance possibly to renew its product ranges.

Contrary to the phenomenon, where the timing of acquisition and dropout of a license are very important in order to avoid being left with unsold stock, the licenses for the classics are often renewed for ten-year periods (a good example are the carnival costumes of Zorro) and investments, both for molds and advertising and promotions, are spread over several years of distribution.

Revenues grow more slowly and may stand at lower levels, but in principle, longevity fully compensates this problem. In addition, a license of this kind does not require investments that could throw the company structure into trouble. The product is of fundamental importance for the licensing of classic characters and brands, both for the licensee that, having to keep a product on catalog for a long time, must ensure quality and durability of the product, and for the licensor that otherwise would see its property damaged permanently by low profile products.

Chapter 5: Greater Europe

Here are some of the major licensors and their most successful properties, of course from the licensing point of view, particularly in the recent years.

Entertainment Characters:
- Disney with its world famous Properties: Mickey Mouse, Donald Duck & Co., Winnie the Pooh, Princesses.
- LEAR and the invincible Gauls: Asterix, Obelix & Co.
- Marvel: with Spiderman and the Superheroes
- MATTEL: with the fascinating brand Barbie and Hot Wheels
- SANRIO with the sweet kitten Hello Kitty (now a bit declining)
- CHARLES M. SCHULZ: with evergreen Peanuts and Snoopy
- WARNER BROSS: with the Twitty, Sylvester the Cat, Scooby Doo

Trademarks and Brands:
- Coca-Cola, Ferrari cars, Fiat, Playboy, Pirelli

Fashion Brands:
- Armani, Dolce e Gabbana, Fila, Gucci, Navigare, Robe di Kappa, Valentino

Sporting Brands and Events:
- Football teams: AC Milan, Inter, Juventus, Napoli, Italia National Team
- Formula 1: Ferrari
- Rugby: Italia National Team, All Blacks (more appropriately a small "PHENOMENON")
- World Soccer Championship, Giro d'Italia (bicycle race) (now a bit declining)
- NBA: Lakers

5.5 Spain

by Eric Belloso

5.5.1 Introduction

Spain as always been seen as a country for tourism, with great weather, great parties great food, and a great quality of life. Today, those facts offer robust support to an economy that used to be based on the construction business, which used to account for almost 15% of the economy generated in the country. Since 2009, however, the situation in Spain has been defined by a strong decline of its GDP (see the chart below) and as a consequence, a strong slowdown of the consumption that has affected all the economic bases of the country, including obviously the retail and the licensing markets.

SPAIN GDP EVOLUTION

YEAR	% CHANGE
2007	3.5%
2008	0.9%
2009	-3.8%
2010	-0.2%
2011	0.1%
2012	-1.6%
2013	-1.2%
2014	1.2%

To the above mentioned facts, Spain is also characterized by its lack of competition in the retail market. One company, El Corte Inglés (with 84 stores), is monopolizing the department store segment and another one, Carrefour (with 172 centres) is the leader, by far, in the hypermarket/supermarket sector. Besides those two companies, Toys 'R' Us with 54 stores is the top chain in the toy retail business. Those circumstances together (the economic crisis and

Chapter 5: Greater Europe

the retail landscape) are generating a very strong entrance barrier for any brands that want to get into this market. Business creativity, together with great marketing activities, are the options used by local executives to overtake this panorama.

5.5.2 History of Licensing

Like in many countries in the world, Disney and Warner have been the precursors of the Spanish licensing business, setting up the rules of the game back in the 70's. Some agencies, such as Promovip and BRB Internacional, began to appear in the 80's either representing third party properties or creating their own structure thanks to the creation of their own animated series (such as "David the Gnome" or "Dogtanian" in the case of BRB). Since then, the number of agencies evolving in the market has increased dramatically resulting in a situation where, honestly, some of them are having problems surviving.

There are possibly three key recent moments in the history of Spanish licensing that should be pointed out. The first one is the start-up of the DTT (Digital Terrestrial Television) and the multiplication of TV channels that allowed many more TV-driven products to get into the market. The second one is the elimination of advertisements in the national TV channel TVE. This fact has been fundamental to the introduction of preschool properties in the market, as previously, none of the channels were interested in broadcasting these kinds of products as the audience and rating calculation was only taking into consideration children from 4 years old. With this measure, series such as Caillou, Pocoyó or most recently Peppa Pig, have all enjoyed very successful business stories. The third change has been monitored, as everywhere in the world, by the technological revolution with, from one side, the huge penetration of internet, (Youtube is the 4th most viewed "TV channel" in the country) and the strong presence of smartphones and tablets that enable the App market to explode. It is estimated that 55% of mobile phone users in Spain are using smartphones, hence the mechanism to reach a very important audience is already in place.

5.5.3 Licensing Today

Spain, like the majority of European countries, can be defined as an old nation not just through its history but more importantly through its citizens. A look at the population pyramid below shows precisely the demographic problem that the country is and will be facing in the close future.

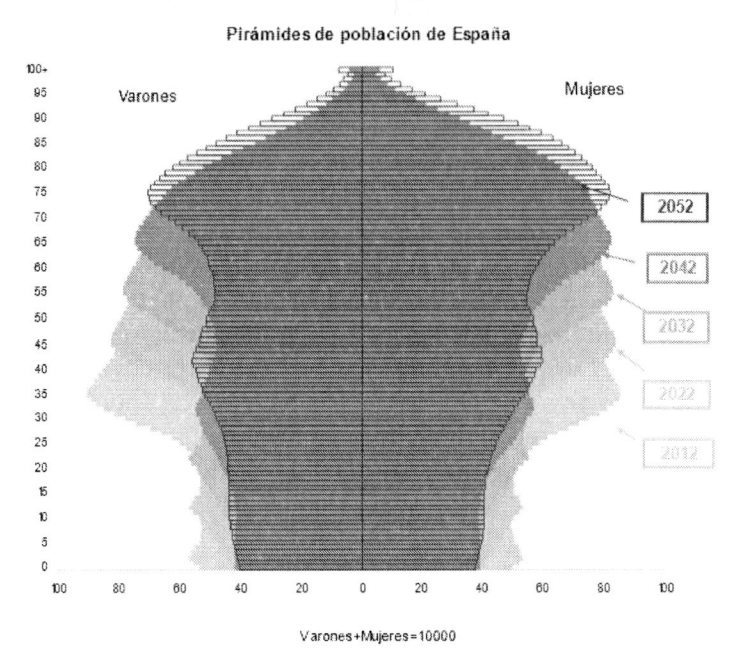

Pirámides de población de España

Varones — Mujeres

2052
2042
2032
2022
2012

Varones+Mujeres=10000

Apart from all the economic and demographic aspects that this pyramid implies, from a licensing standpoint, this chart shows that the young adults are gaining more and more significance with respect to consumer power, hence the importance of sport licensing and fashion brands. This pyramid also assumes that children have a stronger economic power within the home. With many Spanish families having more than one child, children are considered in many cases as the king or queen within the home and usually receive more money to spend from their parents. As a result, their power of decision-making inside the family is increasing – a study demonstrated that 15% of the cars sold in Spain were bought considering the influence of the children. This on a licensing perspective means that the number of toys and licensing products that each of them can receive is maintaining the business at reasonable levels.

Another aspect to take into consideration when making business decisions in Spain is that the current economic crisis strongly decreases the acquisition power of consumers. Here is a chart that shows the variation between Consumer Price Index (IPC in Spanish) and salaries.

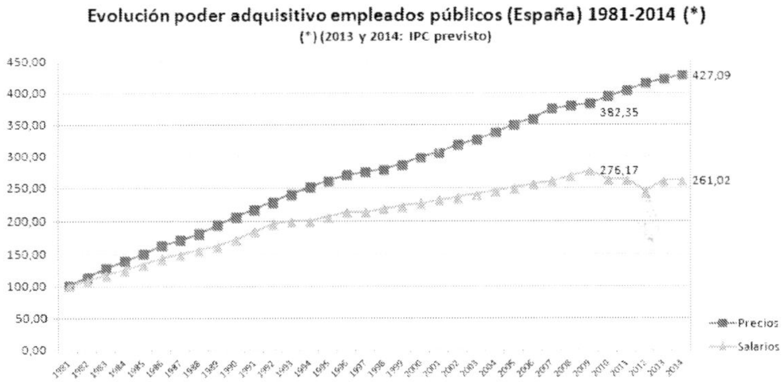
Evolución poder adquisitivo empleados públicos (España) 1981-2014 (*)
(*) (2013 y 2014: IPC previsto)
450,00
400,00
350,00
300,00
250,00
200,00
150,00
100,00
50,00
0,00
427,09
382,35
276,17
261,02
Precios
Salarios

This chart takes into account salaries for public employees but could be extrapolated for private companies. The average gross salary in Spain is estimated at €23,730 which translates in monthly net is roughly €1,637. However, the latest studies also show that 1 out of 3 Spaniard is what is called "mileurista" (they earn €1,000€ a month). This basically means that to create a licensing mass market phenomenon, the consumer price of any licensed product is another variable to consider very carefully.

Analyzing more precisely the Spanish licensing market and taking into consideration all the elements mentioned so far, the following trends are evident in the Spanish marketplace as of 2013:

- Disney properties are everywhere and could be, without any doubt, defined as the leader in this market.
- Sports licensing, and more concretely football (soccer in the US) with the brands of Real Madrid and Barce-

lona FC are solidifying their dominant positions in the market. As their target audience is young adults, they can afford to position their products with a higher price in the market.
- On the preschool side, Peppa Pig is dominating the market with great ratings on TVE (Clan) and is a very important presence in all the main retail outlets.
- Properties based on Internet /App-driven content, such as Angry Birds, are also very well-located in the majority of the stores.
- Other strong properties include the major fashion brands (Armani, Ralph Lauren, Tommy Hilfiger) and their licensed products in the high end area. Cinema licensing with properties such as Spiderman, Despicable Me or classics such as Star Wars can also be bought in the majority of the shops.

Even if Spain has always been a great incubator of artistic talent, internationally the result has never been significantly recognised. Companies such as Inditex (Zara) or Mango are the only visible tip of the iceberg and this circumstance is also true of the licensing world. The most famous Spanish properties that have seen some licensing success abroad are Pocoyó (from Zinkia), Jelly Jam (from Vodka), Chupa Chups (the famous lollipop brand) and obviously the above mentioned Real Madrid and Barcelona FC on the sport licensing side.

Having said that, even with strong internal competition, the Spanish market has always been eager to embrace US and UK properties, which are usually very well-perceived by the consumer and seen as aspirational. Introducing a product line in Spain that has been successful in one of those two countries gives any property a competitive advantage in the market in front of buyer (either from TV channels or from the retail).

In the toy business, Spain has the highest rate of sales from licensed toys vs. non-licensed. Following a study from NPD, 30% of the total toys sold in this country are licensed driven versus 27% in the UK or 20% in Germany! However, another characteristic of Spain is that brands do not last generally forever. Besides the above mentioned Disney, Real Madrid and Barcelona, TV and retail support cannot forever sustain the brand in the majority of cases.

In analyzing the market during the last ten years, the result is that Pokémon has been the top property in the market from 2000 to 2003. Then "Los lunnies" a local preschool show launched in 2003 by TVE has been the retail reference for another three years. From 2006, Sponge Bob has been the reference in the kids market, together with Pocoyo and Caillou from 2008, in the preschool market. Papito Feo made a huge penetration into the girl segment back in 2009. All of them lasted two or three years in the market. Nowadays, Peppa Pig is taking the lead. The future will tell us how long this property will last, but a general feeling in the market is that the short-term trend might change because of the entrance barrier mentioned earlier in the retail world and the recent introduction of technology-driven properties. In the first case scenario, retail avoiding the possibility of taking huge risk with new properties should imply that they'll maintain their already existing franchise. On the second case, once a company will be able to create awareness with its IP, control the broadcasting platform and renew its content quite regularly to keep it fresh (both on the platform and in the market), the result in term of licensed products should follow and therefore, great results could be expected.

There are no official figures related to the extension of the licensing market in Spain, nevertheless some studies show that we might be talking about a business rounding € 2 billion in retail sales yearly. This evaluation is made taking into consideration an estimated €700 million market (retail sales) in the licensed toy business and considering that the clothing, shoes and accessories sectors together, with the above mentioned toys, should represent close to 60% of the overall market. In the same order, there is no official figures related to the importance of the licensing business by category, but we could easily consider that entertainment (covering TV series, cinema and new technology-related products) could correspond to 50% of the market, followed by sports licensing with another 25% and the remaining quarter should be covered by categories such as brands, fashion, music and art. As mentioned before, this result is purely empirical and based on the presence of those categories in retailers such as El Corte Inglés or Carrefour.

Once the decision to exploit a brand in Spain is made, any licensor will quickly notice that the professionalism in this market is another unbreakable characteristic. Such a complex market has dramatically increased the expertise of the majority of the players, and all of them are used to working with complicated rules where brand building exercises and finding the best moment to launch a product are key elements. Besides Disney Consumer Products and Warner Consumer Products, there are a large number of licensing agencies working in this territory. Biplano, CPLG, El Ocho and Planeta Junior might be considered as the biggest ones. And then, there are a number of boutique licensing companies such as Enjoy Brand Licensing, Selecta Vision, Arait Multimedia, Edebé, Luk Internacional, Mendía Licensing, Notorious Brand & People that are taking parts of the pie with some dedicated brands.

The majority of the latest successes in the market have been managed by local companies that do know the specificity of the market that in summary relies on the element mentioned in the previous paragraph: finding the best moment to launch the products on shelves. If too early, the retailers will be ruthless. If the rotation of products does not match their expectancy, they normally never give a second opportunity and obviously, if too late, business opportunities will be wasted. Being in constant contact with the market, either through the retail, study markets or analyzing audience and shares on TV is vital to get into this market.

Finally, when considering travelling over to Spain, bear in mind that most Spaniards are social people. Having lunch or dinner with your counterpart is very common, and you can find yourself either in a great trendy or classic restaurant or eating standing up in front of a bar facing a variety of very appetising tapas. Another thing to take into consideration is that lunch and/or dinner are later than in other countries. Lunch habitually begins from 1:30pm to 3pm and dinner gen-

Chapter 5: Greater Europe

erally begins from 9pm to 10pm. Having wine is also quite normal, moreover during the dinner.

5.5.4 Conclusion

The licensing market in Spain will be, without any doubt, more and more influenced by the content driven through the new devices (mobile phones, tablets, etc.). Whether we are talking about preschool, kids, young adults or adult properties, the majority of the population is influenced by those new instruments. Being able to control the content and the broadcasting (ideally through various platforms) is a key element when considering developing new licensing programs in this country. The competition is high and shelf space is limited, hence the necessity to create a plan that has to be different and easily recognizable by the market. Licensed properties will always have a place in the Spanish market and in the consumer's mind, the differentiation made by a well-known IP will always add value to any products and this is a reality known by all the players of this market. This is a great country to work with and once the rules of the games are understood, the opportunity is around the corner. Don't miss it!!

5.6 The United Kingdom

by Kelvyn Gardner

5.6.1 Introduction

The United Kingdom has a population of some sixty million people and ranks as the world's sixth largest economy as measured by GDP. However, though robust research is hard to come by within the business, the UK is generally considered to be the third largest market for licensed merchandise in the world today, after the United States and Japan. Although it still accounts for almost 17% of the UK economy, manufacturing is no longer a dominant sector. Indeed the service sector, which includes retail, is officially estimated to account for almost three-quarters of UK economic output. As a strong retail sector is vital for the sale of consumer goods, a category which includes the majority of licensed merchandise, the UK's retail strength no doubt contributes to the relatively large size of the licensing business here.

5.6.2 History of Licensing

The UK was a relatively early adopter of licensing with notable early successes in the late 1950s onwards and has had more than sixty years for the business to grow. LIMA's database lists more than 500 licensors/licensing agents in the UK, compared to just over 100 in Germany, and around 50 in each of Italy and France, the other major European economies. Numbers of licensees are in similar proportions. With such a large licensing infrastructure, resulting in significant competition for the buying and selling of licensing rights, it's not really surprising to find that the UK punches above its weight in the licensing sector compared to the economy as a whole.

The UK also has a history of staging dedicated licensing conferences, seminars and exhibitions dating back to the 1980s. London's *Lancaster Hotel* has a particular history here, having hosted licensing trade shows on behalf of various organizers on many occasions throughout this period. The current leading trade exhibition, *Brand Licensing Europe* has been an annual October event in London since 1999, and has

Chapter 5: Greater Europe

established itself as a large and significant international licensing trade show, second only in the world to *Licensing Expo* in Las Vegas. Similarly, licensing awards events have featured here for over thirty years, staged by diverse organizations including *The Licensing Book*, *A4 Publications*, *LIMA* itself, and currently *Max Publishing*.

With an established licensing infrastructure, an identifiable licensing business community, an increasing understanding among business as a whole of the value of intellectual property and a vibrant creative and media landscape, the UK is well positioned to continue to be a major international centre for the licensing business.

5.6.3 Licensing Today

The UK population at the last (2011) census was just over 63 million. The UK was split in age terms as follows (source: Office of National Statistics):

Ages (years)	Population	% of total
0–4	3,914,000	6.2
5–9	3,517,000	5.6
10–14	3,670,000	5.8
15–19	3,997,000	6.3
20–24	4,297,000	6.8
25–29	4,307,000	6.8
30–34	4,126,000	6.5
35–39	4,194,000	6.6
40–44	4,626,000	7.3
45–49	4,643,000	7.3
50–54	4,095,000	6.5
55–59	3,614,000	5.7
60–64	3,807,000	6.0
65–69	3,017,000	4.8
70–74	2,463,000	3.9
75–79	2,006,000	3.2
80–84	1,496,000	2.4
85–89	918,000	1.5
90+	476,000	0.8

This data shows that just over eleven million children age 0-14 currently live in the UK, with a gender split of roughly equal proportions. Children have historically been the most important market in the UK for licensed merchandise. Whilst we have no reason to predict that this is likely to change, there is a growing interest in licensing among older age groups, from "traditional" areas like music and films, but also from the growth in App-based licensing (like Angry Birds and Cut the Rope) and sports and sports personalities (like David Beckham). Additionally, family drama and factual TV series with a majority of adult viewers, such as *Downtown Abbey*, *Game of Thrones*, and *The Only Way is Essex* have also broken through into licensing of appropriate consumer goods. I believe that we can regard this as a sign of a maturing UK market, where a thirty-something can enjoy a product based on a popular TV show without embarrassment, or association with "childish" undertones.

Licensing for "grown-ups" has also popped up in merchandise categories not normally associated with licensing. Two notable examples are audio headphones and spectacle frames, the latter generally referred to as "eyewear". Until very recently, headphones have been the preserve of established audio/hi-fi brands like Sony and Sennheiser. During the course of 2012, the share of the UK headphones market taken by licensed brands grew from 11% of the market at the start of the year to almost 34% by the end of 2012 (source: GFK). Many of these licensed brands are music celebrities, and there is evidence that some consumers now own multiple sets of headphones as fashion items, but the growth of the licensed sector is remarkable nonetheless. In eyewear, the UK market has seen a sea-change from twenty years ago when there was virtually no licensed eyewear (often erroneously described as "designer eyewear") to 2013 with a majority of products available in typical high-street opticians stores bearing licensed brands. According to GFK, over 16 major brands (and many other smaller ones) moved into the licensed eyewear market in the UK in the last five years.

The UK population is growing, which should be good news for licensing. However, like all major western markets

Chapter 5: Greater Europe

media outlets have multiplied exponentially over the last ten years. For children alone there are now more than twenty TV channels dedicated to junior programmes. Whilst this encourages diversity, it makes it all the harder for any one property to "cut through" in genuine mass popularity. The arrival also of "on demand" TV services such as the BBC's iPlayer has also deprived us of many "water cooler" moments as Americans call them, further reducing the "live" TV audience for any one broadcast. The market for films, too, is much more competitive than it was a decade ago. The popularity of the DVD format, especially for gifting, has squeezed the timing of big Hollywood film launches into May-August for cinema release, in order to facilitate a DVD launch in October-December, the prime gifting season. Many licensees have turned away from films as too risky as a consequence. Gone are the days when the summer blockbuster would be just that: one, single, summer movie that seemingly everyone would go to see. Indeed, if we go back as far as the early 1990s it was not unusual for UK licensing businesses to have the luxury of observing the domestic box-office returns of a film released in the USA months before the planned UK release, giving them a chance to buy into a proven success.

Over and above traditional media, the growth of firstly the internet and then smart phone and tablet technology has provided for the first time an alternative universe in which brands can become prominent, attract mass audiences and strong consumer followings, and then, as a natural consequence, move into licensed merchandise. We should not underestimate how significant this is. Previously, major retailers would, outside of niche markets, limit licensed merchandise ranges to those emanating from either the TV or the movie screen. Now, web-based properties have proved that it is the new multi-media screens of iPads and other tablets, smart phones, lightweight laptops and good-old PCs that are becoming the source of powerful consumer interest. Youthscape, a leading research report from Swapit, the UK online swapping and trading community for young people, noted that already 32% of 8-16 year olds own tablets, and if tablet ownership continues to grow at the same rate as in 2012, they could overtake consoles and become the primary gaming device used at home in the next year.

The leading protagonists in the UK market to date have been Moshi Monsters from Mind Candy, and Angry Birds from Finnish company Rovio. Each has distinctively different roots, the former a Web-based platform providing an online virtual community for children 4-10, the latter an App for smart phones and tablets with a wide-demographic appeal right up to young adults. However, the recently-coined term "convergence" applies to each, with TV and movie developments being explored. The Moshi Monsters movie has already been announced, along with plans for a new tablet-optimized Moshi Monsters experience available internationally following the launch of Gree's Moshi Village in Japan. Similarly, Rovio are moving into animated shorts for Angry Birds to be followed by a 3D movie in 2016.

In 2013, the major properties that are being licensing in the UK include Moshi Monsters, Angry Birds, Peppa Pig, Disney (specially Disney/Pixar), Marvel, Star Wars, Hello Kitty, Thomas & Friends, Doctor Who. Among these, Moshi Monsters from Mind Candy; Peppa Pig from Entertainment One; Thomas & Friends from Hit! Entertainment; and Doctor Who from the BBC all have UK origins.

The major licensors in the UK include BBC Worldwide, Hit! Entertainment, Entertainment One, Disney, CPLG, TLC and 20th Century Fox. Major licensees include TDP Aykroyds (apparel), Vivid Imaginations (Toys), Penguin Books, Egmont (publishing), Topps Europe (trading cards and stickers), Blues Clothing, Finsbury Food Group, Kinnerton confectionery, Wild & Wolf (gifts), Blueprint Designs (stationery and bags), Danilo (calendars and cards), GB Eye (posters), Smiffy's (dress-up) and Character World (bedding).

The major retailers here include the "Big Four" supermarkets: Tesco, Sainsbury's, Asda and Morrisons; WH Smith; Toys R Us; Argos; Boots; The Entertainer; Marks & Spencer; New Look; Primark; Debenhams; and John Lewis. It should also be noted that the online retail environment is very strong, with Amazon, Play.com, The Hut, Moonpig and others making significant sales.

Chapter 5: Greater Europe

5.7 The Nordic Region

by Fuad Khan

5.7.1 Introduction

When most people think about the Nordic region usually what comes to mind is tall, blonde, good-looking people, the excellent welfare system, snow as far as the eye can see and of course brands like Nokia, Volvo & IKEA. However, the Nordic region is a small and complex area consisting of 5 different countries, languages, currencies and cultures split among several countries and consisting of about 25 million people. So doing business in the licensing industry requires an understanding of the preferences of the Nordic consumers and what characterizes each country. Below are some basic statistics about the countries that make up the Nordic region.

Sweden
Population: 9.5 million
Language: Swedish
Currency: Swedish Krona

Sweden is the largest country and considered the most important market for licensing in the Nordics because a large segment of consumers is here. Big shopping malls are popping up everywhere and e-commerce is booming. Swedes are known to be trend-sensitive, and Sweden is often used as a "first trial" country for consumer products prior to launch. Paradoxically, Swedes are typically very careful, and rarely are agreement executed until all have had their say which often leads to delayed decisions and initiatives.

Finland
Population: 5.5 million
Language: Finnish
Currency: Euro

Finland is the only Nordic that is a member of the Eurozone, connecting Finland to the European Trade market. Even though the population is small, Finland is nowadays the Nordic hub for tech business. Here we find companies such as Supercell, Rovio and Nokia which have put the tech savvy Finns on the map. Finnish people are considered to be very productive, disciplined and ambitious. Its closeness to the Baltics and Russia has made it natural for several retailers and companies to focus their expansion to the east rather than toward the rest of the Nordics.

Norway
Population: 5 million
Language: Norwegian
Currency: Norwegian Krona

Norway is the only country in the Nordic region that is not a member of the European Union. This means that there are no complications for licensees to sell their products into Norway with added taxes, etc. Since sales number of licensed products in Norway have been small, licensing agents with big international brands often overlook this market. However, this has created a strong market for local Norwegian brands to arise and work with Norwegian licensees.

Denmark
Population: 5.5 million
Language: Danish
Currency: Danish Krona

If Sweden has the most consumers, Denmark has the most companies working in licensing. The Danes are very business minded and have a continental way of executing ideas. This has resulted in Denmark becoming a hub for licensees, especially when it comes to textiles and toys. The competition is strong, and the licensees are picky since all licensors want to get into business with these licensees.

Iceland
Population of 300,000
Language: Icelandic
Currency: Icelandic Krona

Chapter 5: Greater Europe

A major conceptual challenge for foreign licensors entering the UK market is the EU regulation on free trade. In short, with rare exceptions the "common market" that is the European Union has no trading boundaries between the member states. Indeed, seeking to impose such boundaries is a serious breach of EU (and thus UK) law. In practice, this means that it is not possible to grant a license for any specific EU country on a single-territory basis. If you license the toy rights for the UK, your licensee has the right under EU law to sell his licensed goods in any and all countries of the EU. This law applies to all EU states, not just the UK, but is often encountered here first by American licensors entering the European market via the traditional UK gateway. Local lawyers have devised language to provide some legal limitations on this very broad-brush regulation, but, nonetheless, newcomers invariably find it surprising.

As stated in the introduction, the UK has a large and well-established community of licensing agencies able to represent indigenous and foreign licensing properties to the UK market. It's also the case that many non-UK domiciled licensing businesses (Nickelodeon, for example) will set up their European or even EMEA (Europe, Middle East, Africa) offices in London. Several UK-founded licensing agencies have grown over the years to become pan-European and even more international, and companies like The Licensing Company and CPLG (Copyright Promotions Licensing Group) are the biggest licensing agencies outside the USA, and even in the world. An IP owner looking for UK representation will find a wide choice of potential partners, from boutique agencies employing two or three staff, right up to these large firms, all skilled and experienced in the field.

Licensing consultants, often referred to as manufacturers' reps in the USA, are fewer on the ground. There are half-a-dozen serious operators in this field in the UK, several of whom have been running successful consultancies for more than a decade. Their services can be invaluable to new manufacturers seeking to enter the licensing market but unfamiliar with the processes and costs involved, and, longer term, to manufacturers who don't wish to employ full-time licensing staff with the consequent overhead cost.

The UK retail scene is dominated by a number of chain stores in every sector: supermarkets, pharmacies, toys stores, fashion retailers, department stores and gift stores. This infrastructure is, on the whole, beneficial to the effective distribution of licensed merchandise nationwide. These chain retailers are sophisticated businesses able to implement the latest marketing, loyalty and "in-store theatre" techniques to win sales from consumers, so are good partners for innovative licensing companies at agency or licensee level. Many successful partnerships have been forged between licensing and UK retail which have brought great success.

The down side to this structure is that the power balance between retailers and the licensing business can often shift uncomfortably in favor of the former. This can put undue pressure for special terms and high margins on the supply side of this balance. Indeed, the growth of Direct-to-Retail (DTR) licensing agreements is an example of this. DTR agreements are formed between a licensor/agent and a retailer with no licensee; the retailer is free to source the product from any supplier. There are benefits to DTR deals on occasion, especially to get business moving in a slow market, but, on the whole, the licensing business prefers the agent/licensee/retail model. Additionally, many UK "high-streets" and shopping centres (malls) have an identical look which is hurting diversity and squeezing out innovative new retailers as rents are often set at a level that only the national chains can afford. At the time of writing this chapter, the UK economy is in the fifth consecutive year of recession, which has squeezed all retailers large and small, obliging them to discount prices more than usual, which, in turn, have hurt margins for licensees.

Chapter 5: Greater Europe

The often forgotten island that gave us Lazytown is also included in the Nordics. I will, however, not go further into details regarding this country due to its small size and population. Sorry Iceland!

The Nordic region, except for Iceland, has been a stable territory even during the financial crisis when compared to other regions in the world. The category that was hit the hardest is the textile industry, and that is still suffering. Due to economic turbulence, the number of independent stores has been decreasing, and today's consumer has a very limited selection of stores to visit at shopping malls around the region. The big retail chains are the ones that have survived, creating a similar offering of product everywhere.

5.7.2 History of Licensing

Licensing is still in its early phases in comparison to other territories like the US and the UK. The market began to grow in the early 1980's, and most of today's licensing companies/agencies got their start in the licensing business by inking deals with brands like James Bond, Pink Panther, Star Wars, Tom & Jerry, Moomin and Peanuts. Disney was the pioneer for consumer products in the region and thoroughly established the Disney properties as if they were a part of the Nordic culture. Disney's ability to control and steer the supply chain from production to end product at retail has proven to be a key to their success.

In the early days of licensing in the Nordics, gaining the rights to TV programming was a good business since the agents and content owners made money from selling the rights to broadcasters. This soon changed as TV stations began having to pay little or no money for broadcast rights because of the increasing supply of quality content from an increasing number of producers. Label slapping onto products was a common sight, as licensees were hoping that the brand by itself would bear the whole product. This, of course, proved to be a bad tactic since the people in the Nordic are used to high quality products.

5.7.3 Licensing Today

As the market changed according to what the Nordic customer wanted, quality increased making licensed products widely accepted. Today, consumers can find licensed products across most categories. Licensees have come to understand the importance of delivering quality products to retailers in order to have a high sell-through ratio. This is true especially when it comes to fashion retailers, where design and trend are important factors. In fact, one common trend for the region is the minimalistic "Scandinavian" design theme which is now influencing the designs of consumer products across all categories.

The main target groups for licensing are children, tweens, teenagers and young adults who are consuming popular culture, toys and games on a daily basis. E-commerce is booming and also acts as a platform for licensed products from outside the Nordic region. The current hot brands are Hello Kitty, Skylanders, Angry Birds, LEGO and of course, the Disney brands, including Marvel and Star Wars.

A good recipe for success so far has also been the franchises coming from Hollywood production companies like Shrek, Ice Age, Madagascar, Toy Story, Kung-Fu Panda, etc. Products bearing these types of properties satisfy the short-term hype around each movie release in the franchise and contribute to the long-term building of the brand. A single movie release seldom gives any reason for a licensee to invest time and money to capitalize on a risky bet.

Some of the bigger licensees, like FIPO Group, Almedahls, Björna ApS, H&M and Skybrands, could make an impact on a smaller brand through their distribution at any of the retailers, like H&M, The Varner Group, Bestseller, Stockmann, Dansk Supermarked, JYSK, KappAhl, Reitan Group, ICA Group, SOK, and Retail n Brands, which have thousands of stores across the Nordics. But in the end it is the consumer that decides what works and what does not. Nordic consumers in general do not have the collector spirit like in the US for example where you have the craze for collecting several figurines, cards etc., from the same brand.

Chapter 5: Greater Europe

Nordic lifestyle brands have learned from their US counterparts like Ralph Lauren and Calvin Klein that brand building through licensing and co-brandings can be successful. GANT and Lexington Company are two players in the market who have grown their businesses by extending their brands into other categories such as perfumes, sunglasses, home textiles, and watches. These kinds of brands are not considered "licensed" as with the character licensed products, since the brands communicate more solid values like quality, price and status. These are the values that Nordic consumers seek when buying products, and this has not changed for decades. Occasionally, the consumer buy an Angry Birds T-shirt or a Hello Kitty mug for their child, but in general, they would rather save their money to buy the more expensive GANT T-shirt. So a key to success among the consumers in the Nordics is to capture these values.

The food and beverage category is on the rise for licensed products, and here it is even more important to design and craft the products so they gain confidence among consumers. Consumers might buy a licensed dairy product but will not re-purchase if the quality is bad, which in turn will hurt the brand. Parents are cautious when buying branded food items for their children because they are often perceived to be of cheap quality and unhealthy. In this case, it might be helpful for the licensor to cooperate with a well-known food manufacturer and co-brand the item. This could win the hearts of both the parents and of the children who want the popular cookies. However, one should be aware of the restricted laws surrounding marketing to children in the Nordics. Today, for example, you only see toy commercials on the networks that are broadcasting from outside the Nordics. Also, direct promotions are forbidden in some countries, so it makes it more difficult for brand owners to engage the consumers through certain in-store promotions.

Among the licensors, there are a few who have a physical presence in the Nordics like Disney and ROVIO. Most other licensors are utilizing the handful of agents/ consultants that are spread throughout the Nordic region. As a brand owner, one must realize that the competition is very tough in the Nordics. It seldom matters if a TV series has good ratings or a movie is backed up with a huge promotion budget. Today it is all about the big picture. Disney is the consumer products powerhouse that has really refined the ability to promote and license a property. I remember when the Cars 2 movie came out and the brand got huge exposure in commercials and most importantly at retail where tons of licensees were showcasing their products. Disney's ability to bring all of the licensing parties together, including licensees, retail partners and other promotion partners, is basically the model which every licensor should follow.

5.7.4 Outlook, Projections and Conclusion

So after this crash course on how the licensing business works in the Nordics today, what do we see happening in the near future? In today's fast-paced and information savvy world, where news becomes old as soon as it reaches a certain number of tweets or shares on Facebook, how will something stick around long enough to grow and be an evergreen brand?

Brand owners will really have to be realistic about their goals for the short- and long-term. Some properties are just meant to be short-term opportunities, and it is a challenge the brand owner must overcome to be able to supply the short-term demand to consumers. The standard two-year contracts with three-month contract approval time and with one to two months product development time typically do not make it. Instead, licensors are advised to create good relationships with retailers, especially e-commerce retailers, and have manufacturers/licensees ready to respond to the next hyped property so that the product can be in place within weeks. This is especially true in the ever-changing fashion industry, where retailers like ZARA can often get a product from drawing table to store within a two-week time frame. This just shows how quick a retail giant must be to deliver the latest trends and fashions in this region. So licensors should consider umbrella contracts with the partners they need in order to secure the possibility to deliver. It is important for licensors to give their partners the opportunity to work with their brands both in the long- and short-term. E-commerce is ex-

Chapter 5: Greater Europe

ploding with double digit growth every year. It is important that licensees handle the larger e-commerce stores like the regular retailers. Before long, licensors will be making direct to retail deals with a specific e-commerce partners on a regular basis.

The Nordic market is not expected to grow dramatically in population size due to low birth rates, but the willingness to buy more licensed product does have the potential to grow. Delivering high quality products and transforming the license into a lifestyle brand are the keys to winning the hearts of the Nordic consumers. The property Minecraft is a good example of a very successful mobile game that created a community around the game and thus the brand. The licensor took its time before launching any big merchandise products on the market and fed the consumers a little at a time with highly relevant and qualitative products. When a consumer buys a Minecraft T-shirt, it does say something about the buyer and that is essentially what brand licensing does — it connects the people who want to be a part of the same brand culture.

5.8 Turkey

by Hakan Tungaç

5.8.1 Introduction

Turkey has been a crossroad for civilizations for centuries. When a European merchant visited Eastern Asia they went through Anatolia. When Eastern silk traders wanted to sell their properties, they used the Silk Road, a series of trade and cultural transmission routes that were central to cultural interaction through regions of the Asian continent connecting the West and East by linking traders, merchants, pilgrims, monks, soldiers, nomads and urban dwellers from China to the Mediterranean Sea during various periods of time.[1] The information contained in this chapter is based upon estimated retail sales of licensed products, for the period ending December 31, 2012, with all channels of distribution reported in Turkey. The conclusions were amassed through statistical and analytical reports, plus my research conducted throughout the years, via discussions with licensors, licensees, licensing consultants and agents. Retail distribution channels include domestic retail chains and international counterparts: department stores, mid-tier stores, specialty/niche stores), mass merchants, supermarket independents and chains, and Internet and TV shopping.

The licensing sector is rapidly growing in Turkey. Manufacturers of licensed products are using the power of the brand and character to sell products. While helping brand owners increase their brand awareness, licensing increases volume of sales, allowing manufacturers to surpass their opponents in this competitive trade arena. It is not easy for Turkish companies to reach to the success levels that some American and European companies with thirty-year licensing histories have reached, but at the same time, with the right

---

[1] Elisseeff, Vadime (2001). *The Silk Roads: Highways of Culture and Commerce.* UNESCO Publishing / Berghahn Books. ISBN 978-92-3-103652-1.

Chapter 5: Greater Europe

licensing tool and the right licensing strategies in this global world, the sky is the limit.

5.8.2 History of Licensing

In the late 1980s, Turkey embraced the open-market economics principal. In the open-market economy, the government is taking a largely hands-off approach to common transactions. Buyers and sellers enter into agreements with each other for their own mutual benefit and are free to set prices and terms of sale as they see fit. As a result, brands like Coca Cola, Pepsi, and Disney have been introduced to Turkish consumers. Up until that moment, people used to drink "Ayran", a drink made out of yogurt, but the globalization and free market allowed exposure to new drinks, new clothing, new cartoons and new fashion.

By the 1990s, Turkish consumers began wanting everything they saw on TV. Women wanted to have the pocketbook they saw Elizabeth Taylor carry, and men wanted to wear the jeans that Michael Knight wore on the Knight Rider series. Kids loved the Disney characters of Mickey and Minnie Mouse, and so parents were compelled to buy character-licensed toys, books, T-shirts and pajamas. Where there is demand, it had to be supplied. Beginning in the late 1990s, many companies positioned themselves to import these branded items into Turkey. Turkey at this time did not have many factories in the private sector. The government used to own all of the factories; therefore, importing those products played a vital role in the early years of licensing in Turkey.

Even though the collapse of the Asian market affected the Turkish economy, the markets in Turkey's emerging economy kept growing steadily. Since the beginning of the new millennium, with the help of a one-party ruling instead of coalition-style government, the economy grew even more. The purchasing power of every household in Turkey rose to levels where people started to buy many things they wanted before. Since there now was a demand for licensed products supported with purchasing power, Turkish manufacturing companies decided to produce them by themselves instead of importing them. Thus began an age of licensing agreements with property owners from the west with manufacturers producing merchandise in Turkey.

Licensing agencies became popular in the early decade of the new millennium. Agencies like Sentries Licensing Company, who represent the biggest brands, i.e., publishing houses, authors, characters, film/TV, music, video games, and software, provide full service and specialize in the licensing of entertainment, corporate, and lifestyle properties, developing a broad range of compatible products on behalf of their clients. These agencies played a very important role by providing licensing assistance to their clients, while aiming to have closer partnerships with the property owners all around the world.

5.8.3 Licensing Today

According to *The Licensing Letter*, the retail sales of licensed merchandise worldwide increased 1.6% in 2012, rising to $153.2 from $150.8 billion. The regions showing the largest annual rise in retail sales of licensed goods were the still-emerging areas of Central and Eastern Europe, up 6.4% in 2012; Latin America, up 4.5%; and the Middle East and Africa, up 4.3%. Asia also saw increases in retail sales of licensed goods of 1.7% in 2012, with strong sales in China, India, Southeast Asia, and Korea tempered by continued struggles in Japan.

As expected, the so-called BRIC countries (Brazil, Russia, India, China) all ranked among the top 10 as measured by their rates of growth in retail sales of licensed merchandise. Collectively, these four territories registered an increase in retail sales of licensed goods of about 8%, far above the global growth rate. Some economic analysts are starting to refer to the world's fastest-emerging economies together as the BRICT block, adding Turkey to the other four. With a 6.9% increase in retail sales of licensed goods, Turkey joined the others in the global top ten as measured by licensing growth for the first time last year. Turkey is a rising economic giant in this region, and Istanbul has the potential to open Turkey to the world.

Chapter 5: Greater Europe

Although licensed merchandise in all areas is gradually gaining ground, the fast moving consumer products (FMCG) market is growing and experiencing expansion like never before. There have been initiatives in this regard from big names like Nickelodeon, who has different licensing agreements (in Turkey) with individual brands. Danone fruit juices, the flagship fruit juice brand from Danone and one of Turkey's leading FMCG companies headquartered in France, recently announced a tie-in with Disney Consumer Products under which Danone will use the image of Disney's most beloved characters, such as The Cars characters, to adorn the Danone juices and nectars packs. These kinds of relationships with Disney or any admired brand help encourage healthy eating choices and lifestyles among Turkish kids and families. With Disney's most beloved characters on fruit juice packs, it has created a whole new experience and excitement for kids.

Looking at the worldwide scenario, it is evident that rapidly increasing buying power and investment demands coming from the Middle East, the Balkans and Western European countries in conjunction with the increasing number of retail chain stores in Turkey has increased the market share of fast-moving consumer goods. The resultant increase in the number of local and international retail chains and the investments of these channels contribute in a big way to improving the quality and the competition in the FMCG sector. However, international companies eager to make headway into countries like Turkey have to deal with a lack of understanding on the part of the consumer regarding the concept of intellectual property rights, which needs to be addressed to the Turkish audience in great detail.

The licensing of entertainment and fashion properties is also growing in Turkey. The extensive use of communication devices such as TV and handheld electronic devices is definitely making people, including kids, more involved with the world's culture. Turkish kids are also watching Sponge Bob Square Pants when they wake up in the morning, and little girls dream of being one of Disney's Fairies, or little boys want to have cars like the ones they see in Disney's movie, Cars. On the other hand, their parents are eager to buy the

New Balance sneakers that Steve Jobs used to wear, or they want to dress like their favorite celebrities who just walked the red carpet. Barbie, Disney Characters, Sponge Bob, Smurfs, Dora, Winnie the Pooh and Niloya are the most popular entertainment properties in Turkey. Adidas, Calvin Klein, Diesel, Lacoste, Levi's, Nike, Puma, Tommy Hilfiger and Zara are among the major fashion brands in the Turkish territory.

5.8.4 Turkish Properties

Until 2014, Turkey had never exported or become famous for its animations. Then "Niloya" happened. Niloya is a top-rated vibrant and upbeat TV series, aimed at girls and boys ages 3 to 8 years. Produced by Bee & Bird Animations, the series centers on Niloya, a little girl with a taste for adventure, and a cast of equally lovable characters such as Tospik, Mert, Murat and her family. It broadcasts on Yumurcak TV, one of the top two children's television stations in Turkey.

Title: Niloya
Production Year: 2013 – 2014
Duration: 5 minutes per episode
Number of Episodes Per Season: 26
Original Language: Turkish
Age Group: for 3 to 8 year olds
Genre: 3D Animation
Gender Orientation: Girls & Boys
Scripts: Turkish & English Scripts are available

Mavi Jeans is another well-known property originating from Turkey. Mavi Jeans is a brand of denim jeans founded in 1991, headquartered in Istanbul, Turkey. The company manufactures jeans for both women and men, targeting a younger age group. Mavi has flagship stores in New York, Vancouver, Istanbul, Berlin and Frankfurt. Another well know property from Turkey is Beko. Beko is a domestic appliance and consumer electronics brand of Arçelik A.Ş. controlled by Koç Holding. Beko is the official sponsor of the

Chapter 5: Greater Europe

Turkish, German, Italian and Lithuanian premier basketball leagues as well as Aris Salonika football team in Greece.

5.8.5 Conducting Business in Turkey

With its 79 million people, Turkey has a dynamic economy. With its privately-owned companies, the Turkish entrepreneurs try to reach to as many customers as possible not only in Turkey, but also in the world. Of course, when we talk about the licensors and licensees from this region, it will be helpful to analyze them with respect to the property types.

Property Type	Major Licensors
Paper Products, School Supplies	Niloya, Can
Character (Entertainment, TV, Movie)	Niloya, Can
Apparel	Benetton
Fashion	Mavi Jeans
Music	Serdar Ortaç
Non-profit (Museum, Charities)	Hagia Sophia
Sports (Leagues, Individuals)	Fenerbahçe, Beşiktaş, Galatasaray
Trademarks/Brands	LC Waikiki
Publishing	Kaynak Publishing Group

Property Type	Major Licensees
Paper Products, School Supplies	Alfa Stationery
Character (Entertainment, TV, Movie)	PAL Toys, Acun Media
Apparel	LC Waikiki
Fashion	Aydınlı
Home Decor	İstikbal Furniture
Food & Beverage	Ülker, Saray
Sports (Leagues, Individuals)	Neco Toys
Trademarks/Brands	Sentries, Aydınlı
Publishing	Zambak Publishing, Sürat Publishing, Timaş

The retail sector in Turkey is maintaining momentum thanks to increasing per capita disposable income, coupled with an ever-growing consumer appetite. The per capita disposable income of US$ 7,745 in 2012 is expected to exceed US $11,300 by 2017. Despite a weakening of the TL compared to major currencies in the last couple of years, robust consumer confidence promotes the overall activity in the sector. Still underpenetrated compared to developed countries, organized retailing in Turkey is developing at a fast pace thanks to nationwide shopping mall investments and the aggressive expansion strategies followed by retail groups. It is estimated that the share of organized retailers in the total retail market, which was around 30% ten years ago, exceeded 40% in 2012. [2]

The size of the licensing industry is about $278 million as of today. Just like in the United States or other major countries in the licensing industry, the licensed product sales for characters, entertainment, TV and the movie industry surpasses all other sales of licensed products. Respectively, Corp./Brands, Fashion and Sports sales follows in product sales.

---

[2] Deloitte Sales Report.
http://www.deloitte.com/assets/Dcom-Tukey/Local%20Assets/Documents/Retail_Sector_Update_2013.pdf

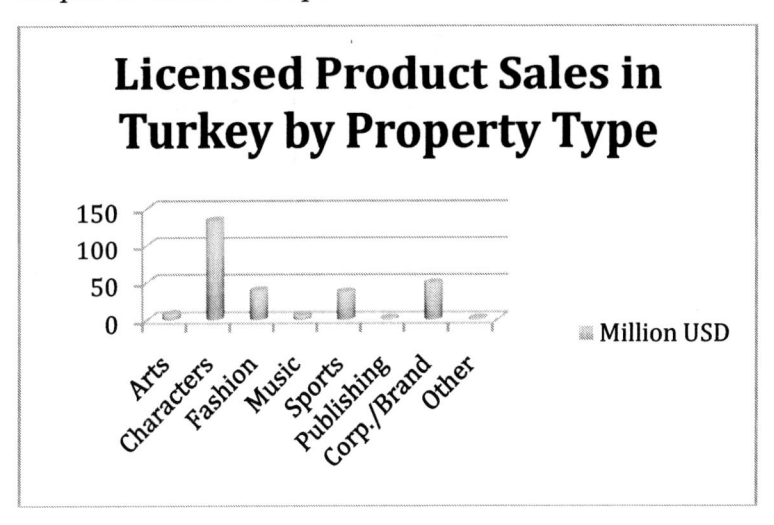

Licensed Product Sales in Turkey by Property Type

[Bar chart showing values in Million USD for categories: Arts, Characters, Fashion, Music, Sports, Publishing, Corp./Brand, Other. Characters is the largest bar reaching approximately 150 million USD.]

In Turkey, the negotiation process may take longer than usual. Turkish business people do not like to be put under pressure and do not like deadlines. Therefore, any attempt to hurry the process will only produce negative results. Being patient is an asset when negotiating with Turkish counterparts. In addition, the financial benefits are not the only aspects of the negotiating process that should be stressed; power, influence, honor, respect are non-financial incentives that will also influence the business decision in Turkey. There are still many family run businesses in Turkey, although there are many big multinationals where a more corporate culture is visible. Turks want to do business with those they trust, feel comfortable with and those who can provide a long-term relationship.

Turkish business people believe that the principal strength of an agreement is in the partners' commitment rather than the actual documentation. Nevertheless, the agreement may be lengthy and detailed. It is recommended to have a local legal expert review the agreement before the actual signing of the contract. However, it is not recommended to bring your legal representative to the negotiation table, as it could be taken as a sign of distrust.

The sheer number of properties coming into the market means it's more difficult to cut through them. The fierce competition in the market is one of the biggest challenges for a licensing professional. Even though it is getting better every year, the battle with counterfeit products is still an issue in Turkey. Therefore, a licensing professional will have to deal with the loss of some royalty income.

The role of local agents, consultants and manufacturer reps varies, but the main role should be having close relationships with the licensor and licensee so that the collaboration process goes smoothly. I would say the best practices for marketing, advertising and promoting licensed products at the local level depends on the property. Marketing is about story telling. If your brand has interesting history and rich heritage, exploit them to the fullest, and present them to your licensee prospects. This tactic is something that you probably do not need to follow when dealing with licensees in your home country where brand awareness is high. But it pays dividends when you do so with your Turkish licensee prospects.

5.8.6 Outlook, Projections and Conclusion

Istanbul has shown consistent growth over the past years in a world in which many economies are shrinking; it is rapidly changing from an emerging city to a world-class economic force in the region, and it represents a preferred touristic destination for many affluent people from various cultures and religions. One of the reasons for partnerships with Turkish companies is the commercial success of the international brands. Turkey is a rising economic giant in this region and Istanbul has the potential to open Turkey to the world. The Turkish licensing industry can handle global icons successfully.

Today, licensing is a relatively new concept in Turkey and is at a nascent stage. While licensing figures are small compared to other international markets, Turkey is fast establishing itself as a strong potential market in the future world of licensing. Brand extensions are flourishing for a number of reasons. More and more companies today realize that one of their most valuable assets is their brand and not just their technology or other tangible assets. A strong brand commands loyalty, positive emotions, preference and associative powers, which are hard to duplicate. The brand is the unique selling point for many products today. Also, in the much cluttered marketplace, where it is very expensive and time-consuming to get brand recognition and brand affinity, many companies choose brand extension licensing to launch new products by leveraging the power of existing strong brands.

Many consumer products marketers believe that the brand has become more important than ever before and many times, the only differentiator in certain product categories. Brands with strong consumer recognition, relevance and loyalty have been successfully extended into new product categories. In fact, for years, brand extension licensing has been used as a strategy to generate revenues. But today, the scenario is changing, with more focus on other benefits that a carefully crafted licensing program can deliver, apart from just royalty revenues.

The next big leap in marketing strategies is brand extensions which are seen as an excellent strategy to enhance and reinforce existing brand equity. Typically, a licensee benefits from the popularity of a particular brand. However, there is also a reciprocal benefit that the licensor receives from the advertising and promotional support by the licensees. Licensing revenues can soon become the most profitable revenues of the company. Because the investment in building the brand has already occurred, there are few additional costs associated with putting forth a licensing program. As a result, a high percentage of revenue is pure profit. [3] Over the last few years, we have seen a lot of change in the Turkish licensing industry. Turkey, once a closed market, now has numerous international and local brands to choose from. Furthermore, licensing is no longer limited to character licensing in Turkey. The licensing industry in Turkey has gained substantial momentum now. The licensors, for sure, stand to gain the maximum, but this has also opened doors for others in the value chain, like independent licensing agents, retailers, advertisers and consumer products manufacturers and distributors.

---

[3] http://www.bradfordlicenseindia.com/gather-experts.php

Chapter 6
Middle East and North Africa (MENA)

6.1 Introduction to Licensing in MENA

by Hussein Ftouni

The MENA region includes the countries of Saudi Arabia, United Arab Emirates, Kuwait, Lebanon, Egypt, Bahrain, Qatar, Oman, Jordan, Syria, Yemen, Morocco, Tunisia, Algeria. MENA has a combined population of 350 Million, 60% of whom are below 16 years old, and share one language (Arabic) and culture.

Licensing Agents. Licensing in the Middle East started with Disney opening its offices in Jeddah, Saudi Arabia in 1993 and in Dubai in 1994. Disney is the biggest licensor in the Middle Eastern region by far due to its coverage of almost all product categories in addition to retail and live events. Disney was followed by Mattel in 1998 which set up office in the Netherlands. Warner Bros. made several attempts to establish their own office in the MENA region but ended up working with a licensing agent for a couple of years. Warner Bros. continued to license in the region through their London office, until 2012 when they appointed a licensing agent based in Dubai. Sanrio also started licensing in the Middle East through a licensing agent in 2006, but then opened their own office in Dubai in 2010. Last but not least, Turner also started their licensing in the region back in 2008 through their London office but then opened their own office in Dubai in 2011. Hasbro, Sony, Paramount, Fox, Nickelodeon, HIT Entertainment, Saban, WWE, Aardman, Nike (FC Barcelona, Manchester United), and the NBA are all represented through licensing agents (MENA has only four licensing agents) whom are all based in Dubai.

Licensed Product Categories. Licensed product categories include: publishing, apparel & accessories, school bags, stationery, toys, wheeled toys and sports items, bed linens, fragrance & toiletries, tableware, partyware, food & drinks, confectionery, and promotions. The concentration of licensed categories in the region is around publishing, apparel and back-to-school. In fact, almost every property/brand represented in the MENA region covers these main categories; printed and 2D products are very common in the Middle East, whereas 3D products are still a challenge for licensees in this area.

Licensing Modules. There are almost all types of licensing modules in the Middle East and they are as follows:
- Manufacturing License
- Distribution License and also called Distribution Permission (DP)
- Direct-To-Retail (DTR)
- Promotion License (Food and Drinks)
- Retail License (Flagship stores as it is the case with Sanrio, Ferrari Store and Maserati Corner)
- Location Based (Lamborghini Cafe, Paramount Hotel and Resort, Trump Hotel, Armani Hotel, Fendi and Versace Residences)
- Theme Parks (Marvel, Nickelodeon, Turner, Lego)
- Live Events (Sanrio, Turner, HIT entertainment, Disney, Marvel)

Licensing Segments. Basically, licensing in the Middle East is concentrated around the character and entertainment segments. Sports licensing is relatively new (FCB, MU, AC Milan, NBA, Moto GP, Ferrari) but is increasing due to the increased popularity of sport in general and of football in particular. Music licensing is relatively new, and Live Nation Merchandise has just appointed a licensing agent in the region. This segment is expected to grow dramatically due to the increased music events and concerts in the UAE (Dubai

Chapter 6: Middle East and North Africa (MENA)

and Abu Dhabi) and due to the increased demand for music merchandise among tweens and teens (i.e., One Direction) in addition to the adult fans for iconic music bands (Live Nation). The licensing of classics, legends and celebrities (The Godfather, Scarface, Ali, Marilyn Monroe) is also growing due to the increasing demand from adult fans and young adults for retro and vintage brands. Charity licensing is well-represented by the organization Whatever It Takes, whereby celebrities donate their artwork to the charity organization and all licensing proceeds go to charity. Already a line of fragrances featuring artwork from George Clooney, Daniel Craig and Lucy Lu has been launched worldwide, and what is remarkable is that this license originated from a Dubai-based company. Mobile Apps, Games and YouTube sensations have also grown quickly during the last three years with Angry Birds leading the trend followed by Moshi Monsters, Trash Pack, Doodle Jump and Talking Friends. Fashion and lifestyle brands are growing slowly (Paris Hilton, Smiley). Brands (Conglomerate, Universities and Automotive) and art brands are almost nil in the region due to lack of awareness as they are culturally not recognized. In a nutshell, character and entertainment properties which are primarily on TV and periodically in theaters (Spiderman, Ironman, Hulk, Transformers, Disney's Pixar movies, etc.) have the lion's share of Middle Eastern licensing due to the wide exposure of TV broadcast and high admission for theaters. However, there are a number of properties that are not aired on TV across the Middle East that have zero awareness despite their high viewing rates in the US and/or Europe.

Licensing Challenges. The following are some of the challenges that lie ahead with regard to licensing in MENA:
- Restrictions --Saudi Arabia and to some extent other Gulf countries prohibit products that feature any symbols which are considered to be offensive to the Islamic religion and culture i.e., skull, angel, nudity, offensive phrases.
- DTR module is yet to be fully exploited as most retailers avoid entering into licensing agreements i.e.,

Basics of Licensing: International Edition

long form agreements, MG, advances, product development and royalty reporting.
- Middle Eastern fashion franchisees are bound to the collections and licenses which the franchisors have to offer and have no power/possibility to take on local licenses.
- Home-grown fashion retailers are still in their infancy stages, and their store numbers are not enough for them to sustain the investment in licenses and product development except for one or two retailers who operate 100+ stores across the MENA region.
- Food and drinks (dairy products and beverages) would go only for the strongest brands (Disney, Marvel, Hello Kitty, Barbie) as they have a track record from past licensees/competitors.
- FMCG manufacturers are reluctant to risk and invest in any new, untested property/brands.
- FMCG manufacturers lack education on licensing and how it could benefit them.
- There is no proper platform or licensing exhibition that could put licensors and prospective licensees into one place for networking and marketing.
- There is no proper platform in place to educate prospective licensees, retailers and promotional partners on the fundamentals and basics of licensing. Unfortunately, manufacturers, retailers and promotional partners in the region are not aware and/or do not attend international licensing shows in London and/or Vegas in order to review new properties/brands and what could be coming to the Middle East. Instead, most wait until the products of that specific property/brand fly off the shelves and then go after it, but in most cases someone else already has the license.

Chapter 6: Middle East and North Africa (MENA)

6.2   MENA

by Christian Zeidler

6.2.1   Introduction

Geographically speaking, the Middle East encompasses a variety of countries, nationalities, languages, and cultures. Definitions may vary but most commonly the Middle Eastern region is defined as the 'GCC' (the so-called Gulf Cooperation Council which is also known as the Cooperation Council for the Arab States of the Gulf) which in itself is a political and economic union of Arab states. The six state members of the GCC are Bahrain, Oman, Kuwait, Qatar, Saudi Arabia and the United Arab Emirates (UAE). At its core, this particular cooperation of states aims to unify economic agreements between the six countries by simplifying trade and other related topics but also by encouraging growth of scientific and technical progress across various industries. Over 40 million people live inside the GCC, led by Arabs as the largest ethnic group. Arabic is the most widely spoken language. However, neighboring countries such as Yemen, Lebanon, Syria, Jordan, Iraq and even Egypt are also often defined as being part of the Middle East. Countries such as Iran, Israel, Palestine, Cyprus and Turkey may be close in proximity but have very little in common with the average, (stereo)typical Middle Eastern nation. This also holds true for the consumer, retailer, and licensing industry in general.

In most businesses, when defining clusters, regions and territories in order to assign management responsibilities, the Middle East most commonly contains the above mentioned six GCC states as well as Lebanon, Syria, Jordan, Iraq and Egypt. This is due to their cultural vicinity of sharing the same or similar language, religion, and traditions. Iran, Israel and Turkey, on the other hand, are often managed in a completely different way and by a different team. Cyprus usually is assigned to the managers that handle Greece which means that it is handled by the European management division.

North Africa on the other hand is, geopolitically speaking, slightly easier to outline than the Middle East. The countries of definition are Algeria, Libya, Morocco, Sudan, Tunisia, Western Sahara and Egypt. The latter, of course, as mentioned before, are often assigned to the Middle East. They all share the same official language of Arabic which, in some cases, is being complemented by Berber and English. Of course, the French language is being widely spoken too, and the cultural impact of France across North Africa is not to be dismissed. Over 200 million people reside in the Northern African states. Other parts of Africa are virtually untouched by the licensing industry due to incomplete retail landscapes, political discord or simply economic disharmony.

Almost always, multi-national companies let their teams situated in Western Europe or Turkey handle both the Middle East and North Africa (collectively known as MENA). These teams are usually part of the Europe, Middle East and Africa (EMEA) cluster. However, in recent years, a few licensors have either started looking at local representation through licensing agencies situated in North Africa or the Middle East while other IP owners have or are considering opening up a sales office themselves.

For purpose of maximizing our efforts to understand the MENA region better, we will exclude the following countries in our definition of the Middle East and North Africa: Israel, Palestine, Cyprus, Turkey and Iran. These countries deserve a chapter by themselves to even remotely capture the state of licensing.

6.2.2 History of Licensing

Currently the regional licensing industry is being dominated by character and entertainment licensing as well as fashion and corporate trademark licensing. Sports and art licensing is insignificant in numbers as of now.

Fashion licensing (alongside restaurant franchising) was among the first business models to establish itself over the last years and decades. In fact, there are many shopping malls across the MENA region that are dominated by international, often US or European brands. Today, a shopping center like the Mall of Arabia in Cairo, Egypt may remind the visitor more of a US mall than anything else. International fashion

Chapter 6: Middle East and North Africa (MENA)

and restaurant franchises can be found aplenty, and the cinemas, too, show the latest Hollywood blockbusters. A day in a Middle Eastern mall can easily be spent buying the latest Tommy Hilfiger apparel collection, checking emails on Apple iPads using "free wifi" over a coffee in Starbucks before continuing to dine in one of the many Applebee's restaurants.

The character and entertainment industry developed more slowly over recent years but can now look at a reasonably successful positioning. One of the first brand owners from the character and entertainment sector to take a serious look at the MENA region was the Walt Disney Company a couple of decades ago. Before Disney entered the market, the consumer was faced with two choices: they could either buy a fake, pirated Disney product or a highly over-priced, actual licensed product brought into the country through parallel importing. It took many years before both retailers and consumers understood and acknowledged the benefits of authentic, licensed product. The Walt Disney Company was crucial in establishing a somewhat properly functioning licensing industry in the region, allowing other licensors to follow. In 2007, MTV Networks International launched, in collaboration with AMG, two free-to-air channels tailored to the MENA region, i.e. MTV Arabia (now MTV Middle East) and Nickelodeon Arabia. Their licensing department was established at the same time. However, only four years later, Nickelodeon Arabia went on a hiatus, and its content can currently be watched on regional channels such as MBC3. A few years later, in 2010, Turner Broadcasting Systems Arabia launched their very own free-to-air channel, an Arabic language version of Cartoon Network, again, with a local licensing bureau attached to its operation.

Other major licensors are either currently being represented by licensing agencies which established themselves mainly in the UAE, Jordan, and Morocco. Alternatively, IP owners are doing direct business, managed remotely from outside the region. Other licensors are rumored to be opening representational sales offices in the Middle East in 2014/15.

6.2.3 Licensing Today

Doing business across the MENA region has its challenges. Political turmoil, fragmentation, incomplete trade agreements and, despite the media's popular depiction of many of these oil-rich states, disposable income is, as a general rule, on the lower side. Piracy is a big issue in many countries as are parallel imports of licensed goods. The status of retail infrastructure varies from non-existing to best-in-class. Cities such as Sana'a in Yemen will have very little organized trade whereas, not too far away, the cities of the UAE boast some of the world's most attractive retail outlets and consumer shopping experiences.

For hundreds of years, the regional retail landscape was defined by the so-called souk (or souq). Initially an open-air marketplace which offered its visitors a variety of products and produce including food, herbs, spices, clothes, carpets and even jewelry and gold, it has over the years evolved. The modern souks now may also sell computers, phones, toys, electronics and other gadgets. In most countries across the region, souks still play an important part of everyday life. Many consumers enjoy the vibrant feel of going to a souk, appreciate a bit of small-talk, as well as being able to negotiate the product price with the vendors. Currently the largest mall in the world, the Dubai Mall in the United Arab Emirates, has managed to cleverly combine the past with a modern approach by building a deluxe gold and diamond souk inside the mall offering mostly lavishly expensive and luxurious items.

So why are many companies considering the Middle East a growing market? Or at the very least, as an attractive location to invest in for future business? The most attractive value the MENA region has to offer to international investors is its large population of children and young adults as potential consumers. Over 135 million people between the ages of 0-14 inhabit the region. Paired with a relatively high international brand affinity and awareness, and, in some cases, matured retail landscapes, the Middle East and North Africa allows for decent product placement. Even though US entertainment brands, TV shows, apps, games and films are some-

Chapter 6: Middle East and North Africa (MENA)

times being criticized for not necessarily fitting into the Middle Eastern and North African cultural framework, retailers and licensees are likely to consider US entertainment properties nevertheless.

When it comes to children's television, there are a few channels worth mentioning which are free-to-air. MBC3, Cartoon Network Arabic, Spacetoon and the Qatar-based Baraem TV and Jeem TV are often considered the leading channels across the region. These channels all show international and regional shows in Arabic language. These channels have a big impact on the local licensing industry. Disney content can be found on regional channels such as the above-mentioned Jeem TV and Baraem TV, or the viewer may tune into a full Disney channel on a Pay TV platform such as OSN.

Most often, the leading, most popular brands of the character and entertainment industry are "classic" brands such as Nickelodeon's SpongeBob and Dora the Explorer, Sanrio's Hello Kitty, Disney's Cars and Princess, alongside Mattel's Barbie and IMPS's The Smurfs. The Smurfs have successfully grown into one of the best-selling brands of the MENA region, since the Sony Pictures movie release in 2011. Marvel's Iron Man and Spiderman franchises have also had some impressive success stories to tell over the last few years. Hasbro's recent appointment of a local agency in 2013 has had positive effects on developing properties such as Transformers, My Little Pony and Monopoly, and the brands are successfully increasing their market share.

Generally speaking though, the region's licensing industry seems to be more interested in classic, ever-green and unwilling risk investment in new brands. Perhaps the strongest "new" brands that entered the market in the last few years with good results are Rovio's Angry Birds and MGA's Lalaloopsy. Cartoon Network's relatively new shows such as Adventure Time or The Amazing World of Gumball have yet to establish themselves as successful licensing programs; due to the shows' unique, slightly off-beat and edgy humor which does not sit easily with the often more conservative buying departments of regional retailers and the risk-averse licensees and distributors. The positioning of these types of brands may

Basics of Licensing: International Edition

take longer than say in the US, where Adventure Time turned out to be a big hit.

Recently some regional character brands have managed to develop into attractive licensing opportunities. Possibly the most famous Middle Eastern character was created by the Emirati Mohammed Saeed Harib who invented the computer animated, three-dimensional cartoon show called "Freej". The show, revolving around four old Emirati women, has had noticeable licensing success, especially in the UAE. It is often being referred to as the Middle East's most successful attempt at creating a regional property from a content and merchandising point of view. Ben & Izzy is another animation series created by Rubicon, an interactive multimedia company based in Amman, Jordan which combined 2D and 3D animation to tell the story of two adventurous kids. The show aired in 2008.

Dr. Naif Al-Mutawa, founder and CEO of the Teshkeel Media Group, created the region's first commercially viable superheroes based on Islamic culture and society called THE 99. Initially a comic book series, the concept worked well, and one of the highlights has been the crossover issues with DC Comics which saw THE 99 fighting evil side-by-side with the likes of Batman and Superman.

A recent, yet successful introduction to the regional animation and licensing landscape has been the popular cartoon Mansour, aimed at 6 to 11 year olds and currently airing on Cartoon Network Arabic. The show was launched on television in 2012, with the creator, Rashed Al Harmoodi, taking a fresh approach to regional animation efforts, marrying situational comedy with action-adventure, while at the same time educating the region's youth on priority issues such as diabetes, obesity, and the importance of Arabic traditions and values. The show revolves around the Emirati main character Mansour and his friends and has been very popular since its launch, and is certainly one to watch. Mansour is supported by Abu Dhabi's Mubadala Development

Chapter 6: Middle East and North Africa (MENA)

Company as part of its commitment to community and social development.

Licensees with an established, regional production facility are a rare find. In fact, besides the food and beverage industry, manufacturing of product is often done in Asia. The services provided by non-food licensees are therefore limited to designing, conceptualizing, and offering logistical services. However, the food and beverage industry has an established footprint. Besides the penetration of international FMCG companies such as Nestle, Mondelez, Pepsico or Mars, regional players are strongly represented, not seldom outshining the international competition in terms of reach and presence. Some big companies to take note of are Almarai, IFFCO, The Savola Group, Americana Group, National Agriculture Development, Cairo Poultry, or Agthia Group to name but a few. The annual Gulfood exhibition which is being hosted in Dubai, UAE is among the largest food expos in the world.

The retail landscape, as previously mentioned, varies from "fully developed" to "hardly existing". Broadly speaking, the retail clusters can be divided into the following:

- Retailer hubs located in the UAE or Saudi Arabia
- Individual retailers located in the Levant area
- North Africa with an often independent network of retailers

The reason many companies inside or related to the licensing industry have positioned their regional head-office in the UAE is because a few large retailers have established not only their central purchasing and marketing teams in Dubai or Abu Dhabi, but in addition a central warehousing unit as well. Some prominent international and regional hyper- and supermarket chains that can be found across the region are Carrefour, Spinneys, Lulu, Waitrose, Hyperpanda, and Géant. Important for the character and entertainment industry are the mostly international specialized retailers and department stores, e.g., Toys R Us, Hamleys, The Entertainer, Hallmark, Debenhams, Galleries Lafayette, and one of the largest

Basics of Licensing: International Edition

groups in the region which is Landmark Group. A very successful local shopping concept that has now even managed to open its first retail outlet in London, is The Toy Store, owned and operated by Gulf Greetings General Trading which also runs the regional franchise for Hallmark. The Toy Store has been active for over 30 years in the Middle East and North Africa and is now considered one of the leading retailers of the region, focusing on kids and family-oriented merchandise.

Unfortunately, having a popular international brand in-hand and a functioning network of distributors and retailers does not guarantee a success in this region. Entertainment One's Peppa Pig, currently a "hot property" in many countries around the world, will have very little chance of entering the market. This is due to cultural and religious norms and the attached stigma attached to the animal. The previously-mentioned Angry Birds franchise did and still does well; however, not in all locations -- on many shelves across the region, the villainous pigs are either not to be found or their visibility has been reduced dramatically. Generally speaking though, the acceptance of global and/or US-based entertainment brands across the region is high. If a little too much "skin" is shown, even if we are talking about a female cartoon character or a toy like Mattel's Barbie, a retailer may be asked by official authorities to remove the offending product from the shelves. This is particularly true for the slightly more traditional countries such as Saudi Arabia, Iraq or Kuwait.

For IP owners who want to fast-track their regional footprint but have not yet looked at opening up a subsidiary inside the region, the best way forward is to use one of the few licensing agencies. This includes some of the independents, namely, 20too – The Premium Licensing Specialist, SEENA, or the Dubai-based Copyright Licensing Agency, or agencies that are part of a media conglomerate, such as MBC3, East West Licensing, and JCC TV.

6.2.4 Outlook, Projections and Conclusions

For the future, the licensing industry of the Middle East will see an increase in entertainment brands penetrate the

Chapter 6: Middle East and North Africa (MENA)

market. As the fashion and the character licensing business slowly edges towards maturity which, of course, will take several years for some countries and even longer for others, the remaining licensing categories, e.g. sports, art, corporate, will become more important. In particular, the sports licensing industry is not even close to exploiting the region's potential, and we are likely to see an increase in this particular category over the next years. Regional character development will increase partly because some previous efforts have been successful (i.e., Freej, Mansour) and partly because large media corporations such as Turner Broadcasting are taking a closer look at developing regional content that reflects the local cultural values but is suitable for an international audience. As evidence of this, the Cartoon Network Studios Arabia in Abu Dhabi, UAE, is doing just that.

Chapter 7

India

7.1 Introduction

by Rohit Sobti

In India, licensing is a marriage not a date. In order to discuss India, it is important to understand that due to the many languages, belief systems and lifestyles, India is really a composite of many different cultures. The country made great strides in raising the literacy level, which in 1947 was only 12%, and today has increased to 74 %. 64% of the population is between the ages of 15-59 years (source MGI Report) and over the last-five years, the country's GDP growth has maintained a consistent growth of 8%.

India obtained its independence about 67 years ago, doing so with a fairly corrupt bureaucracy and democratic system. The liberalization of the Indian economy in 1991 marked the beginning of a new era of growth for the country. The unprecedented economic reforms that were initiated, coupled with favorable demographics, have given birth to a phenomenon within India — the middle-class. According to the Mickensy Global Institute Report, it is predicted that there will be less than 22% of the population by 2025 with income under USD $2000 a year, compared with 54% in 2005.

Until 1991 it was not easy to do business in India, as the country lacked the necessary basic infrastructure. In 1991, Indian Parliament began the process of opening up the economy to churn growth. An important factor was the introduction of computers in to the country, which had a profound and positive effect. By the end of 2013, there were an estimated 865 million mobile phones in the country, which means that about 69% of the population had mobile phones (Source: Market Simplified). Today, there are approximately 180 million Internet connections in the country, which is expected to increase to 443 million by the year 2016 (Source: KPMG

2012 FICCI Report). With the roll-out of 4G mobile service at the end of 2014, the mobile phone market is likely to grow even more quickly than it has in the past.

31% of India's 1.24 billion population live in urban cities, while 69% still reside in villages. The significant growth of India's wealthy population is driving growth in the country, including improvements to the country's infrastructure, transportation (air, rail and road) and greater availability of technology such as access to television, mobile phone and Internet services. (Source – Nationmaster.com). In the last ten years, states like Gujarat, Punjab, Rajasthan and Kerala have shown tremendous infrastructure growth, especially Gujarat which has been dubbed "India's China" due to the significant growth of manufacturing in this region.

The licensing business is relatively new to India, as is only started about ten years ago due in part to the growth of retail within the country. Disney is the dominant licensor in the country, commencing its India licensing operation about seven years back with the licensing of Mickey Mouse and Friends, POOH, Disney Princesses and in the recent years – Cars. Disney's recent acquisition of Marvel has increased Disney's share of the market, as Indians love Marvel characters.

Character licensing is the most popular form of licensing given the success not only of Disney characters, but properties such as Ben 10, Doremon, Power Rangers, Beyblade and Barbie. The market has also produced two successful homegrown properties, Chhota Bheem, a children's property, and Being Human, a (celebrity brand developed by actor Salman Khan, who donates earnings from the property to charity).

In the last-three years, there has been an emergence of Offline Retail Brands such as Stop by Shoppers Stop and Many Brands of Future Retail, growth of E-commerce brands like Free Cultur and New brands by Myntra.com and the first of its kind cinema inspired fashion brand -- Diva'ni jointly created by Yash Raj Films (YRF) and the fashion house, KBSH. The licensing of Bollywood films has also made great progress. As example, the recent licensing effort by YRF for its movie Dhoom 3 created the most significant licensing programme to date for any Bollywood film. Those companies

Chapter 7: India

obtaining Dhoom 3 licensing rights included Mattel, Pepsi, Ceat, Gulf, ICE-X, Krish 3 and Celebrity Brand 'Hrx from actor Hritik Roshan.

The growth of licensing in the Indian market is proof that the country has an appetite for licensed brands, especially those that evolve from television (MTV and Star Plus), films (Dhoom 3, DDLJ, YRF), events (Sunburn), sports (IPL – Cricket League) and celebrities(HRX, Being Human). In a few years it is likely that the list will also include other categories such as gaming, and corporate brands. In the retail sector, offline retail and E–commerce will play a significant role as major retail outlets for sales of licensed products.

The growth of the licensing industry is intrinsically tied to the state of retail, which is the core delivery mechanism for licensed products. As organized retail is at a nascent stage, given that it accounts for less than five percent of country's contribution to total sales, the best is yet to come. Deregulation in retail is almost certain to have a profound effect on providing the impetus for licensing to grow. Currently, the mindset of the offline retail is not licensing-friendly, which means that licensing in India will likely bypass offline retail and will break through to e-commerce. Recently, Walmart announced that in India its strategy will be to establish an online presence first followed by an offline initiative.

India is the fastest growing E-commerce market in the world experiencing a year on year growth of 70%. In the publishing category the biggest online E-retailer, Flipkart.com, accounts for approximately 30% of all book sales in India. What is interesting to note is that the categories of electronics and fashion apparel have had a positive impact on offline retail business, as approximately 28% have visited the offline store after visiting the online store. The Big Four companies of Indian E-Commerce are Flipkart.com (the biggest company, which has crossed USD $1 billion in sales), Myntra.com (largest fashion label brands – USP in creating new brands), Jabong and Snapdeal. Due to cash rich tier 2 and tier 3 cities and low credit card penetration (20 million) e-commerce companies have devised a Cash-On-Delivery model (COD) through which a customer can order the goods without making payment at the time of transaction, and so only upon receipt of the purchase. The COD model is encouraging consumers to buy, as it eradicates the fear of paying for goods that are not delivered and encashing on cash in hand. More than 50% of E-commerce business is generated from Tier 2 and Tier 3 cities, with approximately 20% of the mobile e-commerce transactions coming from Tier 3 cities. This is due in part to the lack of infrastructure and organized retail in Tier 2 & 3 cities where consumers are very aspirational and with a desire to own and wear to branded products. With the emergence of 3-D printers this business is likely to grow as supplier will not have to produce MOQ for the launch of new E-commerce products.

To be a success in India you need to have faith and marry the county, not date it. The success of McDonald's in India is an excellent example. The company invested a significant amount in an effort to understand the Indian consumer, paying close attention to such elements as convenience, reach, price sensitivity, and constant innovation to "Indianize" the experience and keep it aspirational. International licensing companies need to gain understanding of the local market, which is very diverse, and realize that the first couple years will be spent in learning about their target audience. As India is a diverse and developing market, being flexible in structuring licensing agreements is a necessity. Above all, being committed to India will likely bring success in licensing!

Chapter 7: India

7.2 India

by Gaurav Marya

7.2.1 Introduction

Licensing in India all started in the open market with independent vendors on the side of the road selling products to consumers. This practice later evolved to produce small stores dedicated to selling licensed merchandise. Currently, the licensing market in India is experiencing a revolution in terms of organization. According to a recent study by Booz & Co and RAI, the overall retail sector in India will grow at a rate of nine percent during the time period of 2012-2016. The Indian retail market, which stands at $455 billion, is currently dominated by independent disorganized entities, but with more and more organization, and stronger business plans, these numbers will expand at a faster rate. The organized retail sector will see a growth of 24 percent, three times faster than that of traditional retail. This organized segment currently accounts for eight percent of the overall retail market in India.

The current market scenario will see an even more accelerated growth as Indian retailers begin to invest strongly in technology and trained manpower, which will in turn create a stronger customer experience. Currently, the Indian retail and logistics industry employs more than 35 million Indians, nearly three percent of the population. Since November 2011, the market has only seen upsurge, as the Indian government announced various retail formats including multi-brand stores and single-brand stores. While early 2012 saw a 100 percent increase in foreign direct investment (FDI) in single brand retailing, the government also announced a 51 percent increase in FDI in multi-brand retailing, opening avenues for global players like Walmart, Carrefour, Decathlon, IKEA, H&M, Fossil and others. Though there are still some glitches in the government reform, including a 30 percent sourcing clause, which states that at least 30 per cent of the value of procurement of manufactured/processed products shall be sourced from Indian small industries, the market already sees setting up of Decathlon's first store in India along with IKEA opening soon.

The Indian retail market, which began with small moveable shops, now has more than 15 million stores across the country. In fact, many more will have been added by the time you read this. Though the store sizes vary from a small 100 sq ft to some 100,000 sq ft, only four percent of the total stores in India are larger than 500 sq ft.

The Indian retail industry is dominated by the food and grocery category with a 60 percent share followed by the apparel segment, which holds 11 percent of the market. The other industries that are the upcoming categories include jewelry, pharmacy, wellness and mobiles.

The Indian retail industry, which according to a report by Deloitte has seen a growth of 10.6 per cent between 2010 and 2012, is expected to increase to $750-850 billion by 2015. The report suggests that the Indian market will soon see FDI in specialty stores including consumer electronics, footwear, and furniture, as these categories expand and mature. However, the government's FDI policy on sourcing may cause a hindrance to growth of these segments.

On the other hand, though the unorganized sector will expand, flexible credit options and convenient shopping locations will help traditional retail continue its dominance. To conclude, the smaller cities will emerge as the new opportunity sector for retailers as they start facing stiff competition and saturation point in metros.

The coming of modern retail in India will be a boon for the licensing market which is still in its nascent stages and is waiting to spread its wings. The following sections will unveil how the industry has fared so far and what is the way forward.

7.2.2 History of Licensing

Globally, licensing has been a prominent strategy since the 1940s when Disney introduced various Mickey Mouse products including toys, books, apparel and others. In India, licensing took hold only recently with the advent of modern retail and organized markets. Licensing really began in India

Chapter 7: India

two decades ago when Indian conglomerates launched several international brands to the market through licensing deals. For instance, Arvind Brands introduced the properties of Wrangler, Arrow, Nautica, Jansport and others to India. Later, as more licensing deals were signed, other types of licensing started to enter the Indian industry, as the consumer matured and started to create connections with various properties.

India began a phase wherein retail was gaining its footing in the market with the evolution of companies like Ambanis and Biyanis, who introduced the concept of modern retail. The first type of licensing that took flight here was character licensing, which was strongly based on cartoons in the Indian market. Some of the big players that have made their mark in character licensing here include Walt Disney, Viacom, Bradford License India, Dream Theatre, AI Licensing, Green Gold Animation and Cartoon Network Enterprises. The Indian consumer is very familiar with cartoon characters, which appeal to all ages with everyone having his or her favorite. Many licensors cashed in on the connection for the Indian consumer, and it became easier for licensors to capture a gamut of consumers in one go.

The characters licensed by Walt Disney are evergreen. Children's characters like Mickey Mouse and Donald Duck are still popular. Viacom has brought in popular characters from Nickelodeon, like Dora the Explorer and SpongeBob SquarePants. Extend Brands represents classic characters like Popeye the Sailorman, Betty Boop and Baby Popeye.

7.2.3 Licensing Today

Licensing in India has come a long way in the past few years with the coming of new international intellectual properties and success stories of domestic properties. Still in its embryonic stage, the Indian licensing industry contributes only 1-1.25 percent of the global market size of $186 billion. There is still a long way to go with the retail industry getting organized and consumer demand rising. However, India remains a retailers' paradise, with more than a million of brand hungry consumers. As a country, we have only seen global brands entering and making their impact felt in the market. There still lies a dearth of successful home grown brands, a void which being filled in by licensing.

Licensing in the western regions of the world has come full cycle, and now it is time for India to take part in its licensing revolution. Efforts are being made, the results are showing and in the coming years, likely within five years, the percent of India's contribution to the global licensing market will rise

The market in India is currently led by various types of licensing including character, kids, sports, publishing, corporate, celebrity and brands. Although the Indian licensing market has been dominated by international IPs, various brands have also been designed and established in the country, including Chotta Bheem, Little Krishna, Being Human and others. These brands have written success stories in licensing and are some of the strongest contributors to the licensing industry in India.

Gone are the days when Indian consumers settled for one brand and were loyal to it for a lifetime. Consumers have changed; they want variety, a choice of products, and to experiment and then buy what they like the most. The typical Indian consumer is strongly influenced by various media including television, print and digital, of which social media is a strong influencer. Though still a price sensitive market, quality has become one of the important aspects while choosing a product.

When walking into a store, consumers want the full experience, which means every brand that is planning to set its foot in the market needs to work strongly to engage the consumer. Moreover, for brands, the potential target audience lies in kids and teenagers who are well aware of trends and what they want and who also have disposable incomes. A huge opportunity is seen especially in the entertainment segment as the market here is vibrant and easily captures the consuming class, which consumes the brands via television, theatricals and events.

Chapter 7: India

Popular Categories

The conventional product categories still hold the largest chunk of the industry. These categories include apparel, toys, footwear, books, FMCG, and accessories and form a strong connection with consumers. Even though the retail base is not as strong as it could be, brands in these categories are trying to reach the consumer through traditional retail channels. In order to penetrate in to cities beyond metros, licensees are also targeting the traditional retail formats for products categories like FMCG which have a better reach through these stores.

Children's and Corporate Licensing

Kids today are often considered to be the most intelligent consumers. They know more than their parents know, thanks to the exposure they have to technology, internet and television. In licensing to kids, broadcast plays the strongest role, and licensing of broadcast-related properties has gained obvious traction after character licensing became a hit, as the two are inter-connected. Today, Nickelodeon has introduced its new channel Nick Explore and is launching new Ninja Turtles programming which is expected to reach a large audience.

Another category that is growing prominence in the Indian market is corporate licensing. Pepsi and Oxford will be among the first companies with licensing programs in India. Oxford is already on the verge of closing its deal with one of the leading Indian retail conglomerates, while Pepsi is looking to enter the market with a range of apparels, mobiles and footwear.

The demand of character licensing in kid wear is growing with every passing year as the end users – the kids – are becoming more exposed to their favorite characters via different mediums like TV, smart phones, and tablets, which means they can now watch their characters anytime anywhere. At the same time, young parents, who understand which characters resonate with their children, often feel safe in buying them licensed merchandise and are of the general opinion that licensed merchandise represents higher quality goods. For these reasons, there is massive potential for growth in the licensing of kid wear. Fifty million homes spending over Rs 65 a month on branded products translates into merchandising grosses of Rs 25-30 billion a year.

The Stage of Experimentation

With the market maturing and consumers ready to splurge and explore, licensors and licensees are taking steps toward experimenting with new product categories. For instance, recently Disney ventured into the real estate arena as it tied up with Sunteck and Supertech to launch Disney-themed homes. What also is interesting is that product categories including condoms, lingerie and others are being explored. MTV, through Viacom, has launched these products to get to their target audience. i.e., the youth market.

The Role of Local Agents

India has its share of local agents, consultants and manufacturers that helps licensors to make an easy and smooth entry in to the market. These local players have expertise about the culture of the country, understand the legalities involved and are well-connected with the market. This in turn helps licensors to target their ideal consumer. Moreover, these agents also help in creating customer engagement programs that bring the customers closer to the brand. They also ensure that codes of conduct are in line, including maintaining transparency in audits, and ensuring that sales and accounting procedure are implemented and followed.

The growth of the licensing industry is directly connected with the growth of retail, which is the mechanism for delivering licensed products. With organized retail still in its nascent stages, the expansive growth will happen only when this segment expands. This can only be achieved only through deregulation.

Jiggy George, Founder and CEO of Dream Theatre Pvt Ltd, in one of his articles shared:

> A personal example from my journey into the business of brand licensing; while I was with

Chapter 7: India

Cartoon Network, I was offered the role of running the Cartoon Network licensing business and I set up and ran Cartoon Network Enterprises managing the gamut of brands on consumer products owned by Cartoon network and the Warner Bros. brands for promotional licensing. The big challenge then was retail being fragmented and even the major retailers did not have more than a few stores. So, we focused our energies on promotional licensing where FMCG brands leveraged the iconic brands like Tom and Jerry, Superman, and Batman on their consumer promotions. At that stage, the challenge was to educate clients on the value of an intellectual property and tackling ways to monetize the same. The usual refrain from big clients was "our brand reaches more people than yours: you should pay us and look at it as brand building."We thankfully transcended these discussions with partnering with a few majors like Britannia and Cadburys and their case studies and partnerships established that the model worked and licensees benefited by both the financial upside and the brand ruboff. My team launched Cartoon network Enterprises consumer products program and India was the pilot for the Global business and I was fortunate to be part of learning to set up processes and systems to operate a system that could technically transcend geographies and work in any market. The core team was responsible for launching the Power-Puff Girls .The brand had seen a decline globally on consumer products and the network worked zealously to resurrect the brand and we launched a successful consumer products programs. The other highs were launching the Pogo licensing program, launching Beyblade- the biggest selling licensed toys, the

Spiderman movie with Marvel and of course the launch of Ben 10 and MAD.[1]

The Law and Its Implementation

After looking at the growth opportunities in licensing, the Indian market still faces strong challenges with regard to counterfeiting and growing fake products in the market. Counterfeiting is a mother of all menaces which continues to offset the growth of the licensing industry in India. It has been observed that a lot of counterfeit products are available and sold in India even when the particular property is not available in the country or, if available, is not operational in that particular product category. It is a significant challenge that keeps on hitting licensees and licensors. Industry sources estimate that counterfeiting causes a loss of 20-30 percent of business annually. In India, property owners including Disney, Angry Birds, Chotta Bheem, Doreamon, Manchester United, Being Human and others are counterfeited. Of this, Doreamon, Disney and Angry Birds top the charts in product categories including apparel, back to school, footwear, toys and others.

Counterfeiting in India are occurs because of illegal imports, improper distribution networks calling for higher demands and lesser supply; price differentiation, distinct taxation and unorganized retail. The Indian legal system protects property owners from counterfeiting and trademark infringement, and has passed a number of laws to this effect, including:

- Trademarks Act 1999
- Copyright Act 1957
- Patents Act 1970
- Designs Act
- Customs Act 1962

Still a Learning Curve

Licensed brands are still evolving with time as consumers mature and acceptance grows. Some strong brands have had disappointing results, while others have written success

---

[1] http://rai.net.in/blog/?p=483

Chapter 7: India

stories. The key will always be in understanding the essence of your own brand and knowing your consumer. BHPC went wrong with translating its brand in the Indian market, but now with new strategies in place, the brand is likely to make its fresh entry again into the market. While on the other hand, Manchester United, which started off slow in the market, is doing well with consumers at retail with simple jerseys and also Manchester United Cafes where the consumer can connect with the game and the team.

7.2.4 Outlook and Conclusions

Licensing in India is coming across as the sunshine industry as various brands expand their product categories, keep in continuous communication with consumers and create stronger distribution systems. With organized retail taking centre stage for the retail industry as a whole, licensors are trying to explore every possible format for their products. With times changing, new kinds of licensing will gain momentum as new product categories are explored.

The Indian consumer has always been glued to what they are most comfortable with or to what they have known in their lifetime. But with changing times, needs, and approaches, these consumers have gained a new awareness and been transformed to become explorers. Everything that is new and unconventional attracts them. This has been best experienced in retail and licensing. In India, properties which are unconventional have been surprisingly well received and accepted. This phenomenon is best seen in the sports licensing arena. India, where Cricket is religion, has seen games like soccer, baseball, wrestling and others take center stage when it comes to licensing. For example, we have already seen Manchester United stores collaborate with Indus League Clothing, while Arsenal and Liverpool will soon make their entries. The NBA and WWF are other well-known properties in the country. Indian consumers find it more edgy to be associated with these sports; moreover, these brands are strong at customer engagement as well.

Retailers, in the coming years, have to work aggressively along with the brands in order to ensure that product is selling to the right consumer. Ideally, it will result in a back-and-forth relationship where the retailer can also help the brand with customer feedback. This would help both parties enhance product quality as well as add new products that consumers want.

As noted earlier, the market is heavily infected by counterfeits and fakes. What the licensing industry in India needs is to create stronger restrictions and checks on illegal imports, stronger distribution channels so that licensed merchandise reaches consumers before fakes do, stronger implementation of GST and also a more organized retail effort.

Chapter 8

Asia

8.1 Introduction to Asia

by Hubert Co

Licensing is an ever-growing business in Asia. The concept of licensing or intellectual property rights has spread out not only to licensees but to retailers, FMCG's and consumers as well. Being a licensing agent in Asia is tough, but also challenging and fulfilling. Unlike our western counterparts with a more structured pattern on licensed business practices and consumer preferences, our territory has unique traits all our own. Business decisions and consumer preferences are affected by geography, religion, culture, education, product and fashion preferences and many more.

In China, the licensing business is exciting and filled with opportunities. There are several factors that contribute in shaping the China licensing landscape. First is online marketing, which has become a channel for introducing and marketing products. Second the emerging power of the middle class that contributes hugely to the sales of consumer products, and third is the diversity of properties, both local and international. Not only are character brands making a mark in the licensing business in China, but lifestyle and fashion brands are becoming a trend as well. Direct-to-Retail chains are popping up everywhere. Co-branding with Chinese local brands is one opportunity that a lot of properties have started to explore.

Although opportunities may be big and great, it is still a challenge for many licensors in penetrating the market. While a business may have huge potential in terms of merchandising and promotional licensing, other aspects of the business such as a stand-alone store for example may be unsuccessful if you select a wrong business partner. For a time, franchised retail outlets for apparel and accessories were booming in China, so that licensors thought that their business was on the rise. It was, for a certain period of time, until store owners mishandled the business and thus, outlets have closed one by one. This is most probably because each franchisee did not share the brand's vision. It is very important for licensors to choose the right business partners who understand the brand and who help expand their business in China.

China is a huge territory for licensing, but not all cities even with significant populations (especially cities in Tiers 2 and 3) are contributing to the growth of the business. Only Tier 1 cities such as Beijing, Guangzhou and Shanghai are rapidly growing. Hong Kong and Taiwan are still Japanese-oriented, and Korean fashion is starting to grow by leaps and bounds. Hong Kong mall dress-up and character event activities are regular quarterly events in this gateway city to China.

The Philippines has the most matured licensing business among its Asian counterparts. There is a section inside many department stores called the "Character Shop" that sells purely licensed merchandise. Other licensed products can also be seen in various distribution channels such as direct-to-retail, multi-level marketing, FMCGs, QSRs, online marketing. Indonesia can be considered as the next Brazil with its huge population and manufacturing sector in apparel, plasticware, footwear, plush and many more. Singapore and Malaysia are not far behind. They are huge market potentials as is Thailand with many retailers and manufacturing capacity of its own.

Competition in the licensing industry is getting tougher and becoming more intense in this part of our world. Not only are character brands competing for lower minimum guarantees and retail space, but lifestyle, entertainment and even corporate trademarks and game applications such as Plants vs. Zombies and Fruit Ninja are also getting into the licensing business. Local properties in countries that are making a mark in their respective territories and abroad are also getting a share of the market, plus a licensing agent must also think out-of-the-box in order to stand out. A good example of this is the Mr Bean Coffee Shop in Shanghai and Bangkok which has made the property Mr Bean a lifestyle brand.

Chapter 8: Asia

The saturation of brands has an effect in negotiating for high amount of minimum guarantees. Licensors demand bigger amounts which for most licensees are hard to achieve. In retail, not all brands can easily get shelf space. Others will have to compete with bigger properties such as Disney and Hello Kitty which are getting a big chunk of the retail space inside the department stores. Visibility is key, retail promotions such as gift with purchase or purchase with purchase are just some ways to get the customers' attention. With the crowding of brands in department stores, each property must stand out or else, as retailers can easily remove those that are not meeting the sales quota.

Fighting infringements and counterfeit merchandise is also a tough problem to deal with in Asian territories. Educating both the retailers and consumers to buy only licensed merchandise is one way of minimizing infringement activities and achieving the goal. Providing licensed merchandise that consumers can afford could help, too. However, with the growing economy and business conditions in Asia, it is undeniable that the licensing industry will be experiencing growth in the coming years.

8.2   Japan

by Roger Berman

8.2.1   Introduction

Superficially, the Japanese retail and licensing market seems to be paradoxical. On the one hand, Japan is one of the world's largest economies, especially in the retailing and licensing sectors, yet on the other hand, there are many big name cases of failed market entry in retail and, to a lesser extent in licensing. In retailing, some of the biggest international players entered Japan to great fanfare, only to close their operations later. Be it Boots the UK drug store chain, Sephora the international cosmetics chain owned by French luxury conglomerate LVMH, or Carrefour the multinational hypermarket chain, the world's fourth largest by revenue, all closed shop for a gamut of reasons. The explanations are various—lack of preparation, too short-a-commitment, entrenched domestic competition, lack of flexibility to adapt to local market needs, inability to meet the exacting demands of the Japanese consumer—the causes are all classic MBA course fodder. The lack of success for non-Japanese licensing properties mirrors some of the reasons affecting the failed retailers. Several major Hollywood entertainment properties struggled in trying to prosper in the Japanese market with short-term focused chop-and-change strategies using both local agents and then opening their own offices that later were forced to close.

So, why license in Japan? There are plenty of reasons and you can expect at least the following:

- A mature, sophisticated retail market within one of the world's largest economies.
- A diverse variety of IP that meets the needs and tastes of a wide range of consumers.
- Sturdy and effective legal protection.
- Zero or minimal pirating.
- An appreciation for longer-term partnerships over short-term profitability.

Chapter 8: Asia

- A demanding consumer, sensitive to fashion, but strongly loyal.
- Product design, quality, and finish that are among the highest in the world.
- A fashion trendsetter in Asia.

Conversely, certainly do not expect:

- A high growth economy.
- A huge, young consumer demographic—aging society and shrinking birthrate issues are the recent challenges.
- A "Fly-in-Do-a-Deal-and-Fly-Out" business culture.
- An easy market ... Japan requires patience and a continuing commitment.

8.2.2 Licensing Market Characteristics

Although Japan currently does not have an industry-wide licensing survey akin to the International Licensing Industry Merchandisers' Association (LIMA) North American Statistical Study, the Japanese licensing industry traditionally has relied on two surveys separately covering entertainment/character and brands.

The first survey has been conducted since 1999 by Tokyo-based character licensing market research company, Character Databank. Their annual survey of Japanese licensors and licensing agents encompasses character and entertainment properties. Based on annual retail sales, from a peak of ¥2.07 trillion (US$18.19 billion—historic exchange rate) in 1999 to ¥1.53 trillion (US$19.22 billion) in 2012, character merchandise sales have shrunk by 26.1 percent over the lifetime of the survey. But a better way to understand the downtrend is to begin with the 2000 figure of ¥1.68 trillion (US$15.59 billion) which was the start of the more realistic 9 percent decline over the 13 year time period shown in Exhibit 1.

Exhibit 1

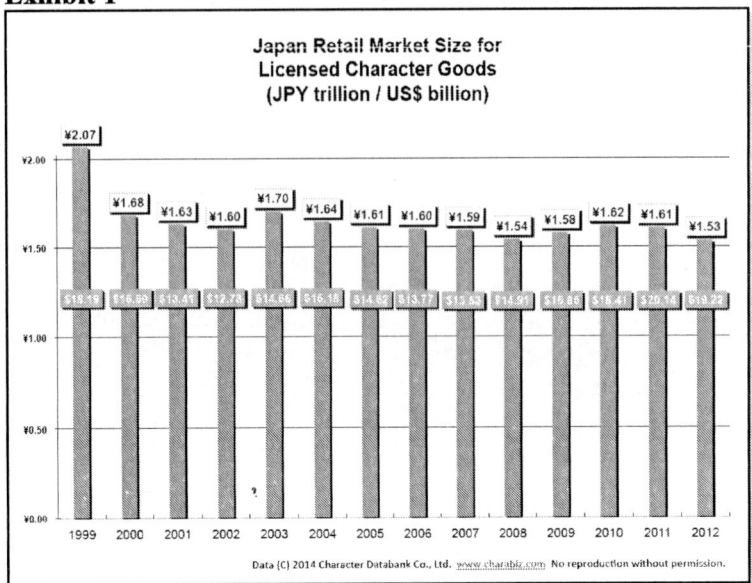

Japan Retail Market Size for Licensed Character Goods (JPY trillion / US$ billion)

Year	JPY trillion	US$ billion
1999	¥2.07	$18.19
2000	¥1.68	$16.89
2001	¥1.63	$13.41
2002	¥1.60	$12.78
2003	¥1.70	$14.86
2004	¥1.64	$16.18
2005	¥1.61	$14.62
2006	¥1.60	$13.77
2007	¥1.59	$13.53
2008	¥1.54	$14.91
2009	¥1.58	$16.88
2010	¥1.62	$18.41
2011	¥1.61	$20.14
2012	¥1.53	$19.22

Data (C) 2014 Character Databank Co., Ltd. www.charabiz.com No reproduction without permission.

The second survey, by major Japanese market researcher, Yano Research Institute, estimated licensed brand sales in 2012 to be about ¥1.32 trillion (US$16.59 billion). Unlike the slower decline for characters, licensed brands have shown a more significant drop in sales over the past decade from a high of ¥1.99 trillion (US$18.44 billion) in 2000 which translates into a 33.7 percent fall over the past 13 years.

Adding the two 2012 figures together results in a combined market, for licensed characters and brands, worth approximately ¥2.85 trillion (US$35.81 billion). Compared to LIMA's own same year estimates for the North American market of $112.1 billion, we see that Japan is about 32 percent of the North American total. This, admittedly, is a less-than-scientific approach using rather generalized, perhaps non-compatible statistics, but this perhaps gives a good idea of the Japan licensing market size.

Major property types are brands, character/entertainment and sports and the primary product categories are apparel/footwear, toys/games, and publishing. Licensed promotions using characters for convenience stores, banks, and in-

Chapter 8: Asia

surance companies are big business in Japan and in many cases, create great, short-term exposure for a property.

Japan is obsessed with rankings and even has a retail chain called "RanKing RanQueen" that stocks merchandise based on sales data of top-selling items in other stores. Character Databank publishes a monthly ranking of top character properties based on purchase value. Exhibit 2 shows the top 10 properties throughout 2012. It is interesting to note the predominance of Japanese properties with only Mickey Mouse, Winnie-the-Pooh and Snoopy as the non-Japanese characters; it is even arguable that preschoolers make no such distinction as to origin.

Exhibit 2

Character Rankings based on Purchase Value (2012)

Ranking	Character	% Share (Purchase Value Base)
1	Anpanman	7.82%
2	Mickey Mouse	6.43%
3	Pokemon	6.00%
4	Hello Kitty	5.70%
5	One Piece	4.23%
6	Pretty Cure Series	4.14%
7	Rilakkuma	3.36%
8	Winnie the Pooh	3.06%
9	Super Mario Bros.	2.67%
10	Snoopy (Peanuts)	2.51%

Data (C) 2014 Character Databank Co., Ltd. www.charabiz.com No reproduction without permission.

Royalty rates are fairly consistent in Japan with merchandise licenses ranging from between 4 to 5 percent of the retail-selling price. This generally equates to 8 to 10 percent of wholesale and 12 to 15 percent of FOB pricing.

There are two market factors that work in favor of licensors and agents in Japan regarding royalty rates. First, setting the royalty based on the recommended retail price is fairly common in Japan due to the lack of widespread discounting.

Basics of Licensing: International Edition

Second, calculating the guarantee based on production volume, not sales, is common. What this means to the licensor/agent is that royalty income is maximized because the royalty is being paid based on what the end-user (the consumer) pays without any discount, and royalty payment is on the full production, alleviating the risk of not receiving royalties on unsold stocks.

Royalty rates for promotional licenses typically consist of a flat fee payment plus a percentage royalty of between 10 to 12 percent of the promotional licensee's purchase price for the premiums or giveaways.

8.2.3 Retail Market Characteristics

Until the recent emergence of China's retail sector, Japan was regarded as the world's second largest retail economy behind the United States. But with ¥137.6 trillion (US$1.72 trillion) in retail sales in 2012 according to figures released by Japan's Ministry of Economy, Trade and Industry, third place isn't bad. Moreover, after a period of flat sales from 2006 to 2011, 2012 marked a modest uptick in growth with 2012 figures 1.8 percent higher than 2011.

Retailing is dominated by the major mass-market chain stores such as Aeon (537 stores) and Ito-Yokado (178 stores). Known locally as GMS (for General Merchandise Stores), they racked up sales of ¥12.95 trillion (about US$162.3 billion) in 2012, a tiny 0.15 percent increase over 2011. Convenience Store chains including the major three—Seven-Eleven Japan (16,375 stores), Lawson (11,130 stores), and Family-Mart (10,581 stores)—rang up ¥9.48 trillion (US$118.8 billion) in retail sales in 2012, representing a strong 11.8 percent increase over 2011. Department stores, whose sales have been in long, steady decline over the years, accounted for ¥6.64 trillion (US$83.19 billion) in 2012 and a tiny 0.32 percent decline from the previous year. Department store sector consolidation has been the key to survival with a slew of mergers over the past seven years. In 2007 H20 Retailing (15 stores) was formed from the amalgamation of Osaka, Kansai-based Hankyu, and Hanshin Department Stores, and in the same year Daimaru and Matsuzakaya formed J. Front Retailing (20 stores). In 2008, two of the strongest and most prestigious store groups in Japan, Isetan and Mitsukoshi, announced their own merger into Isetan Mitsukoshi Holdings (9 stores).

There are a number of key retailers in licensing. For character goods, the primary trendsetter is Village Vanguard (395 stores), a specialty retailer of books, CDs, videos, and a plethora of anything trendy. Merchandise is themed as "cutting-edge global indie" and attracts a diverse range of consumers with a core demographic of male and female 20s to 30s. Their sales FY ending May 2013 topped ¥43.77 billion (US$508.2 million) from stores located in trendy, subculture areas, shopping malls, and fashion tenant stores. The primary appeal of Village Vanguard to licensors is their reputation of spotting hit characters and its influence is such that buyers from other chains visit their stores to see what is trending.

A store very familiar with visitors to Tokyo is Kiddyland (73 stores), Japan's most famous chain store for character goods. Starting from its flagship base in Harajuku in 1950, Kiddyland achieved annual sales of ¥12.1 billion (US$137.8 million) in 2012. Kiddyland also operates standalone character stores: 11 Snoopy Town, 8 Rilakumma and 2 "Character Park" multi-character stores in Kichijoji, Tokyo, and Tenjin, Fukuoka. The customer base is largely female teenagers and mothers with young children.

Plazastyle (124 stores) opened in the Ginza in 1966, originally as a Sony group company and achieved fame as Japan's first import specialty store. Plazastyle also has a licensing division that represents a small range of properties including Suzy's Zoo and Barbapapa thus ensuring quality management and a consistent supply of licensed products to their own retail channels. Plazastyle caters almost exclusively to the young adult female demographic.

Fashion chains also play a strong role in licensing. In upstairs channels, Beams (121 stores; annual sales FY ending Feb. 2013 ¥61.2 billion/US$767 million) and United Arrows (208 stores; annual sales FY ending March 2013 ¥106.6 billion/US$1.04 billion) often launch limited edition branded apparel before distribution begins in the wider market. Both stores are leading upper tier independent fashion and lifestyle retailers with sophisticated urbanite consumer bases. Both operate so-called "select shops" with diverse and eclectic stock selections and, in the case of Beams, merchandise selection is empowered to individual store buyers.

Uniqlo (Japan: 849 stores) has come to dominate value-conscious casual fashion retailing in the past few years, providing similarly positioned Gap with healthy competition. Fast Retailing, the owner of Uniqlo, became the first Japanese apparel company to top the trillion yen barrier with ¥1.143 trillion (US$ 12.6 billion) in global sales in the business year through August 2013. Fast Retailing's stated aim is to become the world's largest fast-fashion chain by 2020. Although its cheap-chic product mix focuses on basics, Uniqlo is proactive in retailing a wide range of IP for t-shirts including entertainment properties (e.g., Disney, Snoopy, Hello Kitty), Japanese anime and manga (e.g., One Piece, Evangelion), and fashion brands such as Laura Ashley.

8.2.4 Licensing Trends at Retail

A number of trends have emerged in Japan over the past few years:

- Fashion globalization - an influx of overseas fashion retailers (H&M, Forever 21, Zara, American Eagle Outfitters, Gap, Abercrombie & Fitch, Topshop, etc.) has led to more direct-to-retail deals, particularly high volume, short-term licenses. Japan's own Uniqlo has also contributed to this trend as well.
- The emergence of "character street" shopping mall zones lined with single-property dedicated, standalone stores such as the Tokyo Station Character Street.
- Aggressive competition by convenience stores has led to more reliance on premium giveaway promotional campaigns using popular characters to differentiate store offerings. Given the high density of convenience stores, such promotions act as excellent media platforms for property exposure.
- Department stores have been struggling to redefine themselves in a shrinking market sector, which has

Chapter 8: Asia

made it more challenging to launch high-end fashion brands.

8.2.5 Media Environment

As elsewhere globally, media is an ever-changing environment with Japanese licensors taking up the challenge of operating in the age of digital property media drivers, such as smartphones and tablet PCs. The influence of TV is waning with the emergence of social media-centric platforms and the gradual shift away from TV is now seen as inevitable. Notwithstanding, the terrestrial free-to-air broadcasters NHK Educational and TV Tokyo remain the primary outlets to ensure the success of children's programming based licensing. Unlike other countries, the broadcast footprint for cable TV remains too small to create traction. Films have not been traditionally successful property drivers in Japan due to short movie runs. The notable exceptions however are series-based franchises Star Wars and Harry Potter, which scored notable successes in merchandise sales. School holiday film specials based on Japanese kids properties, such as Doraemon and Pokemon help to fuel property exposure and keep the franchises current.

Print publishing is still thriving but is in gradual decline. Manga genre dominates the sector with, for example, One Piece, a phenomenal success with over 260 million copies sold. There also is a steady market for children's picture book properties such as The Very Hungry Caterpillar and Peter Rabbit that enjoy a dedicated following from adult female audiences as well as the mother/child demographic.

With Japan as Internet-connected and electronic savvy as it is, it is no surprise that interactive media has blossomed. There has been a phenomenal growth of the social games sector dominated by two platforms: GREE and Mobage with 30 million and 43 million users respectively. The social communication platform, LINE, which has 300 million users globally, has driven the use of licensed character emoticons in online messaging. LINE's own original character series has been the subject of a growing licensing program in Japan. Common across all platforms, Japanese content dominates

Basics of Licensing: International Edition

with overseas IP such as Moshi Monsters, Cut the Rope, and Angry Birds having been largely ignored in Japan so far. The digital gaming market also is seeing a growing overlap and competition between mobile, handheld, and tablet devices in the gaming space.

8.2.6 Licensing Legal Nuts and Bolts

As a mature market, Japan presents no surprises for IP protection. Copyright is valid for 50 years upon the death of the author, with the exception being for film, which is 70 years. Copyright does not require registration and is, of course, non-renewable. Japan is a signatory to all the major international conventions such as The Berne Convention, the Universal Copyright Convention, and the Agreement on Trade-Related Aspects of Intellectual Property Rights (TRIPS). Trademarks are valid for 10 years and are renewable. Ballpark figures for costs per trademark are ¥30,000 for searches, ¥80,000 for applications, ¥90,000 for renewals, and ¥40,000 and upwards for office action responses, if called for. Japan operates on a first-to-file system, so searches are paramount and can save money in the long run. The general rule-of-thumb for licensing is that trademarking in five to six classes covers the majority of important product areas: Class 16 (stationery), Class 18 (leather goods, bags), Class 21 (housewares, glass), Class 24 (fabrics), Class 25 (clothing, footwear), and Class 28 (toys, games). This equals an initial investment of ¥180,000 for searches and ¥480,000, total ¥660,000 (about $8,000).

Unfair competition is another form of IP protection and the Japanese Unfair Competition Prevention Act protects well-known marks in Japan even if they are not registered. Finally, design patents are valid for 15 years and cost approximately ¥250,000 each.

8.2.7 Seven Licensing Pointers for the Japanese Market

Doing business in Japan requires patience and persistence. Japanese companies might sign a contract on the spot but they prefer building trust and confidence first to create strong and lasting relationships. Hence, the Japanese value a strategic over an opportunistic approach. In Japanese culture, "The Seven Gods of Fortune" are a recurring theme. Here are seven pointers that I hope will lead you to fortune in Japan!

1. Adapt—Don't adapt your property, adapt your approach. Flexibility in customizing to local markets has been a key to Sanrio's success worldwide. Hello Kitty has many personas around the world but she is still strongly recognizable as Kitty! The same principle holds true for marketing international IP in Japan.
2. Age It Up—Properties marketed to kids overseas often are also positioned to a more adult demographic. It is quite normal to find young adult women office workers eating their home-prepared lunches from lunchboxes adorned with cute characters such as Miffy or Winnie-the-Pooh. The key age groups in terms of disposable income are: (1) females aged 20 to 34 and (2) the "silver" retiree market. Another emerging demographic is the "Generation X Silver Market" which is the next wave of retirees, born in the 1960s, who will be the first true generation to have grown up with characters.
3. Collaborate—Co-branding is a key trend. Sanrio has widely used this strategy. For example, collaboration between Hello Kitty and Los Angeles fashion boutique, Kitson, resulted in an exclusive apparel offering at Uniqlo called "Hello Kitson."
4. Entice—Japan is an extremely crowded market for character and brand properties. It is important to emphasize the unique factors or "hooks" that an IP presents to the potential audience in order to stand out from the crowd. However common to most successful properties are specific traits that include a strong storyline, a heritage, a track record in other markets, and the "kawaii" (cute) factor.
5. Expect—Manage your expectations and meet theirs in time and quality terms. What you might think of as long-term generally is viewed as short-term in Japan, so setting mutually appropriate time goals can reduce frustrations on both sides. That is, if you're thinking one year, they might be thinking three years. Also, your

standard of quality is perhaps a Japanese consumer's excuse not to buy. It is a well-established fact that consumer expectations in Japan for product quality and service are among the highest in the world.

6. Protect—Copyright is fine but also safeguard your brand with trademarks. Some licensors consider trademarking a cost. That is shortsighted. Consider trademarking as an investment, not an expenditure item.
7. Understand—Conduct appropriate due diligence about Japan. First, recognize the market characteristics with its changing demographic of an ageing society as well as a low growth market as a result of Japan's mature economy. Second, appreciate that Japanese business style is based on building trust with the business partner, it is not simply transactional, and that decision-making can be irritatingly slow. Third, accept that business development is strategic, not opportunistic.

8.3 China

by Tani Wong

8.3.1 Introduction

China, officially the People's Republic of China (PRC), is the world's most populated country. It has a population of over 1.35 billion (1/5 of the world's population) and is 9.6 million sq. km in size. Putonghua is the official language, though local Chinese speak different dialects due to vast geographical area. Renminni (Yuan) is the official currency. The country is a single-party state governed by the Communist Party, and Beijing is the capital city. In 1997 and 1999 respectively, Hong Kong and Macau were returned to China and became the two special administrative regions of PRC.

Since the economic reform in 1978, China has experienced tremendous growth and has become one of the world's fastest-growing economies. As of 2013, it is the world's second largest economy by GDP and the also the world's largest exporter and importer of goods. Total GDP is $9,182 and per capital GDP is $6747.

8.3.2 History of Licensing

Licensing started in China in 1990's. Disney Consumer Products was the pioneer in the field. At that time, most of the licensing business was mainly managed out of Hong Kong. Licensing people chose to travel to key cities such as Shanghai and Guangzhou to meet with potential clients coming from different provinces. The majority of licensing activity happened along the Eastern coast. Dominant properties were mainly Western entertainment characters such as Mickey Mouse, Winnie The Pooh, Tom and Jerry and Sesame Street. These Western cartoon characters all had positive attributes, i.e., were cute, friendly and smart etc. The Chinese even thought that all foreign cartoon characters came from The Walt Disney Company. Japanese cartoon characters were less popular as they were viewed as violent. Thus, most licensing activities were among the established entertainment

Basics of Licensing: International Edition

studios, in particular Disney. Licensing of movie properties was also minimal due to the strict control over the import of foreign movies. At that time, licensing of local properties had not begun.

At this early stage, very few licensees or manufacturers understood licensing. They thought that once they paid a license fee, they received ownership of the property in China, and that they could use the character image in any manner. The product approval compliance rate was very low, and some licensees might never submit concepts for approval. Some were producing licensed products beyond their licensed categories. Even worse, some licensees designed and produced licensed products with their own interpretation of the licensed property.

Retail in China was very fragmented. Traditional distribution channels for licensed products were department stores or licensee owned and operated standalone stores. Following the growth of hypermarket, the entry of Wal-Mart and Carrefour became another market trend in the late 1990's.

Another issue was parallel export. Many Chinese licensees were licensed to manufacture and sell in China but were selling to overseas countries. Many factories parallel exported to Japan, Europe and the United States. Again, these manufacturers thought that they had the rights to sell to the whole world, despite the fact that the license agreement was meant for distribution in China only. They exhibited at international trade shows, took overseas orders and shipped abroad to traders.

Some Chinese companies entered the licensing business to improve their company's profile via licensing. Becoming a licensee of an international brand would give people the impression that the company had international exposure. This helped raise company image, and many companies in the early days just acquired licenses but did nothing in terms of product development and distribution.

Bad debt was another serious issue. Some licensees acquired a license without thoroughly thinking about the geographical area that they had to cover and sometimes committed to a high minimum guarantee. When they realized that the product sales did not meet their expectation, many companies

Chapter 8: Asia

just walked away and did not pay the balance. Some simply closed their companies, and it became very difficult for licensors to track and collect payments. So a large number of bad debts occurred. In order to secure royalty payments, many licensors asked for higher upfront and even full payment in advance. Other companies changed the revenue recognition method from accrual to earn-out. For larger size deals, licensors would request letter of credit or bank guarantees. After all, due diligence was very important and it still applies today.

Other than that, strict foreign exchange control made it difficult for licensors to collect payments. China's government has strict control for remittance of foreign currency out of China. However, many licensing agreements, in particular those with overseas companies, were in US dollars. Licensees needed to go through tedious procedures with different government authorities, including the filing of license agreements (Chinese Version) and paying regional and local taxes, to obtain the permit to remit foreign currency. The translation costs of English to Chinese documents and administration costs for filing caused many licensors to postpone their China entry plans.

Intellectual property protection was a major issue too. Before China's entry to WTO, the idea of IP protection was fairly misunderstood in China. Some manufacturers saw characters on television or from overseas and just copied the images onto their products. On one hand, this scared away many property owners. On the other hand, it forced major brand owners to speed up their Chinese entry plans to tackle the counterfeit problems. It also helped better protect their IP in China for further expansion into other product categories.

8.3.3 Licensing Today

Licensing in China has grown rapidly in the last decade. As mentioned earlier, most licensing activities in China were managed out of Hong Kong in the 90's. In 2004, Disney moved its regional headquarters from Hong Kong to Shanghai. Since then, many foreign brand owners such as Mattel, Hasbro and Nickelodeon began to set up offices in China.

Basics of Licensing: International Edition

Many licensors chose Shanghai as the 1st entry to China as it was a key trading port.

Though many foreign brand owners were interested in exploring the China market, they were hesitant to enter due to the language barrier, cultural differences, a lack of knowledge about the China market, currency control and intellectual property protection. This led to the rise of local licensing agents who acted as the bridge between brand owners and licensees. If the properties came from major studios, local agents were willing to commit a minimum guarantee to acquire the representation. For 2nd tier properties, these agents might pay a lump sum to become a master licensee, and they would sublicense the right to other manufacturers.

In 2000, China released "3000 Whys of Blue Cat," an animated series with an emphasis on science that had over 3000 episodes. The educational nature of this program was widely accepted by both parents and kids. The VCDs were always best sellers. Then, manufacturers started applying Blue Cat images on products and over 1000 Blue Cat specialty stores were opened. It marked the beginning of licensing for China-produced properties and was a huge success at the time.

Another success story involving a Chinese property was "Pleasant Goat and Big Big Wolf." The story was about a group of goats living on the grassland and a clumsy wolf that always wanted to eat the goat. The cartoon became very popular when it was aired in 2005. Due to its success, the producer released a movie in 2009 and it was a big hit during Chinese New Year. The success at the box office attracted many manufacturers to acquire the license. The animation was also aired in Hong Kong, Taiwan, Singapore and other countries. It was the first time that a Chinese animation and its licensing program have successfully expanded outside of China. In 2010, Disney became the master licensee and it was the first time that a China property was introduced under the Disney umbrella of properties.

The success of "Pleasant Goat and Big Big Wolf" triggered many animation companies in China to produce animation. This was further supported by the different subsidy policies provided by central and provincial governments.

Chapter 8: Asia

Since then, the animation industry has grown rapidly. Key provinces like Guangdong, Jiangsu, Zhejiang, Anhui and Fujian have set up animation bases to encourage animation production. Subsidies were further provided by government to animation companies based upon the duration of animation produced. Many companies started animation production to get government funding. In 2010, China surpassed Japan and became the world's number one animation production country. Annual production was 220,868 minutes. However, the majority of the animation was relatively immature. Some successful properties that could further develop through licensing are Momoking, GG Bond, Sweetheart Princes, Happy Heroes, Happy Family, Fruity Robo and Boonie Bears.

In China, the estimated retail sale of licensed products was USD 1.1 billion in 2005. In 2012, it rose to USD 5.2 billion. Entertainment licensing is still the dominant category, which has more than 50% of market share. Corporate brand and lifestyle programs are two fast-growing categories. Following that is sports licensing, particularly after the 2008 Beijing Olympics. This quadruple growth is mainly due to the rapid economic growth as well as the robust development of the internet in China. By 2020, the middle class will rise to 0.6 billion. They have high spending power and look for international brands. They believe foreign brands have better quality and designs and are willing to pay a higher price for them. This huge market potential is very attractive to foreign brand owners to market their brands in China.

Simultaneously, the Internet is changing the lives, lifestyle and consumer behaviour of Chinese today. Two decades ago, there were only around 2,000 Chinese computers that had access to the Internet. According to the Ministry's most recent data, domestic mobile internet users have reached 820 million people, which is more than half of the entire population. It represents an increase of 13% vs 2012 and is almost 10 times as many users as in 2006. More importantly, mobile phone users that are children are increasing rapidly. Nowadays, most Chinese communicate and share information via social networks such as Weibo, QQ and WeChat. The newly risen social media becomes another powerful platform for building a brand in China.

One recent example is "Ali the Fox" which was a cartoon character and started as an emoticon in 2006. It was then marketed online and became a very popular character among young teens and office ladies. It soon launched licensed products on Taoboa which is an online retail platform and received record-breaking orders. This further encouraged Ali the Fox to partner with more manufacturers to launch more products. By analyzing the data collected online, they were able to develop new products that captured the heart of their fans. In addition, the company has begun to organize events regularly to stay connected with their customers and increase fan base. To enrich its content, it also introduced picture books and animations. It has now expanded its reach outside of China and participated in overseas licensing shows.

In the past decade, the Chinese animation industry is developing towards cross-industry, cross-platform operation. It has evolved out of traditional animation and consumer products industry chain platform to online and real entertainment platforms such as edutainment centers and theme parks.

The licensing of movies and related properties has not been 100% effective in China, since the country has imposed import quotas on foreign movies. There are many cases in which a mega hit cannot be released in China due to a failure in passing the censorship regulations. In 2012, China enlarged its quota for imports of foreign films from 20 per year to 34 per year. The extra 14 films are "enhanced" films made in 3-D, IMAX or animations. In order to capture this huge market, many big studios will consider using Chinese artists in the movie or even co-production. The latter is more commonly used by film companies in Hong Kong. An alternative is to import movies for TV channels or online video for free.

The language barrier used to be an issue but is becoming less important. Many young people will study abroad and are well-versed in English. Many living in the cities are educated in and can understand English. They can communicate with the outside world. Many local companies have started acting as licensing agents. Some of them are existing licensees of

Chapter 8: Asia

certain product categories. They then evolve into licensing agents and help brand owners market the brand.. This would help them promote the brand and bring in additional revenue. Others are home video distributors or subsidiaries of TV channels that have experience in dealing with foreign companies. Due to the short licensing history, China does not have a big pool of licensing professionals. It is tough to hire people with proper licensing training. Thus, the performance of different agents may vary a lot. Other than agents, there are also a group of consultants who mainly help manufacturers to acquire license.

In the last decade, many local properties have begun their licensing program. They usually have in-house licensing departments to handle the properties. Some are backed up by TV stations, and some are actually toy companies producing animation to support their toy products. There are also pure animation studios. Again, their main challenge is finding licensing professionals to plan and execute licensing programs. Many tend to hire Hong Kong people to head up their licensing departments and provide staff training. The other may approach existing employees of leading licensors like Disney.

8.3.4 Outlook, Projections and Conclusion

In late 2011, the Chinese government approved a guideline on boosting reform of the cultural sector and cultural development at the sixth plenary session. In 2010, the culture industry represented 2.78% of GDP. In 2016, it is aimed to account for 5% of GDP and become a pillar industry of the national economy. The government will continue to increase support in terms of bank loans, government spending, taxation and land use to foster the growth of the culture industry. With licensing being classified as a culture industry, both central and provincial governments are actively supporting licensing activities locally. One of the examples is to sponsor participation in local and overseas licensing shows. This has a negative impact internally as many provinces host licensing shows locally to obtain government funding. Today, it has almost 50 so-called licensing shows in China but the majority of which are immature. Another new business opportunity is setting up a trademark exchange centre which serves as a trading platform for trademarks though its effectiveness is questionable.

Another form of support from the government is better IP protection in terms of clearer trademark registration guidelines and tighter enforcement of IP protection. Many retailers and shopping malls require proof of license before lending the space to tenants.

Traditional retail may diminish in the coming years, and online shopping become dominant. It is forecasted that most brick and mortar shops will be replaced by online retail in 5 years. On November 11, 2013, the leading online retailer, Taoboa, hit a total transaction of USD5.71 billion in a day. E-commerce is the most dynamic trading platform today. Marketers now do not use traditional marketing activities to build brands. They focus on social media to build fan base, collect data on their preference and offer products based upon their preference. The term O2O or C2B are commonly referred in China today. O2O is "online to offline" and C2B is "consumer to business." The latter allows consumers to develop the products they want by deciding the colour, the fabric used and even where to sell the products via collecting their preferences online. This forces enterprises to keep watching the internet world as a lot of data can be collected from there. And this data will affect the development of the brand.

With the strong economic growth of the country, support from government on developing the culture industry, a better understanding of the licensing industry and improved quality of local animation, we foresee the future of licensing in China to be very promising. Other than entertainment properties, corporate, lifestyle and sports brands, art and music categories also have growth potential in China. It is forecasted that in 5-7 years, China will surpass Japan and become the number one licensing market in Asia.

Chapter 8: Asia

8.4 Korea

by Kyeongwon Kwak

8.4.1 Introduction

Korea is the 12th largest worldwide economy with 50 million people and 17 million households. Over 44% of the total population lives in the Seoul metropolitan area, and those who are between the ages of 0 and 14 make up approximately 18% of the total population. The character merchandising market is estimated at US $7 billion in 2011. Hypermarkets are the largest distribution channels (46% of total character merchandising), and online shopping is expected to drive the future growth of retail. Across all types of media, local and Japanese content dominates due to cultural preferences, strong support from the government, and regulation on TV. Korea is technologically advanced with one of the highest broadband, multichannel, and LTE penetrations that reached 50% in 2013. This advanced technology infrastructure drives consumers to spend much of their time on online games, the Internet, and mobile contents rather than on traditional media.

8.4.2 History of Licensing

Korea has seen its culture industry stimulated after hosting the world-ranking sporting events of the Seoul Olympics in 1988 and the Korea-Japan World Cup in 2002, along with the thriving of World Wide Web infrastructure building in early 2000s. Some animation from the pre-Olympics era is still popular for example the property "Robot Taekwon V", but other properties that have come after the 1988 Olympics are more interesting to the public.

Before hosting the 1988 Seoul Olympics, the Korean government initiated groundwork for the culture industry expansion. Building Theme Parks (i.e., Seoul Land) and making investments in animation production were two of the major changes initiated by the government. Korean studios made most of their profits from OEM, mostly from the United

States in the 1980s and 90s. However, in preparation for the Olympics, the Korean government made great efforts to change the nature of the culture industry from merely supplying OEM to creating content. As a result, "Dooly the Little Dinosaur", "Run, Honey, Run", "Long Long Time Ago", and "Super Board's" began broadcasting on terrestrial TV channels in 1987.

Foreign animations were mainly from the US and Japan, and family-oriented Disney television shows were scheduled on Sunday mornings. Disney's broadcasting on terrestrial TV channels has increased public awareness and loyalty to Disney. In 1992, The Walt Disney Company incorporated its Korean branch, and since then the business in licensing has accelerated.

In early 2000, Internet companies, whose services were at that time limited to providing e-mail, community spaces, and web searching, soon expanded their domain of services to include flash games, short animations and e-cards among other services, and got into fierce competition to win users and customers. "Pucca" and "Mashimaro", properties whose orientation is comic short animation, have gained massive popularity and soon developed their licensing business possibilities.

In 2002, the completion of the Korea-Japan World Cup left a significant impact on many Korean brands. CNN reported on the changes that Korea experienced after the World Cup—a proliferation of online games, e-sports, and tech infrastructure, to name few. This rising attention to Korean culture was followed by an increase in Korean exports of animation, drama, K-pop, and online games. The following year, the Korean drama "Winter Sonata" was sold, and has become a huge public success in Japan. This success offered a glimpse into the possibilities of entertainment-related property licensing. Consequently, "The Great Jang-Geum", "Full House", and "You're Beautiful" were also exported abroad and became popular in Asian countries.

In 2004, Korea unfolded its full-scale K-Pop music-generating promotions, targeting all of Asia. SM Entertainment, under meticulous planning and management, introduced "TVXQ," a South Korean pop duo and experienced

Chapter 8: Asia

great success in Asia. It was the second tide of Korean Wave, following the first Korean Wave generated by dramas. Main attractions such as the pop groups "Rain", "FT Island", and "CNBLUE" have cemented their fandom through both video appearances and their music. This popularity played a key role in the licensing business, adding value to portrait rights. Later, Kara performed the lead role in a Japanese drama, and Big Bang introduced a T-shirt collaboration with UNIQLO Japan.

The same year, Nexon's launching of the multi-play racing game, "Kart Rider" reshuffled the Korean game market from hardcore-based to casual game-based. Kart Rider absorbed the female and youth populations into the online game market. Its membership has reached 13 million, or 26% of the total Korean population. From there, Nexon began a licensing program centered around game properties. Nexon followed with "Maple Story", an online role-playing game, which accumulated sales of 10 million copies.

The TV animation character "Pucca" made its international debut through Disney, after the co-production with JETIX (Disney Channel) in 2005. It was a good example because it showed that well-made Korean animation assets can drive sales in the international licensing market. "Pororo", with EBS participating in production, recently released its 4th season and is one of the hottest animation characters in the licensing market.

Entering the 2000's, the Korean culture industry shows exponential growth in various fields. The once import-dependent market now is capable of producing its own content, and the size of the licensing market is expanding rapidly.

8.4.3 Licensing Today

Leaders in today's domestic markets are the properties of Pororo, Larva, Roboca Poly, Disney, and Kitty. Domestic majors are targeting toddler viewers. TV animation properties are receiving media support by forming partnerships with terrestrial broadcasting companies. These programs need scheduling on EBS and Tooniverse, the top kids channel. EBS, in particular, receives stronger viewership from tod-

Basics of Licensing: International Edition

dlers, whereas Tooniverse is more favored by older kids. Pororo and Roboca Poly, and Crayon Shin JJang and Keroro gained their brand power through broadcasting on EBS and Tooniverse.

"Pucca", "Tickety Toc", and "Pororo" are some of the most famous and internationally recognized assets that are native to Korea. Pucca achieved its international recognition via co-production with Disney Channel. Tickety Toc was an output of the co-production by FunnyFlux and Zodiac Media, then it was presold to Nickelodeon for international distribution. Pororo also received strong media support. With EBS participation, Pororo could eventually make its mark internationally.

Iconix, which owns Pororo and Tayo, is one of the major domestic licensors in Korea. As of 2010, reported annual retail sales of Iconix reached US $500 million, with more than 1,000 product categories. Besides Iconix, other domestic licensors' properties have also established dominant market positions with strong help from the media. The following chart is a summary of some of the top licensors in Korea:

Licensor	Property	Agent
ICONIX	Pororo, Tayo, Chiro	-
VOOZ / VOOZ-CLUB	Pucca, Canimal	-
TUBA Entertainment	Larva, Wingcle bear, Oscar's Oasis, Vicky & Johny	-
GIMC	Cloud Bread	-
ROI Visual	Robocar Poly, Woobi Boy, Chiro	CJ E&M
Disney	Disney Standard Character, Marvel etc	-

Chapter 8: Asia

The following chart summarizes licensee brands in Korea:

Category	Major Licensee
Apparel/Accessory/Fashion	Eland, Samsung, Real company, Wing house, BOB design
Stationery	Barunson, Kumhong, Taeyang
Home	S.K, Eland, BK world, Dongyang CS
Food/Health/Beauty	Lotte confectionery, LG, GS, SPC, CJ, Boryung, Namyang
Toy CE	Aurora, Sonokong, Samsung, LG, Anymode

Domestic retail markets are dominated by 6 retail giants. If considering hypermarkets only, E-mart and HomePlus account for more than 30% of market share each. However, since Lotte owns Hypermarkets, Department Stores, SSM, CVS, Home shopping, Toys R Us, Lotte Cinema, and Lotteria (1,100 stores vs 300 Mc Donald stores) across the country, it is considered the biggest retail influence in Korea. The retail situation in Korea is as follows:

	LOTTE	Shinsegea	Samsung Tesco	GS Retail	Hyundai	Bokwang
Hypermarket	17%	37%	32%			
Department	42%	20%			20%	
SSM	431	129	317	230		
CVS	5,000			5,600		6,000
Home shopping	19%			27%	20%	
Others	Toys R Us Cinema lotteria			Watson		

Source: The maps of business investment 2012

In 2011, Korea's character and entertainment market was reported to be worth US$7 billion. Since 2009, its worth has been increasing at an average of 16% per annum. Ratio between domestic and foreign assets is 51% and 49%, respectively. Hypermarket accounts for 46% of main distribution channels, and online shopping mall does 13%. The importance on these two distribution channels is increasing continually. In Korea, entertainment licensed products are heavily weighed on toddler market. Source: Character Industry White Paper, 2012 (Unit: billion/U$1 = 1,000won)

8.4.4 The Role of Agents in Korea

Almost all foreign companies, except for Walt Disney, do business in Korea through partnerships with domestic agencies. Warner Brothers works with Young & Partners;

Chapter 8: Asia

HIT Entertainment and Discovery work with COCABAN; several Japanese companies have chosen either CJ E&M or DaeWon Media; and Nickelodeon established a joint venture with SBS to do business in Korea. There are a few cases where domestic animation companies have developed projects with broadcasting companies, and other small-scale agencies are also in place. These agents work closely with licensees to develop long-time business relationships. Korean agencies can offer clear-cut marketing approaches and targeting strategies for foreign assets. In order for foreign assets to settle and successfully grow in the Korean market, localization is vital. In this way, licensors must be flexible in accepting and meeting the required demands by the agents. And in the case of TV assets, joint management for broadcasting channels and its schedule is needed.

8.4.5 Outlook, Projections and Conclusion

The Korean licensing market is expected to grow continuously over the next decade because of several factors. The first is the rapidly changing media environment leveraged by YouTube and other social networking services. Not long ago, there was a gap between countries in the media industry For example if an American drama was successful in the US and decided to begin distribution in Korea, there was a gap of 6 months before it could possibly be aired in Korea. But today on You Tube, there is no such gap. As evidence of this, YouTube made Psy a worldwide star almost overnight. On YouTube, people from all around the world clicked on Psy's "Gangnam Style" over 1.5 billion times. YouTube has made it possible for the whole world to connect to the media content simultaneously. This media environment, empowered by the influence of social networking sites like YouTube, is expected to influence the growth of Korean licensing industry in positive ways.

The next possible boost for the Korean licensing industry is the mobile games that are facilitated by smart phones and mobile messengers. Approximately 84% of Korean smart phone users have the mobile game "KakaoTalk" installed on their phones. What is unique about KakaoTalk is that it shows the rankings of the people who play the game and whose contact information is stored in one's smart phone. It allows the users to compete with the people in one's contacts. "Any Pang" is another game that has reached 20 million downloads. With success of its game, Any Pang started its own licensing program through agents. These are just a few examples of the power of mobile gaming in Korea. The growing game market has attracted the attention of entertainment properties. Developers are looking to either make a new game using famous pre-existing characters, or to simply insert famous characters in a game they have already developed.

The third factor influencing licensing is the aggressive overseas expansion by companies with strong sales networks who are looking to expand into the entertainment industry. For example, Eland owns 54 apparel brands, and its operation range includes retails and leisure. In 2011, with 5,200 stores operating in China, Eland recorded sales of US $1.6 billion. Then, Eland took over an animation studio in 2009, and with the acquisition of a theme park in 2012, Eland will continually make its investment in culture industry.

Lastly, the dynamic overseas co-producing of TV animations can also be a key factor in licensing growth. Overseas co-production of the property Pucca by Vooz and Disney, and the property Tickety Toc by FunnyFlux and Zodiak Media, are good examples of successful overseas co-production. Pucca was aired internationally through Disney and Tickety Toc has aired through Nickelodeon.

From 2006 to 2011, the Korean licensing market reported an average annual growth of 9.6%. This was mainly attributed to the rapid changes in the media environment, government support, and the development of the animation and game industries. Today's social networking sites, new available technology platforms and creative collaborations among multi-national corporations will now act as the main driving forces of Korean culture industry development in the next few years.

Chapter 8: Asia

8.5　Southeast Asia

by Marilu Corpus

8.5.1　Introduction

For purposes of this chapter, the countries of Southeast Asia (SEA) will include Indonesia, Malaysia, Philippines, Singapore, Thailand and Vietnam. In Southeast Asia, the country with the largest population is Indonesia with 240 million. The Philippines follows at 94 million and Vietnam is around 90 million. Thailand has 64 million people and Singapore and Malaysia have 5.2 and 28 million respectively. While the size of the population is important in evaluating whether one should enter the territory or not, it cannot be the main determining factor. The following are key factors to consider when entering each of these markets:

- **Culture** - Some of the countries lean strongly towards American culture while others lean towards British culture. Given this, Thomas the Tank Engine and MR Men may be more successful in Singapore and Hong Kong than in the Philippines.
- **Traditions** - Foreign animations that influence children positively are more readily acceptable than others. Parents will screen television programs and not be supportive of programs that do not contribute to the child's well being. Parents want a program that is educational as well as aspirational.
- **Copyright and Trademark Regulations** - Regulations vary per country. There are unscrupulous people who will register trademarks in the hopes that once the owner decides to enter the market, they can sell it to the rightful owner for a good price. This has been a deterrent for some brands to enter the South East Asian market. Also, parallel imports are prevalent with popular brands.
- **Fiscal and Monetary Regulations** -
    1. Withholding taxes: Each country requires the withholding of taxes upon remittance of royalties

or advances. Licensors need not worry about this as once the tax has been paid by the local licensees to their government, the licensee can get a tax certificate for the licensor as proof that tax has been withheld.
2. Foreign Exchange Remittance: Different countries require certain documentation when remitting foreign exchange. This is also due to money laundering issues.
- **ASEAN and ASEAN FREE TRADE AGREEMENT (AFTA)** - ASEAN is an organization formed by the Asian member nations to help each other regarding issues including but not limited to economic growth, social progress, and security and peace. The goal is for the members to discuss concerns in a peaceful manner. Their Leaders attend ASEAN summits to discuss regional issues of that period. AFTA was established so that the member nations could become more competitive with exports in this region. This agreement has imposed the gradual elimination of tariffs in some categories like apparel. It will also allow member nations to gain access to cheaper raw materials reducing their production costs. Ultimately, this will benefit the consumer. However, among the countries themselves, while there are benefits, there will be stronger competition.
- **Local acceptable business practices** - In some countries, giving gifts that are special in one's home country, i.e., local delicacies or handcrafts, especially if that person has a high position in the company, is acceptable. It is not deemed as a bribe. That being said, one must also be aware of the rules of specific corporations which do not allow their employees to receive gifts entertainment of any kind. If you are unsure about local business practices, it is best to ask your licensing agent. Violation of these practices can cause you to lose business. In addition, Asians are very concerned about "losing face" and therefore we must be sensitive to issues or remarks or that can embarrass them.

Chapter 8: Asia

- **Religion** - There may be brands or characters, particularly of the swine and canine persuasion, that may be problematic for religious reasons. Religion and philosophies in Asia are quite diverse.

8.5.2 History of Licensing

The awareness for licensing started in the late 70's and early 1980's. At that time, there were some licensed products present, mostly those imported from Japan for example, Peanuts and Hello Kitty. Sanrio was a licensee of Snoopy through Hallmark Cards Inc., and Hello Kitty, Patty and Jimmy, Little Twin Stars products from Sanrio were exported to countries like Hong Kong and the Philippines. Sanrio was not yet licensing their brands out at that time. They were producing the items themselves. It was not until sometime later that Sanrio would enter the licensing business as a licensor.

Disney already had licensees in the early 80's like JOY-TOY in the Philippines, who did paper products and party goods. Mattel thru BARBIE's distributor started licensing in 1990. Ms Myrna Yao of RICHWELL started with 6 licensees, and now she has close to 50 licensees for the Philippines.

Other than Disney and Mattel, United Media appointed Raymond Mok to represent Peanuts as well as Garfield. RM Enterprises brought the Peanuts characters into Asia in the late 80's together with Hallmark Cards, Determined Productions, Butterfly, Quantasia, among other global master licensees of Peanuts. Garfield too was successful in Malaysia and Singapore through the MPH Bookstores. In the Philippines apparel sold very well in ShoeMart Department Stores.

In summary, twenty years ago, licensing was characterized by the following:
- Retail relationships were primarily the licensee's responsibility. They met their buyers and discussed terms, designs, the purchase order and any advertising requirements. Today, it is the licensing agent's responsibility to work with the retailer on introducing the brand and getting the retailer to accept and pro-

mote the brand, together with funding from the licensee and licensor.
- Advertising and promotions were the licensee's responsibility. Today, some licensors impose The Marketing Support Fund which may lighten the burden of the licensee when the retailer asks for an event. The Marketing Support Fund is a common fund where licensees contribute a percentage of their sales precisely for this purpose. However, the size of the PO may not always be commensurate to the required funding.
- Retail space was readily available, but now, space has become quite crowded given the many brands selling to the same target market.
- Agent responsibility was just to sell the license to companies that had the appropriate distribution channel. Now, the agent is responsible for managing the brand from the early strategic stages to entering the market to sustaining the brand for the long term
- Television was not a requirement as a number of brands were either toy or publishing based (Barbie, Hello Kitty, Snoopy). Today, with no TV, retailers are hesitant to purchase.
- There were very few competitors in the early days of licensing.

8.5.3 Licensing Today

The bulk of the licensing business today is still primarily in the character and entertainment segments with toys and apparel as the largest product categories. The sports industry is a growing segment in SEA, especially soccer and basketball, although popularity is dependent on each territory. Fashion is new but is creating a lot of interest in SEA.

Licensing Agents. In SEA, there are around 5 or 6 licensing agents and master licensees that have offices in the region, with one or two local companies focusing within an individual country. Some licensors, especially the Japanese, have master licensees instead of agents. Representation commissions may range from 20 percent to 40 percent de-

Chapter 8: Asia

pending on the licensor. In exchange for the commission, the agent is responsible for managing the brand, which can include creating the strategy, sales, product development/ brand assurance, initiating marketing activities and promotions through mall and retail events among others.

Below are some of the hurdles a licensing agent may face in the SEA markets:

- It is the agent's responsibility to work with licensees to promote the brand through retail activities and events that will drive sales.
- There are a limited number of licensees in the territory. For example, there may be five bag licensees, but ten children's brands.
- Minimum guarantees, advances and royalty rates in Southeast Asia have not changed in the last ten years. Licensees tend to question the royalty rate and the size of the minimum guarantee especially for a brand that is not well-known in the territory.
- Retailers look at shelf space as very valuable estate. They normally want what is hot.
- Some licensors collect a Marketing Support Fund from the licensees, which is a percentage of sales. This is to ensure that there is a budget set aside for retail activities.
- Terrestrial Channels are still the way to go for Southeast Asia. Cable Channels are very limited.
- There are not a lot of sources for hiring licensing personnel, so if a licensing agent wants to hire, he or she may have to hire from other agencies or invest time and resources into training new personnel.
- Agents sometimes have to deal with licensors who are not familiar with the market and yet insist on what they want which can actually compromise the brand.

Retail. Shelf space is very limited. As a result, retailers will make every effort to be sure that the brand sells as well as give themselves options if the brand does not. Consequently, retailers prefer terms such as Consignment, concession or

OTR (Option to Return). This allows the retailer to free itself from the burden of inventory management as well as payments. In general, department stores strategies are changing. Many have upgraded and are bringing in in higher-end brands such as Armani Kids, Gucci, Burberry, Baby Dior, Ralph Lauren, Hugo Boss and Paul Smith Junior. Some of these retailers have reduced the space of entertainment characters to make way for these high end brands.

In addition, most retailers want to have exclusive programs to be distinctly different from other retailers of the same level. Retailers are always looking for the next hot thing. Each retailer needs to have something that the other retailer does not. They want EXCLUSIVE. Most DTR opportunities today are apparel promotions with companies such as Bossini, Chocoolate and the like. Although Hong Kong-based, they do regional promotions.

Licensees. In today's market, there are more brands than licensees available. As a result, agents need to be resourceful in finding new companies that have adequate distribution channels in their territories that they can trust. Adding to the challenge is the fact that many licensees only want the currently hot brand. However, there are also those who want a classic evergreen brand that do not have highs and lows, but just nice consistent sales for the longer term. In most cases, licensees do not want to take risks. They normally consult with their buyers before they commit to a brand.

Popular Consumer Trends. Fashion and lifestyle brands have become prevalent in SEA with the presence of fast fashion stores like Forever 21, Uniqlo, H&M, Zara etc. These stores do collaborations with Disney, Warner Bros, Toei, Marvel, etc. Collaborations are becoming more frequent. In the last few years, we have seen fashion brands switch from the wholesale model to a licensing model. Paul Frank, TOKIDOKI, David and Goliath are a few fashion brands that follow this model. In addition, fashion designers have extended product categories into home furnishings and accessories. This trend has been aided by the popularity of cooking programs with the Food Network and the Asian Food

Chapter 8: Asia

Channel. People are becoming more aware of different cuisines, restaurants and entertaining.

In SEA, Western, Japanese and Korean brands are quite popular. Television plays a key role in the success of children's brands as most retailers make this a prerequisite before they buy merchandise. Classics like Barbie and Hello Kitty are still quite popular as well as pre-school brands like Sesame Street, Thomas and Dora. The popularity of Superheroes is heightened by movie releases. They sell to both kids and teens, male and female.

SEA has had some domestic successful properties as well. About three years ago, "Upin Upin," a Malaysian production broadcast in English, became quite popular in SEA. It is about brothers who live in a neighborhood with children of the same age. The licensing program, though regional, lasted for a couple of years. In the Philippines, soap operas that are produced by the local television stations have licensed into basic categories like stationery, notebooks and bags.

Major Licensees: Companies in Hong Kong that do regional deals are Bossini, Watsons, Convenience Stores like 7/11. Quick Service restaurants like Jollibee, KFC, McDonalds. FMCG like Mead Johnson, PUREFOODS, Selecta, Merchandise Licensees are Honeybarn, Megcorp, Vendermac, Four Ps, Kids and Teens, to name a few.

Major Retailers: Throughout SEA there are department stores, gift and novelty stores, toy stores, health and beauty aid stores, hypermarkets and convenience stores as well as book stores. Indonesia is mostly dominated by the retailers PT Mitra Adiperkasa who own Seibu, Sogo, Debenhams, Kidz Station, Starbucks and Zara. Mid-tier to mass retailers are: Matahari and Ramayana. Mass Market is covered by Hypermarket and Carrefour. The Mini-Mart sector is dominated by two major players, ALFAMART and INDOMARET which have approximately 9000 stores each. The leading book store is Gramedia. In Singapore, Orchard Road is the main shopping area. Takashimaya, CK Tang, Isetan, Metro, BHG, OG, John Little, and Robinsons. Popular bookstores are Page One, Kinokinuya, Times Book Store, Popular and

Basics of Licensing: International Edition

MPH Bookstore, Specialty stores like Action City, Precious Thots, and Toys R Us. Other retailers are Giant, Carrefour, convenience store Seven Eleven and Cheers. In Malaysia, the retail headliner is Parkson Department Store, which has about 40 stores all over Malaysia. Other players are Isetan, Jusco, Tru, Metro and Carrefour. In the Philippines, SM and Rustans Department Stores cover the mid to hi-tier market, while Robinsons is mass to mid-tier. Key apparel stores are Bench, Penshoppe, Kamiseta, Bayo and Gingersnap. While not a retailer, Avon takes a large portion of the market through direct selling. With the success of Avon, companies like Sara Lee and Natasha have followed suit. Thailand has the two major department stores of Central Department Store and Paragon/Emporium.

Other than department stores, retailers are taking on popular fashion brands and importing them to their territory. In the Philippines, SSI has opened Tiffany's, Ferragamo, Gucci, Tory Burch, Kate Spade, Kenneth Cole, Zara, Massimo Dutti, Debenhams and Starbucks. Uniqlo, H&M and FOREVER 21 are able to take the best locations in shopping malls everywhere as they bring in the customers.

8.5.4 Challenges of Doing Business in SEA

Relationships are very important to Asians. In some cases, they do deals on a handshake, especially if they have known each other for a long time. Sometimes they may buy a brand that is not so popular, to keep an ongoing relationship. What is challenging is that Asians have different backgrounds, histories and cultures and so we cannot all be looked at as the same.

Below are some factors to consider when deciding to license in SEA.

Television Exposure. A pre-school property must be on air. In the Philippines, TV stations are required to air an hour of pre-school programming. Given that this is a requirement, one would think that all the pre-school programs would be broadcast. But since there are quite a few pre-school brands, not all are aired. In addition, it is imperative to have coordination between the TV station and the licensing agent. For most television stations who buy programs, one hardly ever gets the schedule or airing times, as this information is confidential. Also, there are television stations too that air programs every day instead of once a week, thus not allowing the licensee enough time to go through product development and sell at retail. Before they know it, the 52 episodes have already been broadcast and are not aired again for another 6 months.

Retailer Relationships. Buyers in department stores have different brand preferences. Thus the presence of the categories in the department store could be spotty. The marketing fund for the brand is used only for one or two categories as not all the buyers appreciate the same brand. It would be best if the brand was across key categories within the department store. The key selling seasons of a retailer are back-to-school and Christmas. If the property is a movie, licensors and their theatrical counterparts follow the American schedule. This schedule does not always work as back-to-school in some countries is in May or November. Therefore, this affects the product categories that are sold when the movie opens. The selling of movie merchandise is not maximized, an so movie properties are still high risk for some licensees and retailers in SEA.

Licensor Expectations. Sometimes the licensor does not understand the territory and may have unrealistic expectations. If a brand is successful in the United States or Europe, it does not automatically mean that the same will happen in SEA at the same speed. Some countries, it takes time for a brand to be accepted given the number of brands pitching for shelf space. Some new licensors with new properties who enter the licensing business may not have the adequate knowledge to manage and implement a licensing program.

Choosing the Right Licensee. The licensee invests in the brand and has to deal with the requirements of the retailer like discounts, rebates, fees, etc. Any delays especially with time-sensitive launches or movies can upset the relationship with the retailer. Therefore, the licensee must be financially capable otherwise they will not be able to meet retailers' needs. Also, it is not uncommon for licensees to sign agreements without reading them. Every licensor has different rules and guidelines therefore it is important for the licensee to read and UNDERSTAND every paragraph, especially the breaches.

8.5.5   Outlook, Projections and Conclusion

Shopping is a very popular pastime in Asia. Mainland Chinese travel around SEA. Wealthy Indonesians shop in Singapore. Tourists from the Middle East shop in high end malls in Malaysia. Because of this, retailers continue to upgrade the brands they sell, not just for adults but for kids too. Online shopping sites like Zalora have also become quite popular. We believe that this trend will continue across department stores in SEA. Another trend for the future is apps and mobile phone applications. Over the years mobile phones have come to be used as still cameras, video cameras, organizers, small game consoles, datebooks, mini TV's, etc. It is now very easy to download apps from one's phone, and this appears to be an area destined for growth and exploitation.

As can be seen, licensing has been around for many, many years in the United States, and around the world. With all the advances in technology, fashion trends coming and going, changes in consumer behavior, one thing remains constant: licensing is still a very viable and credible marketing tool for companies to use in the development of their products to create a distinct difference from their competitors. The proof is in the increasing number of new brands that are introduced every year in the region.

Chapter 9

Latin America

9.1 Introduction to Latin America

by Elias Hofman

The region often referred to as *Latin America* is defined as those countries of the Western Hemisphere south of the United States, especially those speaking Spanish, Portuguese and French. Latin America encompasses a vast area of approximately 7.5 million miles, and its principle regions are Mexico, Central America, South America and the Caribbean. With a population estimated at more than 604 million, the region's combined GDP is valued at $5.16 trillion dollars.

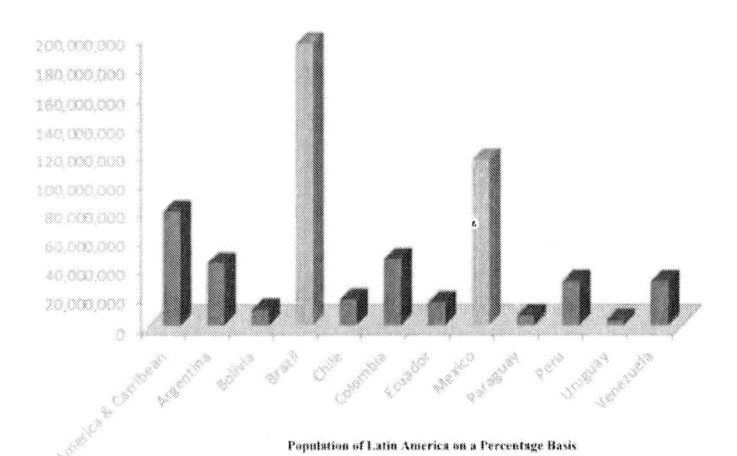

Population of Latin America on a Percentage Basis

Comprised of 20 separate countries, the two principle markets in Latin America are Mexico and Brazil. In terms of contribution to the region's GDP, total population and generation of royalty income, these two markets account for roughly 60 percent of area's gross GDP, contain about 51 percent of the entire region's population, and contribute to well over half of the total licensing royalties produced from the Latin American market. Based on GDP and population numbers, other key markets within Latin America include Argentina, Colombia, Venezuela, Peru and Chile. If however, the list of additional key Latin American markets were based on the generation of royalty income, the list would be comprised of Chile, Peru, Argentina, Colombia and Panama.

Population in Latin America

Brazil	195,632,000
Mexico	118,419,000
Colombia	47,130,000
Argentina	41,350,000
Peru	30,476,000
Venezuela	29,760,000
Chile	16,841,000
Ecuador	15,779,000
Guatemala	15,440,000
Cuba	11,163,000
Haiti	10,671,000
Bolivia	10,517,000
Dominican Republic	9,745,000
Honduras	8,578,000
Paraguay	6,849,000
El Salvador	6,635,000
Nicaragua	6,216,000
Costa Rica	4,667,000
Puerto Rico (US)[5]	3,641,000
Panama	3,605,000

9.1.1 Media

Irrespective of geographical location or local cultural influences, the one consistent factor responsible for the success of most licensing programs is the awareness of the property. In this respect, Latin America is not an exception to this universal rule. Therefore, to evaluate just how "licensing friendly" this market is or can be, it is important to understand how pervasive the distribution and use of media are, such as television, the Internet and social media, as these are important factors in generating property awareness.

9.1.2 Television

Currently, there are more than 1,500 television stations, servicing somewhere between 140 to 150 million television households throughout all of Latin America. However, some countries in the market are dominated by only one or two television networks, for example Mexico. In other countries such as Brazil, Argentina, Colombia and Chile, where until the 1990's television broadcasting was controlled by the government and/or operated as public networks, the easing of government control has given rise to many commercial broadcasters. The largest commercial television groups operating in Latin America are the Mexican network Televisa, Brazilian-based Globo, Argentinean Channels Group Telefe and El Trece (Channel 13) and Colombian-owned Caracol and RCN.

In a number of Latin American markets, the growth of subscription television has been significant. In almost all markets, distribution of pay television is concentrated in the key cities of each market, and is relegated to those higher up on the socioeconomic ladder. Using Brazil as an example, there are some 15 million subscribing homes, reaching 45 million viewers, which equals a penetration of over 25% of the total television households in country. 78 percent of pay television views are classified as "A" and "B" level consumers, with 61 percent located in only two of Brazil's 26 states – Sao Paulo and Rio de Janeiro.

Of the 140 -150 million television households throughout Latin America, over 60 million households subscribe to pay television. The percentage of households watching subscription television varies rather significantly by country. In markets such as Argentina and Colombia, pay television is received by 78 percent of all television households. In sharp contrast, distribution of pay television in Ecuador reaches only 13 percent of all television households.

Pay Television Usage by Country

Country	TV HH	Pay TV Penetration %	Pay TV Penetration TV HH
Argentina	12,957,740	78%	10,164,426
Brazil	54,260,000	23%	12,479,800
Chile	6,455,161	60%	3,842,730
Colombia	10,974,248	78%	8,559,913
Ecuador	3,073,933	13%	403,395
Centro America	5,605,196	48%	2,688,567
Mexico	25,475,684	41%	10,495,982
Panama	1,063,409	30%	319,023
Peru	8,582,986	63%	5,432,758
Venezuela	6,200,000	66%	4,092,000
Dominicana	1,500,320	32%	480,102
Puerto Rico	1,186,147	46%	545,628
Uruguay	1,703,049	37%	630,128
Total region	139,037,873		60,134,452

9.1.3 The Internet and Social Media

Use of the Internet has made remarkable growth across all of Latin America, with the largest percentage increase occurring since 2009. It is estimated that the Internet population of the region is about 260 million users, which is equal to about 43 percent of the total population. Like the distribution of subscription television, the predominant users of the Internet are disproportionally from the higher side of the economically advantaged, and tend to be concentrated in the dominant markets of each country.

Chapter 9: Latin America

Internet Usage by Country

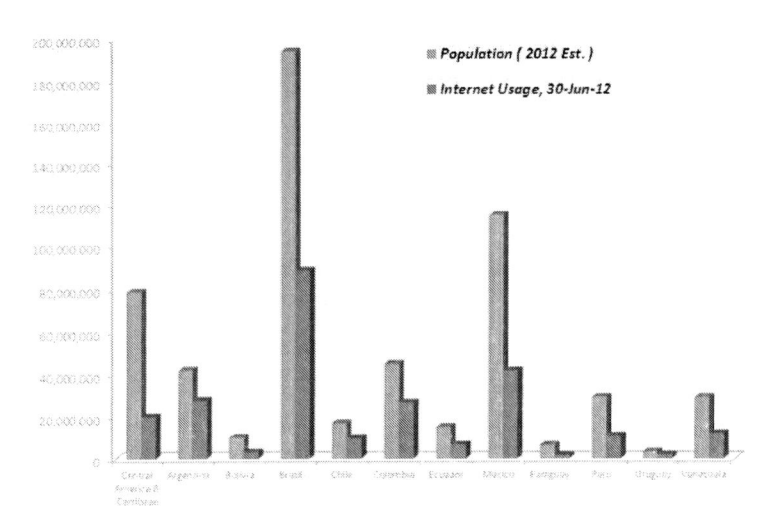

The single largest Internet market is Brazil, which is now the number three market behind the United States and Japan. There are close to 50 million households and offices throughout Brazil that have Internet access. It is estimated that Brazilians rank number one with regard to the number of hours they spend online per month, averaging 77.6 hours. The top five most popular websites are Google Brazil, Facebook, Google You Tube and Universo Online.

The use of social media has also made great strides across Latin America in the last several years. Facebook remains one of the most popular social media websites, which boosts a user base of close to 190 million subscribers. Based on the numbers above, it should come as no surprise that 79 percent of internet users in Brazil access social media networks.

9.1.4 The Retail Market

The level of retail development is not consistent across Latin America, as some markets are more sophisticated than others. Overall, retailers are becoming better educated about market trends. The retail landscape is comprised of a variety of different retail formats that vary in popularity from market to market, but in most all markets, the vast percentage of licensed merchandise is sold through hypermarkets, discount stores, supermarkets, department stores and better specialty stores.

In recent years there has been a considerable increase in the use and popularity of DTR licenses. A number of larger retails – mostly those operating multiple retail outlets in a single market – have witnessed a number of successful DTR licensing programs. This is a trend that is very likely to continue to grow in popularity among retailers in this sector of the world.

Like most other markets, there is a reasonably wide selection of both licensed properties and products, with a heavy emphasis on properties and products that are aimed at the infant and children's market. Across most of Latin America, promotions are an important category for licensing, with food products, such as snack foods and beverages, being the dominant product category.

Below is a list of the most popular product categories for licensing in a number of key markets:

Mexico: apparel, stationery, toys, back to school, publishing and promotions
Chile: toys, apparel, stationery, party goods, DTR
Argentina: back to school, apparel, stationery, publishing, home video/DVD
Colombia: back to school, apparel, stationery, footwear
Peru: back to school, apparel bedding, party goods, food & beverage
Ecuador: promotions
Panama: stationery, apparel, bedding, gift & novelties, baby accessories
Dominican Republic: back to school, live shows, promotions
Venezuela: promotions, live shows

Although a large percentage of Latin America felt a considerable impact from the economic downturn that began in 2008, many markets have or are now experiencing considerable growth. In the recently published United Nation's *World*

Chapter 9: Latin America

Economic Situation and Prospects Report, it states that over the next two years Panama and Peru will be the two fastest growing economies in Latin America. Growth of the Panamanian GDP is forecasted to expand by 6.9% this year and 6.6% next year. Peru's economy is predicted to increase by 6.1% and 6.3% during this same period. Panama and Peru are not the only Latin American markets likely to improve over the next twenty-four months. In addition to Panama and Peru, financial gains are projected this year for Bolivia (5%), Paraguay (4.6%), Guyana (4.5%), Haiti (4.5%) and Chile (4.4%). The following year it is anticipated that this trend will continue with economic growth by Bolivia (5.1%), Haiti (4.8%), Paraguay (4.7%) and Colombia (4.5%). In regional terms, the report notes that growth in Latin America (including the Caribbean) is forecasted to increase by 3.6% this year and 4.1% in year two. The report attributes these gains to the gradual economic recovery of the economy, sound macroeconomic policies, and resilient domestic demand.

Perhaps the best example of a Latin American market that has experienced considerable growth over the last four years is Brazil. Looking at Brazil today, it is easy to forget that the country, and other markets such as Argentina, were near financial ruin in the mid to late 1980's, as hyperinflation made doing business nearly impossible. From an economy that routinely removed the last three zeroes of its currency, froze funds and bank accounts, and made reliance on black market exchange rates a daily factor of life, to its current state as a leading economic power, is an amazing journey.

A brief introduction can hardly do justice to opportunities that Latin America has to offer. In closing, we invite you to *por favor, ven y experimenta por ti mismo la belleza de América Latina*

9.2 Brazil

by Marici Ferreira, Ana Kasmanas, and Glenn Migliaccio

9.2.1 Introduction

Brazil, in South America, is a country of more than eight million square kilometers, divided into five regions: (1) the North, (2) Northeast, (3) Center-West, (4) Southeast and South, and (5) the Federal District. It has over 5,000 municipalities and a population of over 190 million people. Well-known for its developmental phase, Brazil has gained prominence in the global economy, but the country still faces challenges that are far from being solved, especially in social areas, despite generally stronger and more stable economic conditions. Per capita income in 2012 was R$ 22,400 per year, and the Human Development Index (HDI) was 0.730. Brazil occupies the 85th position among the 187 countries analyzed (data released by the United Nations Development Program in March 2013).[1]

The Brazilian economy is based on agriculture, livestock farming, mining, and industry. Gross Domestic Product (GDP) in 2012 was R$ 4.403 trillion (exchange rate: US$ 1.00 = R$ 1.98, on 03/01/2013), up by 0.9 percent year on year, and the balance of trade produced a surplus of US$ 19.43 billion.[2]

To the surprise of academics and politicians, in the last three decades Brazil transitioned from having a pyramid-shaped social and economic distribution, with a broad range of poverty at the base, a small middle class, and a smaller peak made up of the highest social class. The model has now changed, to a diamond, in which the base is narrower because social class D has shrunk, with social class C (the middle class) growing, having consequences for lifestyle and con-

---

[1] Brazilian Institute of Geography and Statistics (IBGE)
[2] United Nations Development Program (UNDP)

sumption. The peak, in turn, also has widened slightly, with more rich people joining the elite.[3]

Today, social class C consists of families who have a monthly income of between three and ten times the minimum wage. This income, for a large part of this population, was reached in recent years due to several factors, among them policies to eliminate poverty, and social inclusion by recent governments, along with economic growth of the country as a whole. With increased purchasing power and the use of various forms of credit, the new middle class has shown a keen interest in new technology, consumer goods, and everyday items. The group has boosted consumption, improving its standard of living and driving the domestic market for manufactured goods, as well as trade and services. Studies by the Getúlio Vargas Foundation (FGV) and the Trade Federation (Fecomércio) forecast that the ascension of social classes D and E will continue for at least eight years—50.5 percent of the population is now in social class C. These are new data that should be considered by governments when adopting public policies. Moreover, it is extremely relevant for planning, marketing, and social studies.

The new situation for the majority of Brazil's population (that is, the 95 million Brazilians in the middle class), means that there are prospects for sustainable growth for Brazil, with less dependence on the external economic situation. In the last 10 years alone, 31 million Brazilians have joined the middle class, with an increased level of education and purchasing power among consumers. Besides the large number of new jobs, both formal and undocumented, women also have begun working, increasing household incomes. Product variety has become part of Brazilians' daily lives.[4]

9.2.2 The History of Licensing

Walt Disney's characters began to appear in Brazilian newspapers in the 1940s, after Disney him- self visited the country and created José Carioca. At that time, Snow White released a record on the Continental label. Editora Abril, now

---

[3] Getúlio Vargas Foundation (FGV)
[4] Trade Federation (Fecomércio).

Basics of Licensing: International Edition

one of the largest media groups in Brazil, began by publishing comic books featuring Donald Duck, licensed by Walt Disney. A little later, characters such as Mickey Mouse and Donald Duck began to appear at birthday par- ties, printed on t-shirts, and used in new chocolates. Licensing was controlled from the New York office until the 1960s, when Disney offices (Redibra, founded by Elcan Diesendruck) and Hanna Barbera offices were opened in São Paulo.

In 1968, Mauricio de Sousa began licensing his characters. It was the first licensing of characters created in Brazil. The characters Blu and Franklin became dolls manufactured by Duplex. Then Mauricio de Sousa's characters began to appear on blankets and sheets. In 1970, the elephant, Thunder, began to appear in commercials for Cica tomato paste. Increasingly, brands, characters, and celebrities grew in importance for companies, making them more competitive while generating value for consumers.[5]

9.2.3 Licensing Today

The principal licensing properties in Brazil today, include: Angry Birds, Barbie, Ben 10, Carousel, Cocoricó, World Cup 2014, Dora the Explorer, Galinha Pintadinha, Jolie, Monster High, My Little Pony, Patati Patatá, Disney Princesses, Rio 2016, Smurfs, Monica's Gang, UFC, Batman, and Brazilian and international soccer clubs. Popular, homegrown, Brazilian properties attracting significant licensing attention are: Cocoricó, Galinha Pintadinha, Jolie, Patati Patatá, soccer clubs, and Monica's Gang.

Unlike the United States, Canada, and much of Europe, there is no official information on the size of the licensing sector in Brazil, and most available figures for the Brazilian licensing market are estimates. Key local licensing operations include:

Licensors—BR Licensing, Cartoon Network, Disney, Exim Licensing, Globo Marcas, Hasbro, Kasmanas Licencia-

---

[5] Licensing-Como utilizar marcas e personagens para agregar valor aos produto (Sebastian Bonfá and Arnaldo Rabelo). M.Books.

Chapter 9: Latin America

mento, Mattel, Mauricio de Sousa Produções, Nickelodeon, Redibra, Sanrio, and Warner.

Licensees—Bauducco (food), Biotropic (soap and shampoo), Brandili (children's clothing), Brinquedos Estrela (toys), FestColor (party pieces), Fini (candy), Foroni (notebooks), Grendene (footwear), Grow Jogos e Brinque- dos (toys), Havaianas (flip flops), Kimberly- Clark (hygiene and personal care), Lunender (adult apparel), Lupo (socks and underwear), Regina Festas (party pieces), Riclan (candy and chewing gum), Sanremo (household products), Sestini (backpacks, bags, lunchboxes), Top Cau (chocolate), and Yellow (toys).

It is estimated that 500 companies now work in licensing, or are licensed, in a market that offers about 500 licenses, and of which 75 percent are foreign. Responsible for the paperwork in the sec- tor, there are about 50 licensors and licensing agents operating in Brazil, creating approximately 1,300 direct jobs.

An estimated 70 percent of the licensing market is made up of properties related to entertainment, 20 percent are corporate properties, and 10 percent of licenses are related to sports. Other key licensing categories include: tools, apparel, stationery, toys, footwear, health and beauty, and food.

In recent years, the market has been growing steadily, at an average of 14 percent per year. In 2012 licensed products in retail earned R$ 7.5 billion, 45.8 percent of which was generated in the first half, compared with 54.2 percent in the second half of last year.

The main product categories in terms of revenue generation in the last year were: apparel, footwear, food and beverages, school, and toys. Personal items, sporting goods and publications grew more in 2012 than in previous years and properties related to digital games, corporate brands, and sports began to emerge with an interesting offering of brands.

Brazil is now the fifth-largest country in revenue from brand licensing worldwide, behind the United States, China, Canada, and Mexico. This ascendancy has a number of positive aspects, such as:

- Plenty of room for growth in several areas
- Increased number of Brazilian brands on the market
- A growing shift away from TV as the primary medium with which to promote brand visibility
- Growth of e-commerce as a channel for more segmented brands
- Better structure of the sector via publishing of "Licensing Brasil" and the new board at the Brazilian Licensing Association (ABRAL)

Conversely, as may be expected, certain less beneficial trends arise from this frenzy of brand proliferation, including:
- Lack of professionals with expertise in licensing and the rise of "hacks"
- Small base of companies that make use of licensing
- Lack of knowledge in retail of the benefits of licensing as a branding tool[6]

Brazil's economic and fiscal peculiarities are totally different from those in the United States, Europe, Asia, or even other countries in Latin America. The economy today is stable, but has endured a turbulent history, and much depends on who controls political power. This is a recurring reality, which foreigners from consistently stable political locales may have difficulty grasping in a business context. What exists today may change tomorrow, if the government so decides. In addition, the local tax system is exceedingly complex and very different from the single rates that often are paid separately in other countries. Explaining this to foreign business partners is especially difficult and time-consuming.

Regarding intellectual property, there has been the recent case of the iPhone brand registered by Gradient in Brazil and in the first instance Gradient won, even though the famous brand was created by Apple. If a brand is not registered at the

---

[6] The Brazilian Licensing Association (ABRAL).

national industrial property institute (INPI) in all the most important categories and if the art created by some- one is not registered at the college of fine arts in Rio de Janeiro, the risk is run that an opportunist will register it. With Brazilian law, the risk is that legitimate brand owners will lose to the opportunist in court.

9.2.4 The Role of Local Agents, Consultants, and Manufacturers

Local agents must represent their licensors well and comply with professional principles and guide- lines, but they also must know how to navigate the particularities of the Brazilian local sector. Agents have to be sound intermediaries between the licensor abroad with its requirements and the licensed company in Brazil and, all of this, with great diplomacy. When a need for a local licensed company is well founded, no matter how demanding the licensor, it generally will defer to local knowledge if an agent's recommendations are strategically consistent, original, and where trust in the relationship has been established.

The biggest problem agents have is managing the urgency that Brazilian licensed companies have become renowned (or infamous) for, with the licensor's more regulated and bureaucratized practices abroad. The advice offered licensees is to plan further ahead so as not to miss out on good licensing opportunities just because of time constraints.

9.2.5 Best Practices for Marketing, Advertising, and Promoting Licensed Products at the Local Level

Being in touch with the consumer, creating a relationship, investing in stocks, etc., all maximize results in any licensing campaign. Communications, announcements, and actions that show the power of a particular character or property, which exploit their attributes as well and involves the target audience are certainly good practice. Retail campaigns with tabloids, point of service (POS) materials, exhibition at the POS with several lines of licensed products, and campaigns with awards and free gifts are practices that typically generate positive and profitable results.

9.2.6 Retail Sector

The Brazilian retail sector has been through pro- found changes in recent years, becoming increasingly competitive. The sector, which used to coexist with high inflation rates, has been growing and developing a new range of strategies that are not just meant to reduce prices and costs. Brazilian retailers have been looking to increase their regional coverage, opening specialist stores, and increasing the presence of groups and chains nationally.

The sector, whose largest companies and suppliers are still concentrated in the South and Southeast, with the exception of electronics suppliers, is calling still for more major structural changes. Such changes lead to improvement in relationships in terms of the supply chain, which is beginning to target not only the commercial area, prices, and payment methods, but also better management in the flow of goods. Alongside family-run standards, corporate governance is being improved through the use of information technology that standardizes the management of companies and their degree of professionalism. Currently, there is a growing use of labor-saving technologies and better-qualified professionals, factors that are essential for a sector that often suffers with less skilled labor and high staff turnover.

Overall, retail involves highly seasonal activities and high turnover, as well as being very susceptible to economic policies that affect the macroeconomic scenario and income and employment indicators. So, a growing Brazilian population and economic stability are important factors for the growth of supermarkets and hypermarkets, as well as other retail activities.

According to a study by the market research firm GFK Custom Research Brasil on the sales of 75 kinds of products in the Brazilian retail sector in 2012 compared with 2011, sales of a list of 14 items focusing on entertainment, including toys, sports foot- wear, games, flat-screen TVs, laptops, and smartphones, rose by 5.5 percent in the year, to R$ 61.3 billion. Sales of durable goods as a whole increased by only 1.8 per- cent in 2012, in the region of R$ 97.4 billion.

Chapter 9: Latin America

"Virtually all the categories that make up the entertainment sector are growing. There is indeed faster development in this segment, causing it to gain in importance, especially driving the sales of toys and high-tech items," says Simone Aguiar, Manager of the Retail Business Unit at GfK.

According to the company, out of the 75 categories surveyed, games grew the most between 2011 and 2012, with 133 percent growth. Other segments with high growth were electric fryers (86 percent), tablets (85 percent) and hair clippers (81 percent).

The fastest-growing region was the Northeast, at 8 percent, followed by São Paulo state (not including the city), at 5 percent. This, incidentally, became the main location in Brazil in terms of total revenue, accounting for 19 percent of total sales. São Paulo state loses ground to the capital city itself in the entertainment sector, where the largest city in the state accounts for 25 percent of Brazil's revenue.

Another trend identified by GfK is the growth in general stores, a sector that includes hypermarkets, department stores, and e-commerce without physical stores. The segment grew by 19.5 percent in revenues, while specialty stores fell by 2 percent in revenue last year. General stores are gaining ground, now accounting for 22 percent of sales in Brazil.

For the next few years, GfK believes that the focus for consumers will be on products that have an appeal in terms of sustainability, as well as the increase in consumer potential for people living in informal settlement towns and communities on the outskirts of cities, especially for major and small appliances. "The government's announcements on tax incentives for local manufacturing of high technology items, especially 3D TVs thinking of the FIFA World Cup and the Olympics, also indicate that consumption will increase," says Aguiar.

9.3 Colombia, Chile, Ecuador, Peru, Venezuela and Central America

by Luis Salazar

9.3.1 Introduction

This chapter will cover licensing in the countries of Colombia, Chile, Ecuador, Peru, Venezuela and Central America (Costa Rica, El Salvador, Guatemala, Honduras, Panama). Latin America is wide, and there are great economic and cultural differences across the different countries, forcing licensors and licensees to adapt work and methods to each country and region. For purposes of this chapter we will divide the region into five sub-categories: Chile; Colombia and Peru; Central America (which includes Costa Rica, El Salvador, Guatemala, Honduras and Panama); Ecuador; and Venezuela.

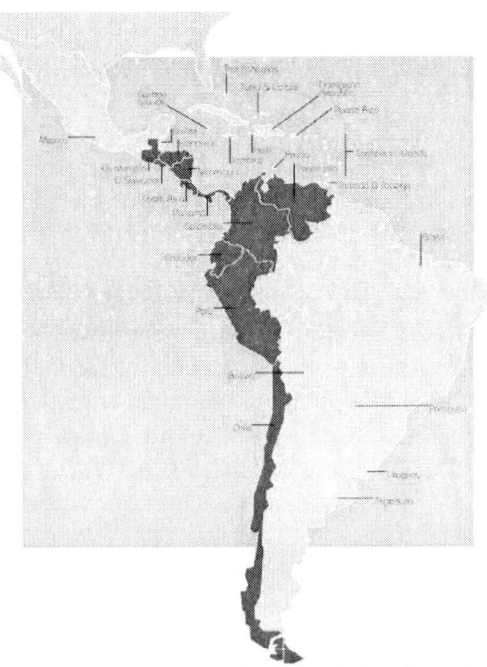

The first category, Chile, is a well-developed and fairly stable economy that offers the licensing business many opportunities in terms of market conditions: modern laws to

Chapter 9: Latin America

protect intellectual property, very low duties, and a low barrier for the entry of foreign goods, as well as a developed and modern retail market in which every licensing company could compete. The second category groups Colombia and Peru together, because both have constantly growing economies (for more than 10 years now) making an impact with their strong growth in retail business mainly due to foreign investment. However, the legislation in these countries is still weak regarding the licensing business. In the third category, we find the Central American region: Costa Rica, El Salvador, Guatemala, Honduras and Panama, countries that have small economies and different legislation, making it difficult for the licensing business. In the fourth category, we have Ecuador, a country with a protectionist government and unstable politics that imply constant changes in legislation and economics causing an unstable environment for long-term business planning. Finally, there is Venezuela, a country with an unstable political situation, a growing inflation, high unemployment and a lack of clear laws defining the industry, resulting in an irrelevant market for licensing opportunities.

South American Countries	GDP growth (Annual % - 2013)	Population (2012)
Colombia	5.1	47,704,427
Chile	4.7	17,464,814
Ecuador	1.2	15,492,264
Peru	4.4	29,987,800
Venezuela	1.09	29,954,782
Costa Rica	5.1	4,805,295
El Salvador	1.9	6,297,394
Honduras	3.9	7,935,846
Guatemala	3	15,082,831
Nicaragua	5.2	5,991,733
Panama	10.7	3,802,281

*Source: The World Bank, Cesla (Centro de Estudios Latinoamericanos)

9.3.2 History of Licensing

Our company, Compañía Panamericana de Licencias (CPL) started in the early 1980's and was one of the first to the start developing the licensing business in Latin America. The first companies to enter the region were Warner Bros. Consumer Products, represented by The Licensing Company of America with three agents for this region, and Disney with two agents, one agent to handle the Peruvian and Chilean market from Argentina, and a second agent to handle the rest of the region from Colombia.

In the early days of licensing in Latin America, selling a license was very complicated because the potential clients were used to using the brands for free, without the license rights. In fact, most of our initial clients were companies that had been using the brands or properties without any official licenses. The market was really small, and did not offer many opportunities. At that time, licensors were looking mainly for profitability. Very few of them were taking care of their brands and were not monitoring strategies, arts and designs or brand assurance guidelines.

In the early 60's, we mainly licensed the entertainment properties of the few movies and free TV channels that were available in the Latin American region. Now, the entertainment industry in the region offers many options to consumers. As an example, in each country, audiences now have free access to 5-7 broadcast channels, and more than 100 cable TV channels, creating a great opportunity for character licensing properties based on these movies and TV shows. In addition, new trends are emerging where licenses are now not only being sought for the characters from these movies or television shows, but also for the brands, celebrities, art and sport properties, toys and, most recently, video games properties.

The licensing business is stronger than ever in Latin America, and keeps attracting new companies with promising opportunities. More and more players are entering the licensing business market, providing more options for the final customers. Nowadays, we need to provide a full range of services to companies, including advice and guidance for the choice of the brand, design styling and strategies for the release of the products. It is extremely important that we work closely with retailers and licensees to achieve success. For all of this, studios require specialized agents who can help them compete in these markets.

9.3.3 Licensing Today

As we mentioned in the introduction, some market conditions in the area could be considered as barriers to entering the market with licensing business. Depending on the country, there are significant differences in legislation protecting intellectual property, often leading to a "black market" for products featuring brands and characters without the license rights. This leads many consumers to think: "Why should I pay for the right to a license if I can have it for free?"

Some of these experiences can be directly attributed to the informal business environment in Latin America, sometimes making it difficult for international businesses and companies to collaborate with local companies. Also, it is important to mention that some countries suffer from political instability, impacting laws and business regulations and making long-term planning difficult. Such circumstances also have a direct impact on the economy (i.e., the Venezuelan annual inflation rate is 57.3%) and affect demand for consumer products.

Although the market is still in the process of development, it is important to mention that the licensing business is growing, and legislation is being introduced frequently to better regulate the markets in the Latin American region. Growing economies imply a better and wider access to television, cinemas, internet, and video games. The result has been a stronger presence from the entertainment industry, raising awareness and impacting demand for licensed product.

It is important to mention that the growing market attracts many new players, wanting to represent brands and market their licenses. Licensors and licensees need to take into account the complexities of the Latin American markets. It is important for international licensors to seek the help of experienced, local agents or partners before they decide to begin licensing.

Although the majority of licensed properties are imported from the US, Europe or Japan, some strong properties originate from Latin America. For example, Brasilian Monica's gang from Mauricio de Sousa Produções is a great example of a licensing success, competing among the great licensing companies of Warner Bros and Disney. Argentinean Mafalda is is another example of a successful property originating from Latin America, but with a very poor licensing program.

Disney, Warner Bros, Cartoon Network, FOX, Dreamworks, Twentieth Century Fox and Mattel remain the most important companies in the licensing business for the Latin American Market. The most popular properties are: Looney Tunes, Baby Looney Tunes, Justice League, Rio 2, The Simpsons, Ice Age, Ben 10, Smurfs, Bajoterra, El Chavo, Monsters Inc., Princess, Angry Birds, Toy Story, and Barbie. The licensing industry works hand-in-hand with the entertainment industry, always looking to satisfy their audiences and leading the way for licensors to reach out to their clients.

One of the most important partners in a Latin American licensing relationship is the retailer. Retailers have played a big role in the licensing business's success, offering new channels for the commercialization of licensed products. With the expansion, as well as the creation of new department stores in Latin America, many licensed products have found their way onto the shelves, and more importantly, to the end costumer.

South American Countries	Retailers (2012)
Colombia	911
Chile	2,102
Ecuador	777
Peru	1,072
Venezuela	262

Chapter 9: Latin America

Central American Countries	Retailers (2012)
Costa Rica	275
El Salvador	269
Honduras	173
Guatemala	253
Nicaragua	87
Panama	178

Though the Latin American market is now considered big and relevant enough for the licensing business, there are still some areas that have yet to be developed, representing new opportunities and challenges for licensors and agents. For example, publishing is very strong internationally in the licensing industry, but is still a very small market in this area. Also, many licensors develop properties dedicated to infants, yet those product categories have yet to conquer the Latin America market as TV channel advertisers do not invest in this age demographic because of the risk for licensees who would want to acquire the property. The toy category is another category that is under-developed in the region. Mattel and Hasbro are the two most important players in the business having almost 80% of the market share in the region.

Fifty years ago there were two companies competing in the region for licensing TV properties, and two agents for each country. Now, over fifty licensors have a presence in the region with more than twelve agents representing TV properties as well as movies, artists, brands, design, sport properties, video games, and toys licenses. The licensing market in our region is much more sophisticated and complex than it was before and now requires highly experienced professionals with the best knowledge in order to reach success. The rapidly growing economies in Latin America are very promising for the future of licensing, led by a growing demand for consumer products every day more eager to identify with new brands.

9.4 Mexico

by Elias Fasja and Dalia Benbassat

9.4.1 Introduction

¡Bienvenidos! Mexico is a welcoming territory for licensing entrepreneurs ... highly sensitive to global trends and extremely quick at reacting to consumer needs and demands. Mexicans enjoy life, family and friends, promote social interaction and are traditionally hefty consumers. Due to its size and copious population, Mexico represents a zesty opportunity for brand owners willing to expand their licensing business into our region, although the country's infrastructure and commercial and retail structures may allow only a handful of those to be successful.

Mexico is the world's eleventh ranked economy in GDP and ranks 55 in the World's 2013-2014 Competitive Index as published by WEF. It is the second economy in Latin America, next only to Brazil, and thanks to sensible improvement in business development conditions, financial stability and business sophistication, Mexico is considered one of the world's big emerging markets. Mexico is intensely populated by over 112 million people; this implies more than 22 million households and a large percentage, slightly shy of 30%, of young consumers under the age of 14.

Not unlike other economies in the region, wealth is very unevenly distributed, and more than 36 million people continue to live in poverty. Lack of significant work opportunities has led to migration, self-employment and the proliferation of an informal economy. More than 30% of economically active people in Mexico are part of the informal sector which in turn represents more than 60% of the country's retail economy, a major topic in today's political and economic agenda, as well as a challenging and undeniable opportunity for licensed products.

The larger portion of the population is situated in the C and D socioeconomic levels and average GDP per capita is still one-third of the US. As result, most retail activity takes place at mass level, whether at the so-called "modern channels" (mass retail chains such as Walmart or Soriana, hypermarkets, warehouses and convenience stores) or the "traditional channels" (which include wholesale, thousands of independent retailers and the very large informal market).

Most economic activity is concentrated in the larger cities, such as Mexico DF, Guadalajara, Monterrey, followed by Puebla, Toluca or León. Home of the country's largest corporations and headquarters of the main retail firms, exception made of Soriana. Distribution of goods to the entire territory becomes an important challenge as well as a highly competitive asset for those who master it.

Approximately 30% of GDI stems from International Trade. Mexico has extensive trade agreements with 40 countries, however approximately 85% of exports take place with the US only. It is easy to see how influenced our economy is by the US economy and how strongly impacted we are by its ups and downs.

Mexico remained afloat the world economic turmoil – was able to maintain price stability and moderate internal deficit. Financial Institutions have proven strong and credit has remained available for qualifying corporations; foreign investment progressed and economy registered growth even through the years of crisis.

Recent changes in Federal Government have slowed economy down as several structural reforms are being crafted and slowly approved, in particular related to energy, education, labor and taxes, which are expected to reestablish competitive pace.

The intense combat against the drug cartels and the outbursts of violence and levels of insecurity in several neuralgic points of the country have also impacted negatively on the international perception of Mexico as a market apt for investment, and have brutally hit tourism, one of Mexico's largest sources of income, next to oil. This is an important setback against the otherwise promising macro-economic landscape, and remains a high priority for the current administration.

Latin America, remains one of today's world's economic engines, next to Asia. And Mexico, despite its significant challenges, stands among the region's best.

As a licensing professional or IP owner, you should consider the following challenges which affect our industry in particular:

- *Rampant piracy and very little anti-piracy* enforcement – A degree of progress has been achieved in recent years and thanks to the work of large IP protection activists in the territory, the IMPI or Mexican Institution of Intellectual Property, a number of new laws have been approved to protect IP owners from infringers and turn piracy and counterfeiting into a federal offense. But piracy is not bound to disappear anytime soon, it is rather something to live and deal with. Especially because the illegal market is aware of the overall shy nature of licensors' anti-piracy programs.
- *Concentration of Retail in fewer hands* – Large retail conglomerates are becoming the rule, and strategic acquisitions have narrowed down the number of players in Retail over the last few years. The reach of these retailers has widened, but not so the space they devote to new brands.
- *Concentration of Telecommunications in few hands* – in particular TV broadcast is controlled by two incredibly large firms which offer limited screen possibilities for new content and very tight entry filters. This once more reduces viewers' choices and affects entertainment licensing in particular. Penetration of alternative media, albeit expected to continue growing, is still limited (pay TV reaches only 44.3% of total households with a 29.4 estimated share1 and broad band is estimated to match a similar number). Significant change is however expected through the boost of smartphones and other mobile devices, and the surprisingly big participation of our country in social networking (i.e. Mexico has the second largest base of Facebook users worldwide accounting for forty nine million users).

Not unlike other territories, new technology will play a big part in how licensing evolves in Mexico the years to

Chapter 9: Latin America

come. (Source: Consejo Latinoamericano de Publicidad en Multicanales. Data: 2013 The Wall Street Journal)

9.4.2 History of Licensing

Licensing as an activity started out in Mexico in the second half of the twentieth century with fashion brands. Brands were then basically split by Licensors by category and scattered among several licensees, who acted in total independence with little to no coordination among them.

The first brand to be developed as a full concept - including shop in shops and stand-alone stores - was the French label *Cacharel,* conceived and negotiated in 1976 by the late Mr. Jacobo Fasja and headed by son Elias until 1992, who would years later found Tycoon Enterprises.

Through the 70's and 80's, character licensing in Mexico was mostly a Disney and Hanna Barbera sanctuary, followed in the late eighties by a number of Warner Bros.' basic merchandising programs. On the girls side there was mainly Barbie. Sports licensing was still at a very early stage, basically with NFL and MLB products.

None of these brands had their own consumer products operation in the territory, but were represented by small agencies or individuals. Disney was in the hands of Mr. Bustamante, Warner Bros. and Ninja Turtles were represented by Mr. Armando Malo (owner of Grupo Innovación), Hanna Barbera was represented by Mr. Gallard, and Mattel by Mr. Olivier.

By the late eighties the Mexican government began entering globalization trends, relaxing its policies for foreign corporations seeking to establish their own operations locally and opening the borders to imported goods which had been restricted until then. This had a very positive effect on the development of Licensing in our territory.

NAFTA (North America Free Trade Agreement) was signed by US President George H.W. Bush, Mexican President Salinas, and Canadian Prime Minister Brian Mulroney in 1992 to facilitate trade among the three countries. It was ratified by the legislatures of the three countries in 1993.

Basics of Licensing: International Edition

Tycoon Enterprises started operations in 1990 as the licensing agent for Mexican TV classsic "El Chavo del Ocho", followed soon after by Twentieth Century Fox "The Simpsons" as its first International client. In the few years that followed most large independent brands resorted to Tycoon for professional representation. Tycoon became the first fully established Licensing & Merchandising Agency to offer local licensing expertise at world-class standards, and remains to date strongly positioned in Latin America.

In 1992, The Disney Co. took over their Mexico consumer products operation. Warner Bros. followed the same steps a few years later, and as result of the merger with Turner took the licensing of Cartoon Network properties (handled by Tycoon until then) in-house too. And before the end of the same decade, Barbie and NFL, which had achieved big relevance also under Tycoon at that time, decided to take their CP operation in-house.

By that time, all the agents listed above with the exception of Tycoon had left the licensing scene. ITC from Brazil was the first non-Mexican agency who tried to conquer our market bringing the representation of "Peanuts". Owner Mr. Peter Carrero first hired a personal friend who regrettably passed away shortly after and then partnered with entrepreneur Mr. Enrique Altamirano, owner of Efectos Especiales and creator of Burundis, a domestic property born from social expression cards which enjoyed several years of success. Mari Carmen Rotter was GM of the operation then. The partnership didn't see the turn of the century.

A few years later, two new players entered the field: Mr. Ronald Dickins with the agency Globo Rojo, later known as Licensing and Promotions, representing initially Power Rangers, then a roaster of several other properties, and Union Internacional owned by Dr. Hideo Hayase K., which represented Dragon Ball during a long and very successful window (then other "anime-related" brands).Both agencies closed their doors in December 2012.

Another three foreign companies opened branches in Mexico and continue in operation: from Peru Compañía Panamericana de Licencias "CPL" (formerly Losani), EXIM Licensing, originally from Argentina, and Losani's spin-off

Chapter 9: Latin America

P&L Global, also Peruvian, all of which have enjoyed significant success.

At the turn of the century, Televisa – a dominant media group in the territory – set out to explore the business potential of licensing and merchandising, leveraging its privileged position among young audiences. By the end of 2003, it named ex-ITC licensing expert Mari Carmen Rotter – Maca – to lead the CP operation, which would manage their own properties as well as third party content too. Their first relevant move in this direction was closing an output deal with Nickelodeon which included all major platforms.

Following global corporate strategies, also Hasbro took its CP operation in-house, and so did Cartoon Network/Turner (who had parted from WB a few years before and was again in the hands of Tycoon).

A few others have ventured into the licensing field since and have built small but respectable operations. However it has become clear that in order to grow and gain a position in this business, you need schooling, experience, professionalization, and a solid portfolio which can be sustained over time.

Setting up a licensing agency in the early days was quite simple and unsophisticated. Licensing agents were mostly former advertising executives and possibly an assistant, who in certain cases was their own spouse. Deals were made "fist come first serve" with little attention to product quality or distribution capabilities, minimum guarantees were negotiated in random ways, several categories bundled in one deal with little care for segmentation, etc. Young, albeit smart, people were handling sales with almost no experience, and licensors were not demanding anything other than new deals and good numbers; no strategy, no retail, no forecasts, etc.

The more structured offices back then would be Disney and Grupo Innovación (agent then for Warner Bros. and Ninja Turtles). But overall the market was still "naïve"… it was the licensing and merchandising kindergarten, and a business with small risk and high ROI. Triggered possibly by a very successful Ninja Turtles merchandising program, we can consider the late 80's and beginning of the 90's as the starting point for modern character licensing.

Basics of Licensing: International Edition

Besides the shifts in International commerce mentioned above, another factor that significantly contributed to this was the resurgence of character-based consumer promotions, which had been banned by President Luis Echeverria (1970 – 1976) and which ban was lifted at the end of the eighties. Such moment was leveraged by huge companies like Frito-Lay and later by Grupo Bimbo, through massively successful self-liquidating and instant-win promotions. Promotions have since become a strong tool at building awareness for licensed brands in the territory.

The first large character-based retail activation happened in 1994, when Liverpool, the largest departmental retailer, reached an agreement with Tycoon Enterprises to develop their Christmas campaign around The Flintstones characters following their movie success. The terms were: Liverpool would give all Flintstones licensees the opportunity to participate and those, whose product performed well, would remain thereafter. In exchange, the retailer would have the right to develop and portray all marketing and POP assets at their own cost and expense. Needless to say, everyone was happy. The following couple of years, under similar conditions, promotions were made first with the Tom & Jerry characters, and then with Looney Tunes, both including a "purchase with purchase" plush promotion.

In 1997, Disney CP broke in, changing the rules significantly by investing a huge marketing sum, including a very impressive street parade. This established a very hard standard to meet and marked the end of the "age of innocence". Ever since, branded retail promotions have become the financial burden of licensors, agents and licensees. Given the early resistance –at times lack of interest- from foreign licensors to invest in local retail, and the absence of standardized Common Marketing Funds, such activities remained only Disney's privilege for a long time. It took several years for licensors to realize the centrality and relevance of investing in local retail.

Slowly but steadily, a growing number of properties broke into the market, and the environment turned increasingly competitive. Licensors became more and more demanding with their agents in terms of more sophisticated services, on-

Chapter 9: Latin America

going financial forecasting and re-forecasting, more seniority in brand managers, dedicated retail work, high yield in exchange for very limited investment in brand building. As the offer of new properties grew in the market, retailers in turn became more selective as well and at that point, the licensing business in Mexico broke into a new era.

9.4.3 Licensing Today

Licensing in Mexico today is a tough and demanding business which requires much more than good will, it needs well-built and sophisticated structures, strong retail relationships, strategic thinking and tons of leverage. The retail environment for licensed product has become quite challenging in great degree due to our retail structure.

Departmental penetration in our country is calculated to be only 40 square meters (430 sq. ft.) per every 1,000 people. Few names compose this sector: Liverpool is the largest high end departmental retailer in Mexico with 65% market share against Sears 20% and Palacio de Hierro 17% (by sales). In the mid-tier we have Suburbia, a soft line retailer owned by Wal-Mart and departmental Coppel only. With regards to mass market, Wal-Mart's share is in the 58% range, followed by Soriana 20%, Comercial Mexicana 12% and Chedraui 10%.[7] Besides these few albeit large formats, there are basically no multi-brand retail chains, therefore no significant "alternate" market for licensed goods within formal retail. This scenario leaves little room for second or third-tier brands, outside the very top, and becomes very demanding with those who make it to the sales floor, namely very high performance and stringent negotiation terms. Small brands have a hard time facing these conditions.

Supporting your brand to get the desired exposure and promotion with the leading chain stores, requires large marketing investment and needless to say, strong and capable

---

[7] As of 10/2012 according to El Economista citing Monex consumer behavior analyst Paola Sotelo.

Basics of Licensing: International Edition

licensees who are in turn reduced to a number of selected vendors. So despite this being a wonderful country of over 110 million souls, the number of possibilities for sound licensing success is unexpectedly limited, and concentration in the "power brands" is very high, as we shall discuss further ahead to more detail.

Major Properties.
Infant / Pre-school: Disney Classics, Disney Princesses, Pixar characters (such as Toy Story or Cars), Plaza Sésamo (Sesame Street co-production for Latin America), Nickelodeon's Dora the Explorer.
Girls: Sanrio's Hello Kitty, Mattel's Monster High & Barbie, musical band One Direction and Universal Pictures' Despicable Me.
Boys: Disney-Marvel Superheroes, Rovio's Angry Birds, Universal's Despicable Me, WB's Superman, Cartoon Network's Ben 10.
Young Adults: 20th Century Fox's The Simpsons, Disney-Marvel Superheroes, sports brands such as soccer clubs Real Madrid or Barcelona or local clubs America or Chivas.
Young Women: Sanrio's Hello Kitty.

Properties Originating from Mexico.
Televisa's TV series *El Chavo del Ocho*, illustration/social expression originals *Distroller* and *Fulanitos*, Internet-born *Huevocartoon*, and world-known artist *Frida Kahlo*.

Major Licensors.
Major licensors who have local direct operation in Mexico are Disney, Cartoon Network, Mattel, Hasbro, Warner Bros., NFL and of course Televisa.

Major Retailers.
High-End / Department stores: Liverpool (and sister-stores Fábricas de Francia), Sears, Palacio de Hierro.

Chapter 9: Latin America

> Mid-tier: Suburbia (mostly soft-lines) & Coppel (includes department stores and footwear specialty)
> Specialty: Office Depot, Office Max, Sanborn's (mostly gift & electronics), Martí (all sports).
> Mass Market: Wal-Mart Group, Soriana, Comercial Mexicana, Chedraui (each group with corresponding supermarket and hypermarket formats).
> Price Clubs: Sams, Costco, City Club.
> Convenience Stores: OXXO, Seven Eleven, Extra.

There are no numbers officially pronounced to date by any of our authorities with regards to Licensed sales or Licensed revenues deriving from Licensed sales in our territory. Market Analysts must yet address our sector to more depth and device a way to align criteria so that our industry can be measured effectively and consistently year by year.

PROMARCA, Mexico's Licensing Association, in collaboration with all its members, carried out the first serious attempt to assess a number to our Industry's worth, and in April 2013 published that:

A total of $1.7 Billion USD was generated from RETAIL SALES of Licensed Goods over the course of 2012 in MEXICO alone. This number is not expected to be precise, but to portray a reasonable idea of our industry's print in local economy.

Product Category	Percent	Retail Sales (billion US)
Apparel	14.0	242
Footwear	3.6	62
Home	10.2	177
Promotions	8.4	146
Accessories	14.6	254
Electronics	0.3	5
Food & Beverage	4.9	85
Paper & School Supplies	16.4	285
Publishing	2.4	41
Personal Care	6.8	118
Toys & Games	17.0	295
Videogames	1.4	25
	100%	1,735

Source: PROMARCA (Asociación Mexicana de Licenciamiento y Promoción de Marcas).

The mix is vastly dominated by Character and Entertainment Brands, followed by Fashion, Sports and other. Expected yearly growth rate: 5%

9.4.4 Codes of Conduct

When doing business in Mexico you should aim for a very positive experience. Save for few inevitable exceptions, expect to deal with trained professionals who, even when new to licensing in particular, are thoroughly prepared in their fields, aware of major global trends and often can account for International experience. Business is normally conducted in a collaborative and friendly tenure, where good will is expected to prevail.

Personal relationships are a key to business success in Mexico, where trust plays an important component. Mexicans prefer to do business with people they can relate to rather than with impersonal organizations. Since trust is something that needs to be developed, it is not uncommon that business meetings are followed or combined with dinner or more ca-

Chapter 9: Latin America

sual gatherings, where other associates or even family members are invited. For licensors who are at times worlds away, this role is played almost in its entirety by the agent, who will act as a cultural bond and interpreter.

Possibly due to this personal aspect of business relationships, you may find that deadlines and contractual obligations are somewhat taken more lightly when compared against other more stringent cultures. So contracts and other written documentation are always recommended, laying down to absolute clarity the extent of obligations as well as the consequences of breach. Compliance is often reactive rather than proactive, so reminder letters or even penalties become a stronger incentive than elaborate agreements.

Mexicans regard their business relationships as those of mutual and corresponding responsibility. Expect a great deal of service against royalties paid, and licensors to do their share of hard work: meaning to significantly promote the brand in the market and provide sufficient MKT tools to engage retail successfully. Licensees feel inherently it is them taking the higher stakes, so respectful manners are expected at all times and a level of aid in times of trouble. Don't expect to have sustained business in Mexico based on threats, unilateral decisions or indifference.

Mexican licensees are creative and practical, they will factor in the reality of their market and devise ways to offset the challenges related to economy and infrastructure, but will feel frustrated when licensors take too long to approve their materials or issue a customs letter... which seem like simple endeavors when compared to the hurdles they must embrace... They expect their business to be taken as seriously as their counterpart's, and need answers to arrive timely. They will respond very positively to licensors who seem accepting to their outlook and show true interest in their business and in their market.

9.4.5 Unique Challenges

Piracy remains a constant threat for our industry. Informal economy indexed at 60% of Mexico's overall economy, it provides a very large and prolific soil for IP infringement.

Whether it is done by local manufacturers producing goods to the lowest standards and quick supplying any rising demand, or by counterfeiters smuggling merchandise in through our highly permeable borders, coming from foreign licensees' stock or factories far away... piracy is rampant, and despite authorities' best efforts and sensible achievements, nothing says the situation will significantly improve, largely due to its social and political implications. Pirated goods hit first. Normally respond better to local taste and needs. If we are to defeat piracy, we must defeat this principle first. Shorten leadtimes. Understand context. Enable licensees to reach consumers sooner with product that is right for their market.

Concentration of Retail. Mexico is affected with this global shift. Volume is strongly concentrated in the mass-retail segment, composed by very few players who are becoming even fewer as result of consolidation or acquisition by larger groups. Despite their big size, these retailers are normally risk averse as far as brands are concerned, and all aim at the same top-notch properties which will presumably help them secure market share and maintain square foot margins high. So we have more of the same stores, but same number of brands, or proportionately... less. With fewer decision makers, competition to attain shelf space becomes fierce for licensees and pressure for in-store investment increases dramatically not only on licensees but on licensors too. As result, chances for emerging or niche brands are seriously reduced – on one hand the entry filter is tight; on the other the requirements for investment are high. Besides, without the big retail players, the critical mass needed to start up production become very hard to reach, and moving into independent retail brings you face to face with the challenges related to informality, as described above.

Execution in Retail - Larger IP owners have developed the right sense of relevance of retail activation and in-store investment. However despite retailers' size and degree of sophistication, execution of programs within these retailers is inconsistent and often results in loss of significant resources out of mismanagement. A flock of merchandisers and promoters is undoubtedly a critical recourse for proper execution in store, and maximization of money invested.

Shifts in Currency Rates – Mexico's economy is highly dependent on the US economy and as result the Mexican peso is often qualified as it relates to the US dollar rather than any other currency in the world. Most licensors have resorted to signing their agreements in US dollars as a security measure, and most licensees have come to accept it. However it represents and additional risk for licensees which they inevitably factor in when submitting projections and negotiate minimum guarantees. During severe shifts in exchange rates, it is not uncommon to see cash flow slow down, and licensees request caps are placed to secure their balancing payments from growing out of proportion.

Jurisdiction – Especially when dealing with major retailers in terms of Direct to Retail deals or Promotions, jurisdiction can be a deal breaker if the Mexican jurisdiction is rejected by a foreign licensor. Be ready to deal with it and to find creative ways to settle.

Withholding Taxes – As Mexico has double-tax treaties with several countries (35 until August 2013), non-treaty countries will be faced with high withholding rates. It is important to prepare yourself on the subject and hear your agent's advice.

Countries with which Mexico has running Double Tax Treaties as of 2013:

Países con los que México tiene Acuerdo para Evitar la Doble Tributación			
Alemania	Corea	Irlanda	Portugal
Argentina	Dinamarca	Israel	Reino Unido
Australia	Ecuador	Italia	República Checa
Austria	España	Japón	Rumania
Bélgica	Estados Unidos	Luxemburgo	Singapur
Brasil	Finlandia	Noruega	Suecia
Canadá	Francia	Nueva Zelanda	Suiza
Chile	Grecia	Países Bajos	Sudáfrica
China	Indonesia	Polonia	

http://www.promexico.gob.mx/es_us/promexico/Acuerdos_para_evitar_doble_tributacion

New Regulations in Advertising for Kids - The rising index of obesity in our general population, and especially concerning children, has become a focal point in Mexican politics and economics. Given the sensitivity of the matter, the government has tried to restrain consumption of foods high in salt, sugar and fat among young ones and the Marketing of these products to kids has been heavily tyrannized. As in other countries, self-regulation can become an effective prophylaxis to avoid legally imposed advertising restraints, however this is a threat that remains and may affect the use of licensed brands and characters in this sector in the medium term. Here, the creative use of licensed characters in positive health promoting messaging becomes essential, as is the advice of local agents or councils.

9.4.6 Role of Local Agents

The agent is the business and cultural ambassador between the parties involved in the licensing transaction, namely, the licensees, licensors and retailers. Experts in their market and well acquainted with local trends and fashions, agents bring to the table the right skills and the needed relationships to enable successful business to happen.

The agent's job begins by making an accurate brand diagnose and by identifying the true extent of possibilities that a particular brand has in that particular market. This can only be done *from within* and via deep understanding of the marketplace, its dimension, the opportunities it entails, its challenges...It is the agent's role to help licensors decipher the rules of engagement with local trade in order to build successful relationships which can be sustained over time. By understanding the market's dynamics and its main actors, the agent should be able to come up with a route that leads to good business with the smallest possible risk. In order to attain this, the agent should be fully immersed in the brand it represents, and fully aware of its strategic goals in the short and medium terms. Alignment with the licensor's core objectives is an essential condition for successful licensing.

Agents bring two priceless assets to the negotiation table: one is *perspective*, which stems from experience in the marketplace and often from working with several other brands. It is not uncommon for licensors to subjectively compare local deals to what they have domestically, however true benchmark comes from agent's knowledge of *who is who* in the local scene, and what each category should be worth. The other is *trust* – the personal angle to the licensing relationship and the ability to build strong relationships with clients. As said in the previous chapter, trust, and a sense of mutual accountability, is key to successful business in this territory and probably as engaging to the licensees as the brand itself.

But these assets will only be of good use if accompanied with *empowerment* and a sensible level of authority to intercede in business decisions and important matters. It is not uncommon for licensors to overlook that the agent's resources and repute are implied in every negotiation, and should be preserved as much as their own, its time valued, its views respected. Sudden shifts in brand direction or decisions which seem arbitrary have a strong impact in the agent's relationships and should be weighted and avoided to the extent possible.

The agent's participation in building the relationship with retail partners is crucial too. Mexican retailers will require a great deal of service, creativity and perseverance. Knowledge of retail timing, core purchase seasons, when a new brand should be introduced, products presented, promotions planned, etc., are questions which can only by answered by a dedicated agent, working off the ground.

It is the agent's task to line up licensees' interests and often other anchor partners (i.e., master toy licensees or home entertainment/theatrical divisions), and coordinate a unified approach to retail in order to negotiate premium spaces and other activations.

Another area of great contribution by agents is the conveyance of trends applicable to product development and design: which colors fly off shelves and which tend to be left behind; is "minimalist" a good treatment for this market, or is saturation what gets the eye? Again these are important questions that can hardly be answered by someone miles away, who at times has never been to the market in question or knows very little about it. When you are designing product that is expected to perform on a local level, licensors must acknowledge the territory's uniqueness, and be open to benefit from local success factors.

Visiting Mexico for in-depth market recognition and first-look at its retail structures and consumers is indispensable. This road-trip is critical not only for licensing managers but for the creative teams supervising product development. Hiring Mexican or Latin talent can help abridge the cultural gap and ease the road to approved deals or approved product, as long as communication lines are clear and tasks are not duplicated.

Empowering the agent in this area, and allowing him or her to do product approvals – proper training preceding - would not only mean quicker completion, but also product that is a better fit to our market. Considering that large licensors such as Disney or Warner Bros. can procure on-site approvals and immediate responses to product development queries, the long and intricate processes where each phase must be checked by three layers of people, at times in different parts of the world, becomes a large competitive disadvantage.

Agents should be expected to monitor licensees' performance, competitors' activity, identify threats, keep licensor duly informed of relevant signals and advise accordingly. It is

Chapter 9: Latin America

a complex job that has multiple battlefronts, whose interests must be reconciled and protected for long term success.

What should not be expected from agents and constitutes a very common misconception is that agents create demand. Desire for product is generated by the brand itself, and by the nature of its connection to consumers, whether aspirational or emotional. Agents may build very successful licensed programs based on such connection, on such bond. But cannot create a bond where it does not exist. Demand remains the licensor's responsibility.

9.4.7 Marketing, Advertising and Promotion

The success of a licensed brand in Mexico is linked to a number of factors:
- The brand's intrinsic connection to local audiences/consumers
- Level of exposure and recognition
- Depth and extent of creative resources
- Investment in Retail
- Continued introduction of relevant content

All of the above are first and foremost the responsibility of the licensor, and without them, promoting licensed product would be pointless. Any brand striving to be successful must first be sure to count with the needed grounds (the substantial bond with consumers) as well as the ammunition to convert this equity into sales.

Depending on the nature of the brand, a specific marketing plan must be developed. Today a CMF, or common marketing fund, is not an attribute of the "big brands" but a must-have for any brand making a serious approach to this market. 1 to 2% of sales are rates normally accepted by licensees on top of royalties, in the understanding that significant activity will be expected in return, whether in the shape of advertising, promotion or retail activation. Licensors are bound to contribute with an amount just as big as the amount accrued by licensees, or more if it is an emerging brand requiring so. The best use for a CMF is probably investment in retail exhibition and activations, since retailers need motivation, and consumers need an undeniable in-store signal telling them what is hot!

Retail activities will include a combination of the following: roadshows to introduce licensed product, crafting of retail incentives (such as promotions or special exclusive offers), design and production of signage and customized fixtures, branded walls or corners, participation in circulars and tabs, and activities in-store, such as character or celebrity appearances, contests, and other shapes of BTL activations.

These activities which generate traffic are highly regarded by retailers, especially if they can be replicated in several of their many stores, but are *hardly ever* paid for by the retailer. Retailer may contribute with larger orders or by using proprietary media, but even when they do, proper execution is not guaranteed, so as result hiring independent merchandising services is advised to supervise materials reach their destination and meet the purpose intended for.

Retail activity has become a strong differentiator for serious brands but also a very high standard for smaller brands to reach and has tightened the way into shelves even further.

For brands with less established recognition, advertising becomes more relevant, as consumers must know legit product exists and where to find it. A specific plan should be developed using the media platforms that are most suitable and more effectively reach that segment.

ATL is expensive so very few licensees will resort to it in an individual level. Cable is more affordable but penetration is still limited and audience often pulverized among the many channels. So in general printed or outdoor advertising is preferred, in particular billboards and buses circulating main avenues, as well as ads in magazines targeting core demographics. But individual acting by licensees remains the exception rather than the rule... and the participation of Licensor, or its agent, is very relevant.

Looping in several licensees – often linked by category – in catalogs or brochures which can be cross promoted among partners is a good way to gain exposure without too high expense and by using anchor partners strengths (i.e., toys or home video partners...).

Chapter 9: Latin America

Brands owned by large media conglomerates allocate a significant amount of resources towards their consumer products business, with initiatives that help drive traffic, promoting licensed product via ads or editorial placed on their broadcast, publishing or online platforms. This is an *undeniable competitive advantage others are bound to meet*, even if with dissimilar resources.

Participation at trade shows is probably the activity which licensees participate in more profusely. Examples include *Expo Papelera* (for school and stationery goods - takes place in March every year*)*, *Intermoda* (fashion – January/July), *Confitexpo* (confectionery and party - July), *Sapica* (footwear & leather– March/August), *Salpro* (gift - August), *FIL* (books - December) and several others… besides expos directly conducted by retailers as trademarked events (i.e. *Expo Walmart, Expo Chedraui* and such…) important at promoting brands inside these organizations.

Promoting licensed product effectively depends on the right understanding of the brand's DNA and that of its core consumers, so it feels natural and coherent. If the brand stands for fun – promote in fun places and in fun ways; if lifestyle, participate in top fashion shows and seek endorsement from fashion celebs; if event driven, use the event to gain visibility; etc.

If the intent to promote is serious, licensors must dedicate the resources. Rely on experts and invest in additional talent. And even if agent's participation in advertising and promotion strategies is crucial at decision making, different skills and liaisons are needed for professional public relations and advertising services, digital media management and so on… so whether you are acting as the licensor or as licensee, don't expect these to be packaged-in within licensing services, unless previously outlined and separately compensated.

9.4.8 Retail

High-End - possibly like anywhere else in the world is mostly focused on large international fashion brands, with amazing in-store displays or "shop in shop" concepts. High end is very selective when it comes to licensing and will

Basics of Licensing: International Edition

choose only the premium properties and will require at least a certain degree of exclusivity. Volume at high-end is normally not that high, although it builds good equity and makes for great launch platforms.

Mid Tier – perfect for multi-brand exposure. Aspirational by nature, dedicate significant floor space to licensed brands. Mostly soft-lines.

Specialty Stores – very strong in their own segment, in particular BTS supplies, toys and sporting goods.

Convenience Stores – mostly for male shoppers and impulse buying, one of the fastest growing formats in the country. Significant due to the number of outlets, these formats are relevant selling points for licensed food & beverage and consumer good promotions, as well as small accessories which require small display.

Mass Market – comprised by the large self-service chains, supermarkets and hypermarkets. This is the terrain of mothers and family, where most of licensed volume is generated, and therefore it is a highly competitive soil. Strong licensed brands presence in apparel, toys, food and beverage, accessories, home and BTS.

Wholesale or "Traditional" – comprised by thousands of small independent shops, boutiques, catalogues, grocery shops or "mom & pop's" or even street stands, where a large amount of licensed sales take place, albeit hard to measure due to their proximity to the informal market...

And of course the big, untamed, informal markets, which are calculated to comprise over 60% of our overall economy, which greatly profit from illegal use of trademarks and remain the largest area of opportunity for brand owners.

9.4.9 Outlook, Projections and Conclusion

The need to invest in POS is increasing. While at some point retailers were looking to offset costs by allowing IP owners to "brand" their seasonal displays, today, Licensors' rising interest in obtaining these spaces have turned them into such coveted opportunities, often disputed between several brands, that a "price tag" has been placed on them!

High-End Departmental Stores. Concentration of high-end departmental stores will continue to imply smaller shelf space for the ever growing number of brands in the character licensing sector. In their constant search for differentiated brands and products, will they be able to move away from the natural demand generated by successful brands and fads without losing business? Will they let the opportunity to have licensed products with high rotation rates slip? Those are questions to be answered only through the experience.

Mass Market. Besides Disney's, there are still few DTR examples of character licensed brands but we are seeing the first stages happening in smaller mass market chains. Wal-Mart's high market share might vary due to the increase of self-regulations which may have an incidence in its new unit's growth rate giving some margin to its competitors. Notwithstanding, new retail chains are not foreseen to emerge in the medium term, the acquisitions by foreign firms (among them a couple of South American ones) which have a higher sophistication in terms of merchandising, might be happening sooner or later.

TV. In terms of kids programming, there's a dramatic dominance of Televisa in free TV which seems difficult - albeit not impossible- to challenge by a new network. In any case, in my opinion, it will take a good long time before it happens. Pay TV has being growing at a faster pace the last few years but it still cannot compete with Free TV in terms of share and ratings, not to say that very few examples of successful licensing programs have derived from the property exposure limited to Pay TV. According to Nielsen Ibope, between 2008 and 2013, the Free TV Audience has dropped from 84% to 72%. As we all know, second and third screens will continue to split kids and adults audiences, diminishing the TV dominance with regards to the exposure of character licensed properties due to its natural time & space limitations.

In order to increase opportunities for TV-driven properties, a cross platform strategy might change the actual scenario and/or Pay TV penetration should increase dramatically its reach at the level of well developed countries.

Theatrical. It is clear that there's a growing aversion to single titles and the market is progressively leaning towards sequels instead, which have proven to be hugely successful. Nevertheless in the short term, the large volume of titles that Disney will be launching to the market each year, adding to its own productions Pixar's titles, Marvel Superheroes and now Star Wars, will represent a big challenge for all stake holders in the value chain of our industry.

The short span between releases inevitably shortens the traditional windows between movies and as a consequence reduces the life of its products on shelf. Considering the nature of the Mexican retail landscape, a fragmented demand would increase the risk of excess inventories – which effects would damage the Theatrical licensing business in the long run.

Digital. Game App properties, represent a large opportunity. Despite the still limited penetration of smartphones, we have seen so far the success of Angry Birds and we are foreseeing more to come as the number of smartphones is growing at a relevant rate. While trying to secure a final launch date or access ratings for TV series in Mexico is usually a difficult task, the daily activity of internet-based property users is measured in a very open and ample way.

When compared to a TV show, apps will not disappear from the mobile screen as long as there is a significant user base around the world, no matter how long it takes to mature in one or another country. It could become soon the major competitor for TV and Theatrical properties if handled properly.

The downside is that not all the new-media IP owners are ready for worldwide success and their resources and licensing experience is still very limited. Therefore, we believe they should rely more heavily on their agent's experience and leave a wider decision margin in them. How wide? Well, it's a good question. This depends on each case, on each brand, a very much on the agent's capabilities.

Competing with the major licensors requires a new POS investment criteria. The traditional economics of cutting down only the agent commission and keeping the reminder

Chapter 9: Latin America

should be modified, allocating an additional portion to ensure retail activities, designated shelf space and social media. Of course, there is many times a "Common Marketing Fund", but when you're launching a property you'll have to think about an upfront investment too, not to mention the need of sophisticated style guides.

Properties with slower return potential, facing the ongoing limited shelf space described, will need to offer Agents higher incentives to "level the field" with the cost / benefit it usually gets from the "Power brands".

The concept of hiring an agent which is not representing major brands so he can focus on a smaller brand might be romantic, but experience has proved it wrong. The leverage a representative has among licensees and retailers lies in the size and volume of the opportunities it brings to the table, the frequency they do business together and the certainty that the agent in question has a track record, and solid/sophisticated structure.

A successful and well-balanced portfolio often proves that the agent you've chosen has all the right qualities. And its larger structure will likely allow him to place more dedicated efforts towards product development supervision, retail relationships and promotions.

To compete with the major licensors who run their own operation, licensors will have to give more autonomy to their agent by means of training and supervision in terms of Quality Assurance and product development, allowing a faster and more efficient "go to market" of the licensed products.

Working this way will allow the agent to judge and approve the licensees' art submissions considering the local culture, avoiding lengthy discussions with their Quality Assurance peers located in a remote country, with good will but often unable to understand each country's taste and specific market needs. No question, such needs are better known by the local expert.

A final recommendation to succeed in Mexico: *Don't forget, to be global, you need to be local.*

Come visit soon!

Chapter 10:

The Licensor—Licensee Relationship

10.1 Introduction

Licensing is a process that is fundamentally based on two separate parties cooperating together to generate a product, service or promotion. The property owner/licensor and the licensee, who will manufacture or produce the licensed products, enter into a licensing agreement that will define the terms of their business relationship. The respective roles and obligations of each party are the focus of this chapter.

The age-old question, "Which came first, the chicken or the egg?" applies when assessing the roles that each party plays in licensing, as well as their relative importance. The fact is, it really doesn't matter which is more important or influential, since both the egg and the chicken perform a vital function in this relationship. Similarly, the willing participation and cooperation of both parties to a licensing agreement are also necessary if the collaboration is to succeed. Like the Chicken vs. Egg question, there is little purpose to assigning greater significance to one party over the other, as each plays a distinctive and integral role.

10.2 The Deal

In licensing, an intellectual property owner grants the right to use the property to a licensee in exchange for the payment of some form of financial consideration. Both parties must invest something up-front in order to profit from the relationship. The licensor has already made an investment, by virtue of developing the property that the licensee believes has value, and securing the necessary legal protection. The licensee, upon obtaining the license, is obligated to develop a desirable product, design attractive packaging, and manage the responsibilities associated with manufacturing, marketing, selling and delivering the licensed goods to the retailer and/or consumer.

The premise upon which licensing operates is that each party receives something of value. Often the more equal the values are between the parties the better the relationship. The licensee obtains use of the other party's intellectual property as the basis for development of a product or service that should make it more attractive to consumers. The licensor, likewise, is compensated through the payment of royalties for the use of the property.

Today, faced with rising expenses, a more difficult retail climate, and greater uncertainty as to which licenses will achieve sell-through success, licensees are less willing to pay high advances and guarantees as the standard cost of doing business. With bidding wars over licensing rights that can push advances and guarantees into the stratosphere, and "sure-thing" licenses failing to deliver promised financial returns, many licensees feel warranted in refusing to make a significant up-front financial commitment to licensors in addition to the investment necessary to design, manufacture and market the licensed product.

The prevailing attitude among licensees today is that royalties must be earned through actual product sales, and not from advances or guarantees based on ambitious sales forecasts compiled before the licensed products have ever reached retail. With that said, however, advances and guarantees do serve a purpose and are very significant aspects of any licensing relationship.

10.3   Establishing Payment Terms

Naturally, in the course of negotiating any license agreement, the parties tend to focus most on the terms of the deal that relate to compensation. Licensing compensation typically includes three principle components: the guarantee, the advance and the royalty rate. Despite what one may hear to the contrary, each element is negotiable.

Chapter 10: The Licensor—Licensee Relationship

10.3.1 The Guarantee

The guarantee is an essential part of the formula for financial compensation contained in most license agreements. Although the licensor is entitled to earn a royalty on each licensed product sold, the rationale for including a guarantee is based on the fact that there is no assurance the product will succeed in the retail market or that the licensee will maximize the opportunity to use the licensed property during the term of the agreement. Therefore, the guarantee assures that, regardless of whether or not the licensee is able to successfully or fully exploit the licensing rights held, the licensor will receive a certain minimum amount of money for the rights granted.

The real question is, as it has always been, how do the parties establish a fair guarantee for those rights the licensee acquires? Be assured, a reasonable advance or guarantee is not some budget number that the licensor needs to achieve for his quarterly or yearly balance sheet, or some "ideal" dollar amount that would satisfy a producer or superior. Advances and guarantees must reflect realistic sales projections which, in some measure, are representative of the popularity of the property, the sales appeal of the product in question and, certainly, the current economic conditions of the marketplace.

If you are negotiating for the right to license a popular property, but in a product category that has only limited appeal, the financial terms should reflect both factors. The same is true if the general economic conditions of the market are soft and overall retail sales are down. These considerations must be taken into account in order to arrive at a financial compensation package that is both equitable and realistic for both parties to the agreement. To proceed otherwise creates a lopsided deal that will prove difficult to enforce, is likely to be re-negotiated down the road or, worse, may strain future relations between the licensor and licensee.

Too often, license agreements are negotiated in the heat of the moment, with little thought given to the fact that there will be other properties and opportunities available in the future. It is this same mentality that can lead licensors to push for unreasonable and excessively high advances and guarantees; terms that might meet their own current budgetary demands, but which are otherwise impractical in the context of realistic sales projections or current market conditions.

Likewise, throngs of unwitting licensees frequently overlook, or plainly ignore, glaring pitfalls when driven by impulse. Too many simply lock onto an attractive, potentially lucrative licensing opportunity in spite of the fact that the up-front obligations involved may be unwarranted or place them in a financially untenable position.

10.3.2 The Advance

In order for any property to attract interest from licensees, it must exhibit certain qualities such as originality, appeal and/or popularity to convince them that, if used on licensed products, the property can generate significant consumer sales.

When negotiating the terms of a license, it is reasonable to assume that the property owner has already made a considerable investment of time and money to create the property. This is the licensor's contribution to the licensing process. It cannot be overlooked. Therefore, any fair licensing transaction should include some form of up-front advance as payment for the right to use the property. Typically, the advance is frequently a percentage of the negotiated guarantee that is payable upon signing of the license agreement. As its name implies, the advance (usually) represents a pre-payment of royalties, and thus recoupable — meaning that the licensee can credit the value of the advance towards future royalties due the licensor. Whether the total advance is paid as a single payment upon signing the license agreement, or made as a series of payments within a certain time frame, the amount is always negotiable.

10.3.3 The Royalty Rate

In licensing, the key financial element for the licensor is the royalty — the sum of money the licensor will receive from the sale of each licensed item. Royalties are generally based on a percentage of the licensee's wholesale sales of the licensed products. Like any other cost associated with the

Chapter 10: The Licensor—Licensee Relationship

creation of the licensed item, it is factored into the product's retail selling price, and is a cost that is passed on to the consumer by virtue of the item's retail point.

For almost every type of product imaginable, there is a pre-existing average royalty range. Whether the royalty agreed upon by the parties is within, above or below the average royalty is often a reflection of consumer demand and interest in the property and product. A greater demand entitles the licensor to a higher royalty, while less popular licenses may command royalties that are at or below the average royalty rate.

However, consideration should always been given to the fact that the royalty rate will affect the product's retail price. Thus, charging too high a royalty can actually have an adverse effect if it inflates the retail price above what the consumer is willing pay, or pushes the price above comparable products.

Ideal financial terms are those that provide the parties with reasonable terms, which include an acceptable advance and guarantee paid to the licensor, and a reasonable royalty rate paid by the licensee. Under such terms, the parties should anticipate that earned royalty payments will ultimately exceed the negotiated advance and/or guarantee.

10.4   Product Development

Once a license agreement is in place between the licensor and licensee, the focus shifts to developing the licensed product. This phase requires close collaboration between the parties and specific performances by each in order to create an appealing, marketable and quality product that consumers will want to buy.

10.4.1   Style Guide

A primary responsibility of the licensor is to furnish the necessary guidelines that the licensee will use in developing the licensed products. This material is usually provided in the form of a style guide. The scope and detail of the materials required is totally dependent on the type of property in question but, at a minimum, it must contain enough information for a licensee to be able to create the product, packaging and ancillary materials in accordance with the terms of the license agreement.

The best way to build a strong and readily identifiable licensing program is through the uniform and consistent use of trademarks, images and color palettes, all of which should be clearly set forth in the style guide. It is important to create a consistent look and feel to all aspects of the licensing program, from products and packaging, to advertising and press releases.

10.4.2 Legal Notices

As all merchandising licenses are based on the use of properties protected by copyright and/or trademarks, licensees are required to include such information on products and packaging. Instructions concerning the content, form and placement of such legal notices must be clearly communicated by the licensor.

10.4.3 Forms

Most licensors have a number of standard forms that the licensee is required to use, such as the submission of materials for approval, and the payment of royalties. Materials such as this should be provided to the licensee at the commencement of the license, in addition to adequate explanation as to how and when such materials should be used.

10.4.4 Approvals

Virtually every license agreement requires that the licensee obtain approval from the licensor for all products, packaging, promotional, advertising and marketing materials associated with the licensing product. While the process of submitting samples for approval is always spelled out in the license agreement, it is good practice to also include this information in the style guide to ensure compliance and, therefore, expedite the response time. Failure by the licensee to obtain such approvals is considered a material breach of the license agreement, and provides the licensor with the right to terminate the license agreement.

Chapter 10: The Licensor—Licensee Relationship

As the licensor may request changes to products and packaging, licensees will be well advised to make such submissions early in the product development cycle. Encouraging licensees to submit products at the design level, and again throughout the development process, helps the licensee avoid having to make costly changes or incur significant time delays. Licensors need to pay attention to insuring approvals are handled as expeditiously as possible, and licensees should be encouraged to embrace the approval mantra: when in doubt, ask.

For their part, licensors have an obligation to treat product and packaging approvals as a significant priority. Licensors need to appreciate that licensees frequently operate under time-sensitive production schedules when it comes to developing products and packaging designs. Since approvals must be obtained before production can commence, delayed responses from a licensor during the approvals process can adversely affect a licensee's ability to remain on schedule and lead to costly delays in products reaching the retail shelf – a situation that can produce adverse financial consequences for all parties.

10.5   Approval Process

Sometime prior to, or shortly after, introducing a licensed product, it is customary for the licensee to deliver to the licensor samples of each licensed product. The actual number of samples required by the licensor varies, and is generally negotiable. One factor in determining the number of required samples is the price of the product, and often licensors will consent to receipt of fewer samples for higher priced goods.

10.6   Royalty Payments and Statements

Once the licensed product has been approved, manufactured and delivered to the retail shelf, the licensee is faced with its continuing obligation of providing the licensor with timely payment of royalties due, and submissions of detailed royalty reports. Typically, the licensee is obligated to submit royalties on a quarterly basis, with payment and statements due to the licensor 30 to 45 days after the end of each quarter.

The methodology employed by the licensee to calculate the amount of royalties due from sales of the licensed products is always defined in the license agreement, and does vary to some extent among licensors. The standard practice used by many licensors is to base royalty payments on the licensee's net sales of licensed product. What this means is that the licensee is able to reduce the gross income by deducting agreed-upon costs and credits, which results in a Net Sales figure, and becomes the basis upon which royalties are determined. Close attention must be paid as to what constitutes allowable deductions, since failure to clarify this can easily result in a misstatement of the actual royalties due.

Typically, licensees are also required to submit a royalty report with their royalty payments. As noted earlier, often the licensor will supply a Royalty Report Form that the licensee must use when submitting such reports. Like the question of allowable deductions, there is no "industry standard" royalty report form. Generally speaking, however, the license agreement will detail what type of information the royalty report must include and in what format it is to be submitted.

As licensees are often obligated to supply the licensor with sales information on each licensed item sold, the licensee is well advised to understand exactly what level of detail is required prior to commencing sale of the licensed products. With a firm understanding of what information the licensee will be obliged to supply the licensor at the outset, steps can be taken to insure that such information is routinely tracked, which makes it less difficult and time-consuming for the licensee.

10.7   Product Liability Insurance

In our litigious society, product liability insurance naming the licensor as an insured party on the policy is a must. Though most manufacturers will have such insurance, it is reasonably certain that the license agreement will specify the minimum level of product liability insurance the licensee must carry, coupled with the demand that the licensee add the

Chapter 10: The Licensor—Licensee Relationship

licensor (and licensing agent if there is one involved in negotiating the license agreement) as insured party(s). The licensee will be required to provide a certificate of liability insurance to the licensor, which must be furnished prior to the distribution of any licensed merchandise. Like other elements of the license agreement, the amount of liability insurance coverage is negotiable. The range of required coverage is usually one to three million dollars.

10.8 Terms and Extensions

If the licensee has the right to renew the license agreement for one or more extension terms (licensing term(s) that follow the original term), frequently the licensee is compelled to deliver notice to the licensor of the intent to renew the license agreement on or before a specified date prior to the end of the term. The average time frame for delivery of such notice is usually 30 to 90 days prior to the end date of the license agreement.

The licensee's right to renew the license agreement is (usually) subject to the licensee meeting some pre-determined financial threshold, which is often expressed as a minimum amount of royalty income paid during the term of the license agreement. Like so many other points in the licensing agreement, the requirements that must be met in order for the licensee to have the right to renew the agreement are subject to negotiation. If the license agreement provides for the right to renew, licensees are well-advised to calendar the date that notice is due to the licensor. Failure to provide such notice may provide the licensor with the right to either disallow the grant of an extended term, or change the financial terms of the renewal period.

Renewal terms often require the licensee to pay an advance and/or commit to a guarantee that specifically applies to the new term. If a renewal term advance is required, payment is usually due at the commencement of the renewal term.

Chapter 11:

The License Agreement

11.1 Introduction

The cornerstone of any licensing program is the license agreement that is entered into between the licensor and a licensee, as it will govern the eventual relationship between the parties. A good license agreement can make the program run smoothly, while a bad one can cause more problems than either party needs. It is often the case that once the license agreement is signed, the parties never find the need to refer back to the document again, but should the need arise, its contents and structure become crucial.

License agreements can take many shapes and forms, and it is the rare case that one licensor will use the same form agreement as another licensor. Moreover, while the property owner/licensor typically starts off with a "standard" agreement, negotiations between the parties will ultimately result in a number of changes. Consequently, the final signed agreements may vary significantly from one licensee to another. In an ideal situation, however, the core provisions of the licensor's standard agreement will remain consistent.

11.2 Negotiating the Terms of a License

The negotiations leading up to the drafting of a license agreement are typically handled by the relevant business executives charged with the responsibility for negotiating the license. While there are occasions where one or both parties may be accompanied by their attorneys during these negotiations, the presence of counsel is usually reserved for larger or more complex transactions. Where the licensing executives are experienced and the issues are relatively straightforward, there is no need to involve counsel at this point. The purpose of these negotiations is to arrive at some consensus relative to the business terms of the agreement. There is normally sufficient time later in the process for the attorneys to get involved and conclude the agreement.

The negotiation of a license agreement is like most other business negotiations, i.e., typically, one party is in a stronger bargaining position than the other. Similarly, one party may have a stronger incentive to enter into the license than the other, which can shift the bargaining leverage to the other party.

In negotiating license agreements, leverage is not always about size and power, but more commonly, about a party's need to enter into the agreement, which can be the result of a variety of different circumstances. For example, one party might have a desire to enter a particular market, and the license is a means of accomplishing it, while another party might desperately need to include a licensed property on its products to stay competitive. Whatever the motivations, it is rare that both parties have equal leverage in licensing negotiations.

Prior to entering actual licensing negotiations, the parties should have each fully investigated the other party to insure that they are compatible and can work together in the future. For example, the owner of a famous trademark, such as TIFFANY, should understandably be hesitant to license its famous mark to a manufacturer who has a reputation for producing low-price, low-quality impulse items.

The only sure way to conclude that the eventual relationship will be a good fit is for the property owner to fully investigate the potential licensee. Many licensors require that a potential licensee fill out a "License Application Form" which requires the prospective licensee to provide its full and complete financial information, as well as information concerning other licenses that it may hold or has held in the past. This is a good practice that should be followed by all licensors.

When the licensor obtains the completed application, it should do more than simply read and file it. If the prospective licensee looks good "on paper," the licensor should consider

Chapter 11: The License Agreement

the application as the starting point. It is advisable for the licensor to fully check the references provided and speak directly with other licensors to learn how the licensee performed for them. While past performance is no guarantee of future success, past failures may well be an indicator of future failure.

After vetting the prospective licensee, the parties are then ready to begin the negotiation process. While it is the rare negotiation that covers all of the points that will ultimately be included in the final license agreement, most negotiators will start with the essential elements of the business transaction. If the parties cannot reach agreement on the fundamental business terms, it may not be worthwhile to proceed any further. The following items will typically be discussed in the course of most licensing negotiations:

- What licensed properties will be included in the agreement, i.e., the licensed property?
- Are there any elements of the property that will not be included in the license, e.g., the likeness of an actor.
- What are the specific products or services that will be included in the license, i.e., the licensed product(s)?
- In which territory will the licensee be able to sell licensed products, i.e., the licensed territory?
- In what retail channels will the licensee be permitted to sell the licensed products, i.e., the channels of distribution?
- How long will the licensee be able to produce and sell licensed products, i.e., the term?
- Can the licensor grant similar licensing rights to other parties, i.e., exclusive or non-exclusive rights?
- When does the licensee have to begin marketing and selling licensed products, i.e., the product introduction and distribution dates?
- How much does the licensee have to pay for the right to sell licensed products, i.e., the royalty, advance and guarantee?

It should be appreciated that these are only some of the points included in a typical negotiation, and they will certainly vary from one to the next. Nevertheless, they will serve as a good starting point for most scenarios.

In this regard, it is important that the parties discuss and agree upon the specific licensed property that will be included in the license agreement as well as the licensed products for which the property is being licensed. In defining the property, it's important to define it specifically, e.g., does the licensed property include simply the PEANUTS name, or does it include the right to use the characters CHARLIE BROWN and SNOOPY?

When defining the licensed products, it is similarly important to be as specific as possible and they should be limited to only those products that the licensee is actually capable of manufacturing and selling. Broad definitions should be avoided wherever possible.

For example, if the licensee intends to use the licensed property on T-shirts, the licensor would be well advised to define the licensed products more specifically, e.g., "100% cotton men's T-shirts without a collar from sizes S-XL."

This, of course, leads us to the question of exclusivity. Will the license be exclusive to the licensee, exclusive to the licensee with the licensor reserving the right to produce the licensed products itself, or simply non-exclusive? In recent years, the trend has been toward non-exclusive licenses since they pose far fewer problems if the licensee does not perform as expected or, worse yet, goes into bankruptcy. Additionally, some entities, such as state-funded universities, have a policy of only granting non-exclusive licenses.

There are exceptions, of course, particularly where the licensee is prepared to make a substantial commitment to the program and/or pay a significant guarantee. One way to satisfy both parties is for the licensor to provide "back-door" exclusivity for the licensee by providing that while the agreement is, on its face, non-exclusive, the licensor agrees that it will not during the term of the agreement grant any conflicting licenses to third parties provided that the licensee is not in breach of any provisions of the agreement. Such a compromise protects the licensor should the licensee go into bankruptcy by allowing them to grant other licenses. Similarly, it

Chapter 11: The License Agreement

offers the licensee some degree of exclusivity provided that it is performing under the terms of the agreement.

The parties need to discuss and agree upon the length or "term" of the agreement and the "territory" in which the licensed products can be sold. The term of the agreement is always a difficult negotiation since the licensee will want the agreement to extend for as long as possible, while the licensor will want to limit it to a relatively short period of time. The licensee's position is that it will be investing substantial sums in developing and marketing the licensed products and will therefore require time to recoup its initial investment. Conversely, the licensor is concerned that it will be tying up its valuable property right for a prolonged period of time with no guarantee that the licensee will actually exploit the property.

The typical compromise is to set the term for a reasonable period of time, e.g., two to three years, with the licensee having the option to renew for additional periods upon meeting certain performance criteria. For example, the term might be for two years with two separately exercisable options to renew the agreement for additional extended terms of two years each. There are notable exceptions where longer terms of, perhaps, five to seven and maybe even ten years are the accepted standard. Use of such longer terms, however, are usually reserved for product categories that require the licensee to make a sizeable investment in the development of the product, and/or when the product requires a more extensive development period, e.g., video games.

Similarly, there is a basic difference between what the licensor and licensee each wants with respect to the licensed territory. Most licensors prefer to limit the territory to only those countries where the licensee can demonstrate its ability to distribute licensed products. Most licensees, on the other hand, will want to extend the territory as broadly as possible, usually on the chance that they may expand into those countries in the future. Caution should be exercised when granting broad territorial rights to a licensee, without reasonable assurances at the start of the agreement that it is capable of achieving distribution in each of the desired markets.

Where a licensee requests the rights to a broad territory, but the licensor is uncertain that it can fully exploit them, one possible compromise is to consent to the proposed licensed territory for a limited period of time and impose specific performance requirements on the licensee. For example, if the licensee does not commence the sale of licensed products in Australia within 18 months from the date of execution of the agreement or generate at least US $100,000 in royalties from sales in Australia within 24 months from such date of execution, the licensor shall have the right to delete Australia from the licensed territory.

The negotiation of product introduction dates and first sale or retail distribution dates are also important to insure that the licensee will actually work the license. If such dates are not met, the licensor would have the right to terminate the agreement. Some licensors may tend to minimize this requirement with licensees who commit to paying a sizeable advance and a large guarantee, but that should never be a reason to totally ignore these performance requirements.

The issue of compensation has been left to last in this discussion because to a majority of licensing executives it is the most important provision and, theoretically, consumes the most negotiating time. In actuality, however, the financial terms of many license agreements typically generate the least amount of negotiation. Many licensors have fixed in their minds what they are looking for in terms of financial requirements, taking the normal variances between product categories into consideration. For example, if someone wanted to take a license for a Disney character, the royalty rate will almost never be negotiated—it will probably be the same as in the other 150 license agreements that Disney has granted for that property.

There may, however, be some give-and-take on the advances and minimum guarantees, particularly in tougher economic times. Still, these numbers are heavily based on the licensee's sales projections. For example, if the agreed upon royalty rate was 12% and the licensee has projected a million dollars in total net sales for the licensed product, the licensor will typically apply that royalty rate to the projected sales figure and arrive at an appropriate guarantee and advance based on such projections. Some licensors will require that the licensee guarantee at least half of the projected royalties

Chapter 11: The License Agreement

for a royalty period and then pay half of the guarantee as an advance.

It should be appreciated, however, that these percentages are simply a starting point for negotiation and licensees will (and should) always seek to negotiate a lower percentage for the guarantee, e.g., 25-40% and the corresponding advance. Since the licensor is relying on the licensee's own projections, a licensee would be well advised to be conservative in its sales projections so as to provide a "comfort zone" in negotiating the guarantee and advance.

There often is significant room to negotiate the compensation package when there is little or no history for a particular property type and/or product and, as such, no established royalty exists. In these situations, the parties may spend significant amounts of time negotiating the royalty rate and any advances or guarantees.

There are many strategies used in conducting licensing negotiations. Regardless of the strategy, however, there is no substitute for preparation. In virtually all negotiations, preparation will result in a better deal for the party. For example, if an issue develops concerning the establishment of an F.O.B. rate, the parties should understand and be prepared to discuss: 1) how the licensed products will actually be shipped and sold; 2) the purpose of an F.O.B. rate; 3) the cost of the item on a domestic vs. F.O.B. basis; 4) the impact of the royalty rate on these two forms of costing; and 5) what the other side has historically done on the question and what is the standard in the industry. Armed with such knowledge, the parties will be in a significantly better position to negotiate a rate that will work for everyone.

A technique employed by some negotiators is the "Take it or Leave it" approach, typically when there is a larger disparity in the bargaining leverage between the parties and one side is assuming a more aloof position—some may call it condescending. Many an attorney or executive has heard the dreaded statement, "This issue is non-negotiable. If your client won't accept it, we're done." Translated, that means "Take it or leave it."

A licensee or licensor should NEVER be intimidated by such a threat since it could simply be a negotiating ploy. Unfortunately, there is no accurate way to know for sure what is in the mind of the other negotiator and whether he is serious or simply bluffing. Parties to a negotiation need to follow their own instincts and determine whether they have really reached the end of the negotiations or whether there is more room, while at the same time give consideration as to how important it is to conclude the deal. The best way to test a take-it-or-leave-it response is to simply make an offer and see how it is received.

11.3 Term Sheets/Deal Memos

One of the most effective ways to insure that these oral negotiations between a licensor and a prospective licensee ultimately result in a formal license agreement is through the use of a basic term sheet or deal memo, which is entered into between the parties at the conclusion of their negotiations. The term sheet is normally a one or two page document outlining the salient business provisions that were negotiated, but usually leaves out most of the legal points. When the term sheet is initially prepared, specific business terms, such as the royalty rate, advance, territory, etc., are usually left blank and it serves as a checklist for the negotiations between the parties. At the conclusion of the negotiations, the parties can then insert the appropriate numbers agreed upon during the negotiations.

The term sheet is intended to serve as a preliminary document that memorializes what the parties have negotiated, subject to entering into a formal agreement within a stated period of time. The term sheet should state that the failure to conclude a formal agreement by a predetermined date will result in its expiration. This insures that the term sheet does not become a binding agreement in the event that the parties fail to conclude a formal license agreement.

Term sheets are particularly useful when the initial negotiations are conducted by the licensing executives with the understanding that the matter will then be turned over to their respective attorneys for finalization of the formal agreement. Absent a term sheet, it is often difficult to "conclude" negoti-

Chapter 11: The License Agreement

ations, as there is no formal documentation of the terms that have been agreed to by the parties.

Despite the existence of a completed term sheet, one party may occasionally decide to reopen the negotiations. The existence of a signed term sheet, however, makes it more difficult for one side to try to renegotiate points that have been previously agreed-upon.

Ideally, the term sheet should address the following essential elements of the arrangement:
- Nature of the grant (exclusive versus non-exclusive);
- Clear and specific identification of the property and product(s) to be covered by the license;
- Licensed territory;
- Term or period of the agreement, usually including specific dates for both;
- Renewal options, including any requirements that must be met;
- Royalty rate, advances and guaranteed minimum royalties, and any specific dates by which such payments must be made;
- Dates when marketing and distribution will commence;
- Amount of product liability insurance required; and
- Time period within which a definitive formal agreement will be worked out.

11.4 The License Agreement

When the parties conclude their negotiations, regardless of whether or not a term sheet or deal memo is signed, it is time to memorialize their agreement into a formal, written license agreement. The first question that immediately comes to mind is which party should prepare the agreement?

The answer may depend on whether the license agreement is part of a larger licensing program conducted by the licensor or is a one-shot agreement. It is usually incumbent upon the licensor to prepare the first draft of the agreement, since it owns the intellectual property rights and has a vested interest in preserving those property rights. This is particularly true if the transaction is part of a larger licensing program.

Basics of Licensing: International Edition

The licensor will want to have a certain degree of uniformity among all of its licensees since it will not typically want to have different licensees operating under very different license agreements. Indeed, maintaining some degree of uniformity for a licensing program is important.

11.4.1 Definitions

The terminology used in most license agreements varies often and is almost always a reflection of the attorney drafting the agreement. For a better understanding of the terms most frequently used, Chapter 2 offers a useful reference point.

Different licensors call different things by different names. At the end of the day, however, it doesn't matter what something is called, it only matters what it means. What is important is that the parties expressly define what the key terms mean, and these definitions are typically contained in the first part of every license agreement.

11.4.2 Grant of Rights

The one essential provision in any license agreement is the "Grant of Rights" provision, since this is where the licensor formally grants to the licensee the right to use its intellectual property. It typically identifies the specific elements of the property that are being licensed and for what purpose(s). If the property includes multiple components or elements of artwork, it may be advisable to physically attach the artwork or define the components separately in an attached schedule or exhibit. In some cases, this provision may also identify any specific elements that are not being licensed since the inclusion of both helps to avoid future misunderstandings.

Also expressed in the grant of rights is the type of license being granted, e.g., exclusive versus non-exclusive. To review, an exclusive license agreement is one in which the licensee is the only party that can use the licensed property on the licensed products in the licensed territory for sale in a particular channel of distribution. Note that the grant is restricted by these four parameters: the licensed property; the licensed product; the licensed territory and the channel(s) of distribu-

Chapter 11: The License Agreement

tion. This means that the licensor can grant other exclusive (or non-exclusive) agreements to third parties for items other than the licensed property, or for products other than the licensed product, or for sale outside the licensed territory or in different channels of distribution.

In a non-exclusive grant, the licensee may be one of potentially a number of licensees permitted to use the licensed property for the licensed product in the licensed territory and within the channels of distribution. As noted previously, the trend in licensing is toward non-exclusive licenses, which are far less risky for licensors.

The license agreement should also recite whether the licensee has the right to grant sub-licenses to third parties. In the event that the licensee is permitted to grant a sub-license, it is advisable for the licensor reserve the right of pre-approval, be a named party in the sub-licensing agreement or, at the very least, be notified of such grant. If sub-licensing is allowed, the agreement needs to clearly establish how the sub-licensing revenues will be handled.

Finally, the agreement should provide that the licensee will operate within the licensed territory and not knowingly ship the licensed products to entities outside the licensed territory or sell the licensed products to parties that it knows will ship the licensed products outside the licensed territory. Obviously, this provision is intended to address the issue of gray market goods where goods authorized for distribution in one country are shipped into another country that has not been authorized by the licensor.

One of the most challenging tasks facing anyone drafting an international license agreement that includes countries in the European Economic Area (the "EEA") complying with the anti-competitive restrictions of the European Community Treaty.

In most license agreements, a licensee is granted the rights to distribute and sell the licensed products in particular countries, typically referred to as the "Licensed Territory." By implication (or specific recitation), a licensee is prohibited from selling outside that licensed territory. Licensed territories are frequently restricted to specific countries, e.g., United States, Australia, Japan, etc.

Basics of Licensing: International Edition

When, however, the licensed territory involves one or more countries that are included in the EEA and the license grant is exclusive, a brand or trademark licensor needs to be mindful of the Article 81(1) of the European Community Treaty. Article 81(1) expressly prohibits "all agreements....and concerted practices which may affect trade between Member States and which have as their object or effect the prevention, restriction or distortion of competition within the common market." Article 81(2) provides that any agreement that is found anticompetitive is automatically void.

While, presently, the grant of territorial exclusivity may not violate the provisions of Article 81(1), the grant of absolute territorial exclusivity may very well run afoul of the restrictions imposed by this Article. In order to comply with these prohibitions, many licensors will avoid prohibiting passive sales, i.e., obligate the licensee not to supply to anyone outside the allocated territory or where the licensee is approached by such a potential customer. Thus, the licensee would be allowed to fulfill orders from outside the licensed territory for licensed products when such orders were unsolicited.

Suggested language addressing this issue follows:

> Notwithstanding this Clause, where the Licensed Territory includes one or more countries which comprise the European Economic Area ("EEA"), nothing in this Agreement will be construed as preventing LICENSEE from supplying Licensed Products in response to unsolicited orders from purchasers in EEA countries outside the Licensed Territory or in countries outside the Licensed Territory which have entered into Europe or Free Trade Agreements with the European Community ("Free Trade Countries"), or as preventing LICENSOR from permitting another LICENSEE in similar circumstances from supplying its own Licensed Products in response to such unsolicited orders from purchasers in EEA countries or Free Trade Countries which are within the Licensed Territory. The LICENSEE

Chapter 11: The License Agreement

shall not, however, solicit orders for Licensed Products from purchasers in countries outside the Licensed Territory.

LICENSEE acknowledges that LICENSOR may have granted the right to third parties to distribute Licensed Products in territories outside of the Licensed Territory and that the Licensed Products of such third parties may be exported into the Licensed Territory in breach of contractual restrictions on such third parties which forbid such exports. Notwithstanding any of the other provisions of this Agreement, LICENSEE agrees that in these circumstances, LICENSOR shall not be deemed to be in breach of this Agreement. Nevertheless, LICENSOR will use commercially reasonable efforts to stop such exports.

The licensor may attempt to specifically reserve rights to certain future technologies. This has been a hotly contested issue over the years, particularly involving entertainment and motion picture rights and whether grants of film rights included videocassette and eventually digital rights. As such, many licensors now specifically reserve all non-granted rights including rights in any future-developed technologies that incorporate the licensed property.

There may be cases where the licensee has pre-existing materials that it owns and wants to continue to own after conclusion of the license agreement, e.g., video game engines, etc. The agreement should specifically identify such materials and provide that they will remain the property of the licensee after termination or expiration of the agreement although all elements of the licensed property must be removed.

Care needs to be taken when attempting to impose control over where the licensee may sell the licensed products or the manner in which they may sell and distribute such items, since certain restrictions could conflict with relevant antitrust laws. It is preferable to simply identify those territories or channels where the licensee *can* sell and distribute licensed products rather than identify those territories or channels where they *cannot* sell or distribute. As previously noted, sometimes, inclusion of the official language(s) that can be used when referencing the licensed product will tend to limit the markets in which the product can be distributed. Specification of language rights is often provided for in publishing agreements.

11.4.3 Term of the Agreement

The term of any license agreement will define the relevant time period during which the license agreement shall remain in effect. The term may vary depending upon the licensor's pre-established criteria, or the product category. Many licensors will only grant licenses for a term of two or three years, although as mentioned, licenses for certain product categories, e.g., video games, are commonly granted for longer terms due to the time and/or cost required to develop such products. The terms of agreements that relate to copyrighted materials, e.g., in publishing agreements, are typically tied to the length of copyright protection afforded such properties.

In those instances where the term is established for a fixed period of time, a licensee will frequently request one or more options to renew the license agreement for extended terms. Options are intended to protect a successful licensee from a licensor who wishes to leverage the licensee's success and seek out a new licensee on better terms after expiration of the initial agreement. An option gives the licensee some contractual assurance that, if it has been successful, it will be able to continue the license.

The exercise of an option, however, is generally dependent upon the licensee meeting certain threshold performance-related criteria. For example, a licensor may grant a license for a fixed term of two years with the option to renew the agreement for an "extended" or "renewal" term of an additional two years provided that the licensee has submitted $[X] in royalty payments, was not in breach of any material provision of the agreement and notified the licensor in writing of its intention to renew the agreement at least 30 days prior to the expiration of the term then in effect.

Chapter 11: The License Agreement

11.4.4 Compensation Provisions

The manner in which the licensor is compensated for the use of the licensed property by the licensee and any sublicensees can vary widely. Possible options include:
- A one-time lump sum payment to the licensor;
- Ongoing royalty payments to the licensor, based solely on sales of licensed products by the licensee, with no advance or guaranteed minimum payment;
- Either of the above, except that the licensor is paid an advance and/or a guaranteed minimum royalty payment, which is usually recoupable against future royalty earnings.

The most common form of compensation is a royalty calculated as a percentage of the licensee's net sales of the licensed products. To reiterate, "Net Sales" is almost always a term specifically defined in every license agreement. Though the actual definition varies, it will always be based on the licensee's gross sales of licensed products less certain enumerated deductions. These deductions will change from agreement to agreement. Licensees should pay very particular attention to how the term "net sales" is defined, as this can have an enormous impact on its royalty obligation.

Again, it should also be appreciated that various types of royalties are frequently charged. Each is a function of how the licensed products are actually distributed, such as where the licensed products are manufactured offshore, or in such cases where the licensee may also sell the licensed products directly to consumers. F.O.B. (sometimes called an L.C. or Letter of Credit) rates are typically between two and four percentage points higher than domestic rates, due principally, to the fact that F.O.B. sales are made at a lower price point. In those instances where the licensee has both the right and the ability to sell the licensed products directly to the consumer, the royalty rate may also fluctuate. Direct sales, as this is usually referred to, provides the manufacturer with the ability to sell products at the retail price. Therefore, many licensors will require that the royalty be paid on the higher retail price rather than on the wholesale price.

Basics of Licensing: International Edition

Most licensors require licensees to pay an advance against royalties upon execution of the license agreement, as well as some form of minimum royalty obligation. The advance against royalties is just that—an advance against the licensee's actual earned royalty obligations. It is therefore creditable against the licensee's future earned royalty payments due the licensor. In most instances, it is treated as nonrefundable.

The need for an advance is quite important in the licensing industry, as it accelerates the licensor's cash flow. In most instances, the licensee will not commence the sale of licensed products for months, if not years, after entering into the agreement. Without an advance, some licensors could go more than eighteen months before they begin to see any actual royalties from a licensee. The other reason for an advance is that it serves as a further incentive to insure that the licensee will not simply take a license and then sit idle with the property. By paying an advance, the licensee has made a definitive financial commitment to the program.

There may be some instances where a licensor requires the licensee to pay a non-refundable, non-creditable licensee fee at the time the license agreement is executed for the right to actually take the license. This is not very common but does occur in some categories.

Many license agreements also include a minimum royalty provision that can be either guaranteed or non-guaranteed. A guaranteed minimum royalty, as the name implies, means that the licensee is committed to paying a certain minimum amount in royalties to the licensor over either the term of the license or for a specific period. That way, if the licensed products are a failure, the licensor knows it will receive at least some minimum amount in royalties. In certain categories, e.g., art licensing, licensees will not agree to any minimum guarantee, although they may be willing to agree to a "non-guaranteed" minimum royalty which, if not met, will give the licensor the right to terminate the agreement.

Where licensing occurs in different countries and payments will be calculated in the currency of one country but paid in the currency of another country, it is advisable to specify the currency conversion rate that should be applied and

Chapter 11: The License Agreement

the date of such conversion as the rates will change over time. For example, the agreement may state that the conversion rate will be the same as that published in *The Wall Street Journal* as of the date such payment is due.

11.4.5 Sub-Licensing

Few, if any, merchandising licensors allow their licensees to engage in sub-licensing since they want to control the ultimate use of their properties. While there are certainly ways to control how and what a sub-licensee does with the property, in practice, controlling a sub-licensee is inherently more difficult for a property owner than controlling a licensee.

It should be noted that—as a matter of law in most jurisdictions—a licensee has the right to sub-license its rights in the absence of a specific prohibition in the agreement, which is why most merchandising license agreements expressly prohibit sub-licensing.

There are, however, instances in which sub-licensing is permitted, typically with respect to international rights where sub-licensing can be a valuable substitute for a distribution arrangement. In those instances, the terms of any sub-license grant should be addressed. An alternative to sub-licensing international distributors is a sub-distribution agreement. Under this type of agreement, the licensee would continue to remain obligated to pay the licensor a royalty on product sales on the same royalty basis as for all other sales.

Where sub-licensing is permitted, the license agreement should further address how the licensor will be paid for sales made by the sub-licensee. In many cases, the licensor and licensee simply agree to share the sub-licensing revenues on some mutually agreeable basis. A 50-50 split between the licensor and the licensee of net sub-licensing income (gross sub-licensing income less the cost of conducting the program, or an agent's commission if an outside agent is used) is quite common. Such a formula gives the licensee the ability to deduct its operational costs against such income prior to an equitable sharing of the profits with the licensor.

Another approach to allocating sub-licensing revenue is where the licensor receives the same royalty on the sub-licensee's sale of products as it would from the original licensee for its own sales. In such a situation, the licensee may elect to charge the sub-licensee a higher royalty than it is paying to the licensor and retain the difference.

11.4.6 Accounting Provisions

As mentioned above, one of the most important considerations in any license agreement is the definition of net sales, since this is the basis for calculating the licensee's royalty obligation to the licensor. In most any license agreement, "Net Sales" refers to the licensee's gross sales of the licensed products less whatever deductions the parties agree to permit, e.g., shipping costs, taxes, credits and discounts, and returns. It should be appreciated that the actual definition of net sales will vary from licensor to licensor and, for some, even from one product category to another.

A licensee should make certain that it has the right to deduct non-recoupable "government fees" from its gross sales. Similarly, licensors should not permit a licensee to deduct the cost of manufacturing and/or promoting the licensed product, or the cost of the royalty paid to the licensor.

A common practice in structuring licenses for publishing properties and in certain other industries where unsold goods are returnable is that the licensee will have the right to deduct a "Reserve for Returns" from the royalties due on a per quarter basis. A fixed percentage of royalties, often 20% to 30%, is deducted from the total royalty payment to compensate for the return of the product. Most agreements will require that any reserve deducted must be accounted for in next royalty report. Therefore, if the licensee deducts a reserve of 20% in the preceding quarter when actual returns equal only 10% of the reserve deducted, the remaining 10% that is outstanding will be added to the current royalties due.

Some companies prefer to negotiate a flat percentage for all deductions rather than attempt to individually itemize each one. Such percentages normally range from between 5% and 10% of gross sales. The inclusion of returns in this flat fee

Chapter 11: The License Agreement

deduction can, however, cause problems for some licensees, particularly in industries where returns are commonplace. Similarly, many licensors actually impose a cap on the amount of such deductions.

Royalty accounting for most licensees is typically provided on a quarterly calendar basis with statements and payments due within 30 (sometimes 45) days after the conclusion of the previous quarter. Thus, licensees will normally report and pay royalties by January 30th, April 30th, July 30th and October 30th of each year. In certain industries, such as publishing, royalty accounting is provided less frequently, e.g., semi-annually or annually. Alternatively, in situations where a licensed property is particularly hot or when the reliability of the licensee comes into question, royalty accounting may be required on a monthly basis.

The agreement should clearly spell out what form the licensee's royalty statement should take and the degree of specificity required in the accounting. Many licensors require electronic reporting, in addition to hard copy. A good practice is to actually append a copy of a sample royalty statement to the agreement. Many licensors also require that the royalty statement be certified by an officer of the licensee to underscore the need for accurate and truthful reporting.

Questions frequently arise as to when a royalty obligation accrues, e.g., upon the sale or payment of the item. Many license agreements specifically address this question and typically require that the royalty obligation will accrue at the earliest date possible, e.g., when an order is placed rather than when payment is received.

Another question frequently presented involves the issue of inter-company sales at a discount. Most agreements provide that in such a situation, the transfer will be deemed a sale and the price can be no lower than the typical selling price for the licensed product to a third party. The failure to provide language dealing with this issue can give the licensee the ability to distribute the licensed products at a lower effective royalty cost. There have been occasions where licensees established a bogus entity to purchases the licensed products, which then became the paper entity that distributed them to retail.

The payment question is always an issue, particularly if the licensee is located in a different country. Most licensors require that all payments be made in the licensor's national currency, typically by check or wire transfer drawn on a bank in the licensor's country. This is done to avoid incurring bank collection fees. Currency fluctuations could, however, be a reason for requiring that royalties are paid in the licensee's currency.

A "blocked currency" provision is frequently requested by a licensee, particularly when it is selling product in countries where it might be difficult to get currency out of that country. Many licensors refuse to agree to such a provision, particularly if the licensee knowingly sells into a market where there is the possibility that currency will be blocked.

The agreement should also provide that the licensee will pay interest on any late payments made to the licensor. It is a good idea to establish how interest will be calculated, e.g., 0.5% per month from the date the payment was originally due. Some licensors fix the interest rate at the current cost of money, e.g., prime interest rate, or cite a specific interest index as the basis used to calculate interest due. If underpayments of royalties have occurred over a prolonged period of time, computing interest charges can be complicated due to the fact that interest rates tend to fluctuate.

Many licensors include an acceleration provision in the agreement which provides that, upon termination of the agreement for cause, all outstanding guaranteed monies will become immediately due and payable. This avoids the unpleasant situation of having to wait (or worse yet, chase) a terminated licensee for outstanding monies.

The licensor should have the right to audit the licensee's books and verify the accuracy of the licensee's accounting. Reasonable notice is normally required and the inspection should be at the licensee's place of business during reasonable business hours. The licensor should have the right to make copies of what it is shown during the course of the audit, and the licensee should be required to cooperate with the audit. It might be wise to specify that the audit provision survives termination of the license agreement to avoid conflicts where a licensor elects to audit a terminated licensee.

Chapter 11: The License Agreement

The license agreement should further provide that in the event the audit reveals an underpayment above a threshold amount, the licensee will not only be required to pay the underpayment with interest, but will also have to pay the licensor's audit costs and any attorneys' fees required to collect same. The actual threshold amount will vary from license to license, but it is common to set it as a percentage of the amount actually paid for the period, e.g., 3% to 5%. Some agreements provide that if the underpayment reaches a second, but higher, threshold amount, e.g., 25%, the licensor may also terminate the agreement.

The agreement should further include a provision that requires the licensee to maintain all of its books and records for inspection over a period of time and at a location where they can be easily inspected. A typical time period for retaining records is three years from the date to which they pertain.

11.4.7 Quality Control Provisions

Every merchandising agreement gives the licensor the right to exert some degree of quality control over the licensed products produced by the licensee. There are many reasons for such a provision, although the most important one is that the licensing of a trademark without monitoring the quality of the licensed products is considered "naked licensing" and can result in a loss of the property owner's underlying trademark rights.

Most licensors prefer to monitor the quality of the licensed products even if the property being licensed is not a trademark. They will frequently require the licensee to submit samples of the licensed products for review and approval at various stages of the development and manufacturing process. Such submissions are for the purpose of reviewing the actual licensed products to insure that they meet certain minimal quality levels, as well as to confirm that the licensed property is being properly used and that all appropriate legal notices are included.

In the merchandising area, at a minimum, licensors will typically require a licensee to submit samples of the licensed products at the following stages:

Basics of Licensing: International Edition

- Preliminary artwork depicting the licensed property;
- Final artwork depicting the licensed property;
- Initial prototypes of the licensed products;
- Final prototypes of the licensed products; and
- Production run samples of the licensed products.

While the above may appear to be "overkill," it is important to ensure that the licensee is on the right track in manufacturing licensed products of a type and style that will be eventually approved by the licensor. Such a policy is actually beneficial for the licensee, since it helps identify any potential problems at an early stage and allows the licensee to make the necessary changes and corrections before starting its production run. Making changes at the earliest stages of product development will very often save the licensee both money and time.

A WORD OF CAUTION: most licensees are more than capable of producing the products without any help from the licensor. Ideally, the professional licensor is supportive of the licensee and does not use the approval process to assert artistic control over the licensed product. Reviewing products for quality and to ensure that they comply with trademark and marking requirements is far different from using the process to insist that a certain color is of the proper hue, for instance; unless, of course, such details are necessary to comply with the property's style guide.

In addition to the licensed products, most licensors will require the right to approve a licensee's proposed packaging as well as the placement of any intended advertising. This measure helps to assure that the selected media outlets are of a type and style consistent with the image that the licensor wants to portray, that they properly depict the licensed property and that they contain all appropriate legal notices.

One primary concern of every licensee is that the licensor will unreasonably delay consideration of its sample product submissions. Most licensees are working on very tight production schedules, usually dictated by a retailer. If a licensor fails to act promptly in the review and approval process, it can have a significant negative impact on the success of the licensed product.

Chapter 11: The License Agreement

Professional licensors are rarely, if ever, dilatory in their review of sample submissions, although the actual process does take time. One way to approach this issue in the agreement is to establish a set timeframe for conducting the review and a provision for what happens if the licensor does not respond within such a timeframe. Most licensees want a failure to respond within the set period to constitute approval, while most licensors will insist that such a failure to respond be deemed disapproval. This, of course, is a matter of negotiation and compromise is always possible.

11.4.8 Representations and Warranties

Every licensor will be asked to make certain representations and warranties to the licensee, including:
- Licensor has the right to enter into the subject agreement and there are no other agreements in place that conflict with it;
- Licensor is the sole and exclusive owner of the property; and
- Property does not infringe upon the rights of any third party.

The first two warranties are relatively straightforward. The last one, however, can be problematic. This warranty is tantamount to a guarantee that the licensee's use of the property will not infringe upon anyone else's intellectual property rights. That is a very serious warranty and one that most licensors do not take lightly—particularly with respect to relatively new properties. Such a warranty requires the licensor to conduct extensive trademark and copyright searches to ensure that the use by the licensee of the licensed property will not result in the infringement of the rights of another party.

Most licensors require a licensee to warrant that it will use its best efforts or, at least, reasonable commercial efforts, in advertising, promoting, and marketing the product. It is also not uncommon for a licensor to require that the licensee commence actual distribution of the licensed product by a specific date in order to maintain its rights under the agreement. For example, a toy licensee may be required to introduce the licensed product by Hong Kong Toy Fair 2015 (the

"Product Introduction Date") and actually commence shipment of licensed products by another certain date, e.g., April 30, 2015 (the "Initial Shipment Date" or "Distribution Date"). The licensee's failure to meet either of these dates would give the licensor the right to terminate the agreement.

If the agreement is a worldwide agreement, consideration must be given to the distribution of the licensed product outside the United States. Frequently, the licensee is given one year from the introduction in the United States to introduce and begin selling the product abroad. Consideration may also be given to approaching this on a country-by-country basis. For example, if the licensee has not begun selling product in a particular country by a particular date, the licensor has the right to delete (or "recapture") that country from the license grant.

11.4.9 Indemnification and Insurance

Indemnification means that in the event a third party should make a claim against or sue one party to the license based on the actions (or inactions) of the other, the other party will be responsible for defending such claim and paying any costs or judgments arising from a lawsuit.

In most license agreements, the following cross indemnities are typically provided:
- Licensor will indemnify the licensee against claims based on any breach of the licensor's warranties, including claims for infringement; and
- Licensee will indemnify the licensor against claims based on any breach of licensee's warranties, including claims for product liability.

The first is fairly simple; if the licensee gets sued because its use of the licensor's property infringes the rights of another party, the licensor is responsible and should defend and bear all costs associated with any subsequent lawsuit. This is one of the reasons why it is so important to first clear a property before commencing a licensing program, since the licensor will typically be responsible for any such claim. As stated earlier, there is no faster way to derail a licensing program than to find out that the property being licensed in-

Chapter 11: The License Agreement

fringes the rights of an outside third party. The cost of even defending an infringement lawsuit can easily run into the millions of dollars, and the potential liability is even larger.

The second situation is also very straightforward. If the licensee's products are defective or cause injury or death to a third party, it is the licensee's responsibility and it should be prepared to defend and indemnify the licensor as a result of any such claims. It should be appreciated that product liability concerns are particularly unique to products that are intended to be sold in the United States. Licensees who intend to manufacture and sell licensed products in countries other than the United States may consider these provisions less important, although a major product liability lawsuit can still have an enormous impact on the property and the program.

Most licensors require that a licensee carry product liability insurance to fund its indemnity obligation and, further, that the licensor and its licensing agent be added as named insureds to the insurance policy. In this manner, both parties are clearly covered. There is typically no cost or fee for adding an additional party to such a policy. By extension, most licensors will require that they be notified should the licensee fail to maintain such coverage or, alternatively, change the limits of their coverage. In many agreements, failure to maintain the required product liability coverage gives the licensor the right to terminate the agreement. Obtaining product liability insurance for the sale of product in countries outside the United States can be more challenging.

The licensor should take special care in reviewing these policies, paying particular attention to the licensee's selection of the carrier as well as the limits of product liability insurance. The minimum product liability limits will vary according to the type of licensed product. Obviously, any licensed product that can be considered reasonably dangerous, including knives or lighters or any products that can be ingested, including food products, candy, and drinks, should justify a higher limit of insurance than the standard level of $2 to $5 million per occurrence.

11.4.10 Termination Provision

The termination provision is, perhaps, the most important provision in any license agreement, since it will be the first provision reviewed should a problem develop between the parties. If the relationship between the parties proceeds in the manner both expected at the time they entered into the agreement, there may never be an occasion to review the termination provision in any significant detail. However, in the event that a problem develops in the underlying relationship between the parties, and one party wants to end the relationship, the termination provision will become critically important.

A well-drafted termination provision should give the licensor the right to terminate the agreement upon the occurrence of certain events, including:
- Licensee's failure to obtain the licensor's product approvals prior to the distribution of the licensed goods.
- Licensee's failure to introduce product prior to the product introduction date;
- Licensee's failure to meet the initial shipment date;
- Licensee's failure to maintain product liability insurance;
- Licensee's failure to make the minimum royalty payments;
- Licensee's failure to continuously sell or market products;
- Recall of the product by the Consumer Product Safety Commission;
- Licensee's protracted inability to conduct business; or
- Licensee's repeated failure to pay royalties when they come due.

In addition to the above, both parties should have the right to terminate the agreement on notice (normally thirty days) in the event of a breach of a material provision of the agreement by the other party and the party's failure to cure that breach within the notice period.

It may also be advisable for the licensor to have the option to terminate a portion of the license agreement and reclaim some of the rights being granted without terminating the entire agreement. For example, a licensor might want to reclaim a country where sales did not commence by the distribution date or even a particular type of licensed product that was simply not introduced or sold.

The termination provision should similarly address the issue of what the licensee can (and cannot) do after termination or expiration of the agreement. In most cases, the licensee will be required to cease all manufacture of the licensed products, return all of the licensor's materials and provide the licensor with an accounting of all inventory on hand. Most terminated licensees will be permitted to dispose of any existing inventory for a limited "sell-off" period, provided that the termination was not the result of inferior quality products or improper use of the property. The length of such a sell-off period will vary from agreement to agreement.

11.4.11 Boilerplate Provisions

The use of the term "boilerplate" can be misleading because it implies that these provisions are blindly included in every agreement without thought or consideration. Nothing could be further from the truth. These provisions are very much intended to govern the conduct of the parties and to control how certain events will be treated. That alone makes them practically as important as the provisions discussed above.

Some of the more important "boilerplate" provisions establish:
- Who is responsible for obtaining and maintaining intellectual property protection, both domestically and internationally;
- Who is responsible for pursuing infringers and how any recovered assets are to be divided;
- Manner in which notices are to be given under the agreement;
- Manner in which disputes are to be resolved and what law will control;
- If there are different language versions of the agreement, which one is governing;

- Conditions under which the parties may assign the agreement along with its rights and obligations; and
- Integration of the agreement and amendments.

Intellectual Property Protection

It is typically the licensor's responsibility to obtain and maintain intellectual property protection for the property. This is understandable since it is the actual owner of such property rights, and the licensee is paying for the right to use the property. A property owner should think seriously before allowing another party, particularly a licensee, to assume responsibility for protecting its intellectual property.

The question of who should pay for international trademark protection is not always as clear-cut, however, principally because of the expense associated with obtaining and maintaining such protection. As explained earlier, international trademark protection must be acquired on a country-by-country basis and, as such, can get very costly. Some property owners (particularly smaller ones) are simply not in a financial position to undertake an international filing program without some assistance from its licensees. In such instances, it is not uncommon for the licensee to advance the costs associated with an international filing program with the understanding that it will be able to take a credit against its royalty obligations in the amount of such expenses. Clearly, this approach benefits both parties.

In this regard, the agreement should specifically address how much cooperation between the parties is expected and obligate the licensee to cooperate with and assist the licensor in refining the intellectual property rights protection. This will, of course, help to avoid subsequent disputes involving a refusal by the licensee to execute any necessary documents to perfect such rights.

A "licensee estoppel" provision is frequently contained in license agreements that do not involve patents. This provision prevents the licensee from challenging the validity of the licensor's underlying intellectual property rights. While courts have consistently held that licensee estoppel provisions relating to patent rights violate the antitrust laws, they are allowed in trademark and merchandising agreements.

Chapter 11: The License Agreement

Third Party Infringements

The right to sue infringers typically rests with the licensor. While most intellectual property statutes provide that actions can only be brought by the owner of the intellectual property rights, some courts have held that an exclusive licensee can bring an action for infringement. To address this, many license agreements expressly provide that the licensor is the only party that can initiate an action against an infringer. Some licensors do allow a licensee to bring an action of its own, however, either with the licensor's consent or if the licensor does not act in a timely manner.

In any event, the agreement should not require the licensor to pursue any and all infringements. Enforcement litigation is extremely expensive and there is always a law of diminishing returns. That is not meant to imply that property owners should not take reasonable steps to stop the infringement of their intellectual property rights, but the rule of reason needs to apply. It might simply not be worth spending $100,000 in legal fees to shut down a company that is selling $350 worth of infringing product.

Notices

Every license agreement needs to specifically provide how notices are to be given under the agreement and how payments are to be made, including notices for breach. There are instances where a party might want to include its counsel and its licensing agent in the notice provision to insure that an actual copy of the notice is immediately received and acted upon.

Disputes and Forum

Most agreements address the question of disputes, specifically, what law is to apply and how and where disputes are to be handled. In domestic licensing situations, the governing law is of lesser importance since federal law will typically apply, although questions of contract interpretation can vary significantly from state to state. What is important for a licensor, however, is to make sure that all of its license agreements consistently provide for interpretation under the same state law in order to avoid a situation where a court sitting in one state interprets a particular provision differently than a court sitting in another state. In international licensing, the choice of law provision becomes particularly important and requires thorough review by qualified legal counsel in all involved countries.

How and where disputes will be resolved is also an important consideration. The choice is typically between litigation versus arbitration and where any such proceeding will be held. Mediation is a very effective tool for dispute resolution and a number of licensors regularly require mediation as an initial step in the dispute resolution process.

In international licensing, arbitration is a commonly used method of dispute resolution. There are a number of groups and institutions that regularly handle dispute resolution, including the International Chamber of Commerce (ICC), JAMS International, the British Columbia International Commercial Arbitration Centre (BCICAC, Canada), the International Centre for Dispute Resolution (ICDR), the international branch of the American Arbitration Association), the London Court of International Arbitration (LCIA), the Hong Kong International Arbitration Centre, and the Singapore International Arbitration Centre (SIAC). The World Intellectual Property Organization (WIPO) has an arbitration and mediation center and a panel of international neutrals that specialize in IP disputes.

Assignability and Transfer

Courts typically consider license agreements to be personal and, as such, they may not be assigned as a matter of law without the consent of the other party. Most licensors reaffirm this in the body of their agreement.

An issue that has been of particular prominence in recent years involves the "transfer" of a license agreement, where it moves along with a corporation that was acquired by another corporation. In such event, no assignment of the agreement is typically required. To avoid this outcome (or at least assert some authority over it), many licensors expressly prohibit the "transfer" of the license agreement in the event that control of the licensee changes hands. Some even impose the payment of a "transfer fee" as a condition for their approval.

Chapter 11: The License Agreement

Force Majeure

"Force Majeure" is a doctrine intended to protect the licensee in the event of excusable non-performance caused by an act of God, the government, war, terrorism, fire, flood, or labor troubles. Such a provision will typically excuse such non-performance during the period of trouble and then for a fixed period thereafter.

Governing Language

It is not uncommon in international licensing for an agreement to be reviewed and ultimately executed in different language versions so that the parties can have the benefit of being able to review and understand the terms of the agreement in their native language. Despite the best intentions of their respective translators, subtle differences in wording may occur between the two versions. Thus, the agreement should properly provide which language version will govern should there be a difference between the two.

No Joint Venture

While many licensors commonly refer to their licensees as "partners," they are not so as a matter of law. In fact, most licensing agreements expressly state that the parties are not partners or joint venturers.

Integration

Every agreement typically includes and should end with an integration clause, which provides that the license agreement is the final and entire understanding between the parties, incorporates all prior written or oral agreements between the parties and may not be changed or modified except by written agreement signed by all parties. This provision is intended to restrict a party's ability to rely on any statements not contained in the agreement and effectively "integrates" everything into the final license agreement.

Chapter 12

Best Practices in Licensing Administration[1]

12.1 Introduction

Once all the preliminary steps have been completed, it's time to start the process of developing a licensing group or department. While the procedures outlined in this chapter are aimed primarily at property owners who are seeking to establish their own licensing departments, many of the steps and procedures have equal applicability to licensing agents who are managing licensing programs for their clients.

The first step in the development of any licensing department is the appointment of a leader to oversee and direct its operations. This individual is typically called a "licensing director" although other titles, such as "licensing manager" or "licensing administrator" are frequently used. Obviously, it is important for the licensing director to have some experience in licensing, preferably on a managerial level. While the actual running of such a department is something that an otherwise sound business manager should be able to easily handle, having experience in the industry will certainly accelerate the learning process and will reduce the chance of errors along the way.

If the person selected to run the licensing department lacks actual licensing experience, it might be a good idea for the property owner to bring in a licensing consultant for a period of time to assist with establishing the procedures that will be required to actually run the program. In the licensing industry, experience is important, and there really is no substitute for it.

---

[1] Based on a CLS presentation on *The Fundamentals of Creating and Administering a Licensing Program* by Peter Van Raalte of THE VAN RAALTE CO.,INC., 229 Midland Avenue, Montclair, NJ 07042

12.2 The Licensing Department

In order to begin making the critical decisions concerning the structuring and staffing of the department, the property owner should revisit what the objectives are for developing a licensing program for the property. The three most common objectives are the following:

- Increasing brand awareness through extensions into other product categories and through the associated PR and advertising;
- Strengthening the property owner's trademark and copyright protection through use of the property on ancillary products; and
- Generating additional revenue.

Not surprisingly, most licensing departments are structured in such a way that they address each of these objectives.

While there are many ways to organize and staff a licensing department, perhaps the most effective way is to divide the group by responsibility with everyone reporting to the licensing director. Typically, this would include the following groups:

- **Marketing Group**: Responsible for handling marketing, advertising and public relations;
- **Sales Group**: Responsible for the solicitation and sales of licensing rights;
- **Legal & Contract Administration Group**: Responsible for overseeing legal matters, reviewing and administering all license agreements and supporting the other groups;
- **Finance Group**: Responsible for tracking and collecting royalties, overseeing audits and providing reports to the licensing director, and;
- **Creative Group**: Responsible for developing brand identity, translating brands into images and handling product approvals.

This does not mean that every licensing department requires a minimum of five groups or, for that matter, even requires five different individuals to accomplish these objectives. Many excellent licensing departments are composed of only one or two individuals, each wearing multiple hats and

Chapter 12: Best Practices in Licensing Administration

sharing these different responsibilities. At the same time, other larger departments have more than a hundred people (and possibly more) broken down into groups and sub-groups.

12.2.1 The Marketing Group

The marketing group is responsible for pulling together the marketing material that the sales group will use in seeking out licensees as well as overseeing all marketing, advertising and public relations activities.

Licensing is all about lead times. If a licensor wants to accomplish something in 18 months, steps must be taken today to set the wheels in motion. As such, the marketing group must work with the licensing director to initially develop a merchandising or marketing plan that will serve as a roadmap for the entire licensing program.

Perhaps the easiest way to create such a merchandising plan is by developing a timeline schedule using, for example, the Gantt chart features that are included in such Microsoft Office products as Excel, Visio or Project. Such a schedule should be broken down by product category and, for each category, should identify when: (a) presentations need be made to potential licensees; (b) license agreements must be entered into with licensees; (c) presentations should be made to potential retail partners; (d) products must actually be introduced by licensees; and (e) sales of licensed products should commence. The timeline should also note the dates of all relevant industry trade shows.

In developing the plan, the property owner needs to consider the appropriate lead times that its licensees will need to manufacture, ship and introduce the licensed products, taking into consideration potential delays caused by local customs and holidays, e.g., Chinese New Year (which can have an impact on manufacturing), etc. It should also identify where and when new products in a particular category are typically introduced.

The marketing group also has responsibility for planning and overseeing the group's attendance and participation at various licensing trade shows, e.g., the Licensing Expo show in Las Vegas, and such international licensing shows that are

Basics of Licensing: International Edition

held in markets such as London, Tokyo, Germany, Shanghai and Hong Kong. The trade show schedule should also include category-specific trade shows such as Toy Fair, MAGIC and the Bologna Book Fair. Since attendance at such trade shows is an essential part of the marketing process and occurs throughout the year at various locales around the world, this can be a time-consuming task, if done thoroughly.

Attending tradeshows is one of the best ways to learn about a specific industry and become knowledgeable about the current trends, styles and new developments occurring in that industry. It is also a good place to make or renew contacts with potential licensees and agents. As such, property owners are well advised to consider exhibiting at the Licensing Expo Show, and appropriate international licensing shows, in addition to attending key industry trade shows.

When attending a trade show, it is important to have a plan. Most trade shows are large, but are frequently organized into various sections by category. A great deal of time can be lost by not using the trade show directory to see what sections of the show are worth visiting. Trade show directories are also a valuable resource for use after a show, as they often provide excellent information about those companies who exhibited at the show.

Finally, the plan should include other relevant milestones for the program, including the commencement of any advertising programs and where and when such advertisements would be placed. It should further include planned PR programs, as well as consumer and retail promotions. Also, it is important to time trade advertising and PR programs to coordinate with the applicable trade shows.

Is advertising worthwhile? It can be expensive and should only be undertaken if the property owner can afford it. More importantly, placement is critical. A great ad in the wrong place will not produce satisfactory results. If the intent is to reach companies and decision makers in a particular industry, then consider advertising the availability of the property in trade publications most often read by members of that industry. The message delivered must be clear, compelling, and provide enough information to connect with the desired audience.

Chapter 12: Best Practices in Licensing Administration

Development of a public relations program is also an important component of a property owner's marketing effort. The strategic placement of such marketing materials can be an effective and affordable way to support the property, and an efficient way to build brand awareness. Industry magazines and newsletters (both print and e-mail) thrive on industry news and the marketing group should plan to release a steady stream of communications in order to stay out in front of potential customers.

If the property lends itself to promotional activities, e.g., parties, branded product giveaways at trade shows, etc., these activities should be planned and built into the merchandising strategy as well.

The marketing group is also typically tasked with responsibility for working with both the sales group and the creative group to produce a sales kit that will be used by the sales group in soliciting and closing deals with licenses. A good sales kit will typically include the following components:

- Description of the property to be licensed;
- Style guide illustrating how the property should be used in developing licensed items, inclusion of the available artwork for the property and all pertinent information that the licensee should aware of regarding the development and marketing of the licensed goods;
- Overall merchandising plan to allow a prospective licensee to see how their products fit in with the broader program;
- Demographics of potential purchasers of licensed products;
- Broadcast partners and initiatives, identifying air dates, frequency, etc., including the partners' marketing and support plans;
- Comprehensive retail plans identifying potential retail partners and product rollout schedules;
- Licensor's independent advertising and marketing plans to show how the licensing program interacts with the overall business development agenda;

- Advertising and publicity plan identifying planned trade advertising, public relations, mall tours, costume character program, etc.;
- Sizzle video and/or PowerPoint sales presentations; and
- Boards and sample product concepts illustrating how the property will potentially look when applied to products.

Finally, the Internet cannot be forgotten. We live in an online world, and a property owner should create a website featuring its property and information about the licensing program, or use a social network such as Facebook to promote the availability of the property. This should be a step taken early in the process and responsibility for the development and maintenance of the site typically falls under the marketing group.

12.2.2 The Sales Group

The Sales Group is tasked with the implementation of the merchandising plan by identifying a list of all potential licensed products, a list of possible licensees for each product, and then actually "selling" a license to potential licensees in those categories, using the sales kit discussed above.

The sales groups of larger licensing departments are typically broken down by property, market segment and then by product category, e.g., MICKEY MOUSE licensed merchandise toy products. The theory behind this is that the relevant sales executive becomes an expert in a particular industry, capable of not just understanding its key players and dynamics, but of actually working with the licensee to help develop better product. Selling a license for merchandise sales can be quite different than selling one for promotional sales or directly to retailers, and the value of establishing personal relationships with key manufactures in a product category can be a highly valuable asset.

Finally, the group will include support personnel to assist in making and scheduling appointments and closing deals.

Chapter 12: Best Practices in Licensing Administration

The first order of business for the sales group is to identify those product categories where licensing would be most appropriate and then to develop a list of possible licensed products within those categories. Once done, the group needs to assemble a list of potential licensees for each of these possible licensed products.

This is typically done by researching the particular category and identifying those manufacturers who would be in the best position to manufacture product of the type and quality required by the licensor, and who also have the resources and distribution channels to maximize sales. While every category typically includes a host of choices, many experienced licensing salesmen find themselves going back to the same manufacturers who they have worked with in the past and and who have done a good job.

This is one area where the manufacturer's representatives play a major role because they will approach the sales group on behalf of their clients and actually sell their clients to the property owner.

Potential licensees can also be identified using the LIMA database of licensees at www.licensing.org. The database is broken down by product categories and types of products within each category. There are also a number of industry directories published by the various trade publications. Finally, potential licensees can also be identified by simply walking the various industry specific trade shows, where virtually all manufacturers in a potential category are present, irrespective of whether they carry or have ever carried licensed products. Each of these trade show producers publish a directory which can also be a good source for locating potential new licensees.

Once the sales group creates a list of potential licensees, it must then contact and potentially meet with the most promising manufacturers to discuss licensing opportunities. This is where the sales group must "sell" the license to a potential manufacturer, stressing the benefits that taking a license for the property can offer the licensee. The dynamics of such meetings will largely depend on the property, i.e., whether it's a "hot" property or one that has never been licensed before. Obviously, selling a license for a hot property takes far

311

Basics of Licensing: International Edition

less effort than trying to convince an otherwise reluctant manufacturer to take a chance with a new, untried property. It's no different than a car salesman trying to sell Road & Track's Car of the Year, versus one that has just recently been introduced.

The basic tools of selling a license[2] are fairly straightforward:

- Know Your Property. Do your homework and know all that you can about the property. To the prospective licensee, you are the expert on the property you are selling.
- Know Something About The Category You Are Trying to License. You cannot successfully sell a manufacturer without knowing some basic information about the product category.
- Familiarize Yourself With The Potential Licensee. The more you know about the company you are trying to sell to, the better your chances of success.
- Know Your Competition. Be prepared to respond to questions concerning competitive properties.
- Build Your Case. Know the strengths and weaknesses of your property—no property is perfect, so acknowledge its shortcomings while accentuating the positives. It's important to have the facts and figures relating to your property at your fingertips. Know what you are trying to accomplish before you start your presentation and remember, you are leading the meeting, so know where you are heading!
- Good Presentation Tools are Essential. In today's techno-marketplace, good presentation tools are expected and essential. The better the visual, the easier it is for the prospective licensee to picture the application of your property to his product. Your marketing and sales materials need to be both informative and attractive.

---

[2] Based on a CLS presentation *How to Sell a License* by Danny Simon, President of The Licensing Group, Ltd. 6363 Wilshire Blvd., Los Angeles, CA 90048

Chapter 12: Best Practices in Licensing Administration

- Believe in and Get Excited About Your Property. Enthusiasm is infectious. The more excited you are about the property you are selling, the better it will be received. Of course, enthusiasm will not replace or cover up a lack of knowledge about the property, product category or your ability to sell a license!

The salesman should also emphasize the benefits that may be derived from taking a license, including increased sales, the ability to sell other products in their line, building exposure and awareness of the manufacturer's own brand and product line and opening up distribution into different channels.

Once the list is narrowed down and there is an expression of interest by one or more potential licensees, they are typically asked to fill out and submit a "Licensee Application" in which the prospective licensee provides important information about its company, financial strength, licensing history and manufacturing and distribution capabilities.

The sales group then reviews and evaluates all of these completed licensee applications and ultimately selects the one that appears the best fit for the property. The evaluation process varies from licensor to licensor, but some of the more important elements considered by most include:

- Type of products they are proposing and whether they will be a good fit for the property;
- The company's quality history, e.g., have they manufactured high quality products in the past;
- Size and structure of the company, e.g., is it a major player in the field, or a start-up business;
- Strength of design and manufacturing capabilities, e.g., who will actually design the products and where and by whom will they be manufactured;
- Capitalization and financial strength, e.g., are they sufficiently capitalized to meet the financial conditions of the license and to put resources behind the license, or are they on the verge of bankruptcy;
- Distribution capabilities, e.g., how and in what markets will they distribute the product;

- How the license will fit in with the manufacturer's product mix;
- Sales history, e.g., what are their sales revenues and what percentage of their total revenues will the licensed products represent;
- Licensing history, e.g., have they had prior licenses and how have they done with them; and
- What financial terms are they offering.

It should be noted that financial terms were specifically identified as the last consideration because, for a license to be successful, it needs to be more than just about who is willing to pay the highest royalty rate or the largest advance or guarantee. If the licensee is not capable of manufacturing quality product or does not have sufficient market penetration, the selection of such a licensee can have a negative impact on the property.

Most licensors do not simply rely on the potential licensee's answers in the Licensee Application but will do their own due diligence to confirm various facts. It is quite common for licensors to order financial reports e.g., Dun & Bradstreet, to confirm a potential licensee's financial information and the company's history of meeting its financial obligations. Similarly, licensors will also ask for and check the licensee's references, including bank and credit references, in addition to asking other licensors about their experience with the company in question.

Once a potential licensee has been vetted and is selected, the final step for the sales group is to "close the deal" on the best terms possible for the licensor. Typically, this process starts with the preparation of a term sheet or deal memo which identifies the relevant terms of the transaction.

It is important to keep the entire licensing group aware of how these discussions progress as well as the terms being discussed. In many instances, it might even be necessary for other sections of the property owner's organization be involved or, at the very least, kept advised. The use of a sign-off sheet is a good idea to insure that the sales group doesn't offer terms or conditions that the property owner is simply unable or unwilling to offer. Getting as many people involved

Chapter 12: Best Practices in Licensing Administration

in this process as necessary is important to avoiding an embarrassing situation or, worse yet, one that must be unwound. Frequently, the sales group will work with the contract administration and legal group during this phase.

12.2.3 The Contract Administration and Legal Group

The contract administration and legal functions are typically intertwined as they cover both the legal protection that is required to support a licensing program, as well as the contract administration function. Frequently the same individual or individuals handle both functions.

Trademark Clearance and Protection

The necessity for clearing and protecting a licensing property internationally is covered at length in Chapter 4. Trademark clearance is typically the responsibility of the property owner, even if an independent licensing agent is used.

Prior to actually launching the licensing program, U.S. and/or global trademark search(es) should be conducted to insure that the use of the property by potential licensees will not infringe the rights of any other party. In performing such searches, special attention should be given to third party uses in those classes with the most licensing activity, i.e., apparel, publishing, toys and video games, etc. If there is the intent or likelihood that the property will or can be licensed outside the U.S., then make certain that the trademark search includes those international markets where the property might be licensed.

Assuming that the property is cleared in the key classes, appropriate trademark applications should be filed to commence the protection process.

Licensing Forms

Creating a set of standard forms that will be used for the licensing program is very important and should be done at the very outset to insure uniformity throughout the program. Some of the forms that should be developed are:

- Licensee Application Form
- Term Sheet or Deal Memo
- Basic License Agreement
- Product Approval Forms
- Royalty Report Form

Of all of these forms, perhaps the most important is the company's basic license agreement that will use with all licensees of the program. Special care should be taken in the development of the licensing agreement due to the fact that it will serve as the operative document that will define the relationship between the parties.

It should be appreciated that license agreements are "evolving" documents, meaning that as issues develop and lessons are learned from both good and bad experiences, and most licensors will adapt changes to their standard license agreements to insure that future agreements address such issues. Unfortunately, it is usually not possible to change an agreement that has already been signed with a license. Therefore, significant attention should be paid to the development of the licensing agreement to insure the form is properly prepared in the first place, and will likely mean that fewer changes are required going forward.

This is not to suggest or imply that every licensee will accept the property owner's standard form—most will want some changes and that is to be expected. The goal, however, is to keep the changes to a minimum so that there is a greater degree of uniformity between all the agreements within a program.

Contract Administration

As the name would imply, the group's primary function is to insure that all licensees comply with their obligations provided in the license agreement. The group will have day-to-day management responsibility for the licensing program and, in this regard, will frequently work in combination with the finance and creative groups.

It is advisable to establish strong, workable internal systems from the very beginning to make sure that the program

Chapter 12: Best Practices in Licensing Administration

proceeds smoothly and minimizes problems. The group should control the paper flow of the licensing process, which typically commences with internal approval of a licensee's proposal, through termination of the licensee. In most cases, the group is responsible for the following activities:

- **Preparation and Completion of the Deal Memo.** It is important that the deal memo be routed through the appropriate groups for review and approval.
- **Licensee Review and Evaluation.** This entails conducting financial and risk management reviews for all potential licensees and ultimately selecting the final licensee. An important consideration is recognizing any potential product liability issues.
- **License Agreement.** This includes the preparation, negotiation and execution of the license agreement and any amendments. It is good practice for summaries of the license agreements to be prepared and circulated to the various departments and kept readily accessible.
- **Licensee Administration.** This requires the development of a docketing system and "punch list" of all relevant due dates by licensees which should be circulated to other relevant departments, e.g., product approval dates to creative, product marketing deadlines for legal, etc. Additionally, and perhaps most importantly, it facilitates communications between the appropriate departments and licensees, to insure compliance with the terms of the license agreement.

Established licensing programs may quickly find themselves in a position where they have to track literally hundreds of licensees and licensed products on a worldwide basis, for multiple licensed properties. While some have and continue to do this manually, the better practice is to computerize the operation using a comprehensive contract administration software package that also features a royalty tracking/accounting module. Depending on the anticipated number of licensees the property is likely (or realistically) to generate, investment in product approval software might be a wise in-

Basics of Licensing: International Edition

vestment. Selecting and implementing the right package at the beginning of the program will avoid having to change procedures and systems mid-stream, which tends to cause complications. An effective contract administration software package should be able to:

- Assemble license agreements by the selection of individual clauses;
- Generate summaries of the license agreements and sort these by property, licensee, date, territory, term and product(s);
- Generate form letters or e-mails to licensees for reminders and failures to comply with due dates;
- Track and monitor licensees, licensed products, and submission and approval dates;
- Generate monthly reports, invoices and reminders;
- Monitor licensees' royalty and guarantee payment status;
- Manage all other aspects of the licensees' financial requirements and obligations;
- Track third party participation revenues for disbursements; and
- Produce management, sales, marketing and product approval reports as well as other relevant information anytime, from anywhere.

While some property owners prefer to develop their own, proprietary, contract administration systems, there are a number of excellent third party packages available that will meet the needs of most licensors. These software packages are designed to run on PC's and Apple platforms, and are surprisingly reasonable in price, compared to the cost of actually developing a proprietary program. A few of the more commonly used packages as of this writing include the Universal Rights Management system by Jaguar Consulting; Dependable Rights Manager (DRM) by Dependable Solutions; the Pelican ProFiles suite by Counterpoint Systems, Inc., and the licensing administration program from Octane 5, which also offers the inclusion of a product approval software program.

Chapter 12: Best Practices in Licensing Administration

Companies that market off-the-shelf licensing packages can be found in the "support services" section on LIMA's licensing database at www.licensing.org. Most of the companies listed in this section will provide potential customers with evaluation copies of their products as well as detailed sample reports that the program can generate.

12.2.4 The Finance Group

The finance group typically gets involved once the license agreement is actually signed and licensing revenue starts flowing, i.e., when the advance gets paid. This group is tasked with the responsibility of tracking payments due from both licensees as well as sub-agents in various international markets. The finance group should work closely with the contract administration group, utilizing their software to track all payments due and revenues received from licensees. This group also compiles the reports that will enable the property owner to quickly and easily evaluate the success of the overall licensing program, including the status of individual licensed properties, the licensees and the licensed products.

12.2.5 The Retail Group

In the early days of licensing, licensors would sit back and rely on their licensees to interact with the retail community. Times have changed. Today, most property owners understand the key role that the retailers play in the success or failure of a licensing program, and actively seek to engage them to help licensees maximize the market presence of their licensed products. Consolidation of the retail community has given key retailers enormous power, and securing distribution in one or two of the major chains can be the difference between success and failure.

Many licensors begin presenting their licensed properties and licensing programs to key retailers more than a year before licensed products are actually scheduled to reach the retail shelves, to generate excitement for their properties and pave the way for its licensee's products. Retail presentations should clearly convey:

Basics of Licensing: International Edition

- Property uniqueness, storylines, production quality, and identification of any notable talent affiliated with the property;
- Identification of broadcast partners and broadcast plans;
- Identification of key licensing partners, including master toy, apparel, publishing and video game licensees, as retailers want to know who has signed on to the licensing program – it is a critical part of their evaluation;
- Identification of promotional partners, the amount of advertising support for the property and any potential for developing in-store cross promotions;
- Property owner's plans to leverage assets and/or any relationship(s) that might help promote the property; and
- Advertising and publicity plans for the property to help create consumer awareness.

Some tips for making retail presentations[3] include:

- **Don't Be Vague.** Make sure your presentation has direction and a point of view specifically tailored for the retailer you are presenting to.
- **Allow the Retailer to Take It In.** Once you make your case, allow the retailer to absorb and interpret it for themselves. They understand their venues best and may know details of which you are unaware.
- **Identify Only Your Actual Licensees.** If you are giving out a licensee list, make sure that the licensees are on board since the retailer may contact them.
- **Don't Mention Other Retailers Who Have Passed.** If other retailers have passed on the property, keep it to yourself.
- **Think Out of the Box.** Don't limit yourself to the tried and true. Explore the host of new channels of distribution currently available. They may not be the

---

[3] Based on the LIMA webinar entitled *Presenting to Retail: The Good, The Bad and the Ugly*, by David Niggli, former Chief Marketing Officer for FAO Schwartz.

Chapter 12: Best Practices in Licensing Administration

biggest, but they could ultimately prove to be successful, and could lead to bigger opportunities down the road.
- **Be concise.** Time is precious, so make sure to convey your message in an efficient and concise manner.
- Be **passionate!** Your approach should not be, "I wanted to see what you thought of this property", but rather "I have a new property that is right for you and let me tell you why."

In recent years, many retailers have not been content to simply sell licensed products that were manufactured by conventional licensees but, instead, have gone directly to the property owner and taken on a "direct to retail" licenses for certain products or product categories, which they then have manufactured in their own factories or by another third party for exclusive distribution in their stores. By eliminating the conventional licensee and their profit from the equation, the retailers are conceivably able to offer the licensed products to the consumer at lower prices.

12.2.6 The Creative Group

The creative group is tasked with the responsibility of controlling how the property appears and will actually be used on the licensed products. It is also responsible for the review and approval of all licensee submissions to ensure that the quality standards are being met and the licensee is using the property correctly on its products.

Most property owners provide their licensees with a "style guide" that illustrates how the property should be depicted and used. It is a "road map" for the licensing property and should be closely followed by all licensees. Today, most style guides are delivered in digital format rather than in hard copy and many are maintained on-line for ease of reference by a licensee.

Again, the primary purpose of a style guide is to inform a licensee as to how it may present the property on the licensed products enabling creation the best licensed products possible. It will also assure that there is uniformity between

Basics of Licensing: International Edition

all licensees and licensed products regarding how the property appears on product, packaging and in marketing materials. A typical style guide will include:

- How the property is to be depicted and displayed, what characters or brands are included and/or maybe used, etc.;
- Rules for use of the property, e.g. "Character X should never…;"
- If a character is included, what poses can (and cannot) be used and, the character size ratios;
- Vehicles and environment artwork guidelines;
- The color palette of the property in terms of use on product and for backgrounds;
- Approved logos, hangtags, packaging graphics, and possibly product concepts;
- Product approval requirements that outline when and how a product must be submitted to the licensor for approval; and
- Required legal notices, and where and how they must appear.

Many property owners prepare their own style guides while others outsource the project to companies that specialize in their preparation. There are a number of such entities and they can be found in the "support services" section on LIMA's licensing database at www.licensing.org.

As licensees are brought on board, the creative group monitors how the property is used on licensed products. As spelled out in their license agreements, licensees will be required to submit proposed product, packaging and advertising to the licensor for approval at various stages of the production cycle, and it is the responsibility of the creative group to review and approve such submissions. Also, as noted earlier licensees are typically not permitted to proceed to the next step of product development unless they first obtain written approval of their submissions. In many instances, the failure of a licensor to provide the licensee with approval of a submission means that the submission has been deemed disapproved.

Chapter 12: Best Practices in Licensing Administration

Many licensees involve the licensor's creative group early in the licensing process to ensure that both parties are on the same page when it comes to product development. By reviewing early renderings of product and packaging, potentially devastating problems can be avoided, e.g., the production of products that are unacceptable to the licensor. When the creative group is involved at an early stage, small problems can often be corrected before they become large and expensive issues.

As the licensing program expands, keeping track of and reviewing licensee submissions, can become a time-consuming undertaking. As such, it is advisable for the creative group to work with the contract administration group and its computer systems to docket when such submissions are due and when responses are required. A program with 50 licensees, for example, may have to track and respond to more than 1,000 submissions every year—no easy feat to do manually.

12.3 International Licensing

Licensing is a global business and one cannot simply focus on the country where the property is created and initially merchandised. This is particularly true for entertainment properties and major brands.

If the property is represented in an international market by a licensing agent, the agent should prepare a licensing plan and submit it to the property owner before the commencement of any international sales effort. Such a plan should: (1) outline the list of products that the agent believes would be appropriate for the property, (2) make recommendations of the trademark classes that should be secured, and (3) state what materials will be needed to market the property.

As is the case with most licensing matters, successful licensors work backwards from the date when they expect licensed products to first hit their respective markets. The following steps should be taken in the development of an international program:

- Immediately after the decision is made to proceed with an international licensing program, seek trademark protection in each country where licensing is contemplated as well as those countries where licensed products will likely be manufactured, e.g., China, Thailand, Vietnam, Malaysia, etc.
- The expense for filing trademarks in multiple markets can quickly add up. To control costs, create and assign an order of importance to a list of primary markets and relevant product categories. Using these two lists, commence the international trademark program according to the priority of markets and product categories you established. As your international business grows continue to increase your trademark protection by continuing to include new markets and/or product categories.
- Immediately after a broadcast commitment has been obtained, of when timing dictates:
    o Set up a network of agents in countries where licensing is contemplated;
    o Develop territory-specific tools, e.g., dubbed sizzle reels, translated one-sheet brochures with relevant territory information, broadcast information, global key category partners, etc.; and
    o Identify territory-specific opportunities and work with the appropriate agent(s) to secure them.
- At least one year before the projected launch of licensed products in a particular country:
    o Create sub-agent representation agreements with those sub-agents who will represent the property in their market;
    o Manage the sub-agents through systems that reinforce deal execution, product development, retail commitments and product roll-out schedules; and
    o When and where possible provide support to licensee(s) at key industry trade shows. Using the toy category as an example, support-

Chapter 12: Best Practices in Licensing Administration

ing the property with advertising and/or promotional efforts at trade shows such as the Hong Kong International Toy Fair, and other shows like the London and/or Nuremburg toy shows can have a positive impact on business. Additionally, providing licensees with material such as sizzle videos, posters, costume characters and handouts for use at their tradeshows can be effective and welcomed tools that your licensees can use to promote your property.

12.4 International Agents

A significant difference in operating a licensing program in international territories outside of the property owner's home market is the fact that the property owner may be incapable of doing so. The two most significant reasons are lack of relevant knowledge and the language barrier. A lack of understanding of local market conditions, and/or a database of potential licensees, and an inability to communicate can greatly impede efforts to establish international expansion of a licensing program. This need for assistance to extend the boundaries of a licensing program quickly gave rise to a new segment of the licensing industry – the international agent.

In addition to resolving the potential problems of language and insufficient knowledge of the marketplace, international licensing agents bring the credibility they have established, and therefore the ability to open opportunities that otherwise might be unavailable. Also, based on their experience in the industry, they are frequently able to negotiate better licensing terms than the property owner, in addition to being readily available should such need arise.

12.4.1 Sub-Agent vs Agent

If the international agent acquires the rights to represent the property in a specific territory(s) not directly from the property owner rights, but from the property owner's agent, then technically the international agent is acting as a sub-agent of the property. As the essential duties, responsibilities and obligations are very much the same acting in either capacity, for the purpose of this book no distinction is made between international agent and international sub-agent.

12.4.2 Role of the International Agent

The principle role of the international agent is to represent and build an extension of the property's licensing program in a specific country or region. This includes not only the responsibility of selling the licensing rights to manufacturers within the assigned market(s), but also to facilitate the administration of the licensing program as its local representative.

The advantages of working with international agents are numerous, including: the agent has more direct contact with local licensees; the agent manages the administration of the property; the agent adapts the property to conform to local language and customs, and the responsibility to collect and transfer the royalty income generated from the market is the agent's responsibility.

The following is a list of certain duties and responsibilities that are commonly expected of the international agent:

- Assist the property owner in refining and developing the property into a licensable property;
- Provide assistance in determining which product categories the property owner must file in for trademark protection;
- Develop marketing and presentation materials for use in presenting the property to prospective licensees;
- Identify prospective licensees likely to be interested in taking a license for the property;
- Present the property to those prospective licensees most likely to be interested in the property;
- Negotiate the terms of all agreements between the property owner and the licensees;
- Administer the licensing program, including periodically reviewing all licensee submissions of licensed products and associated advertising, packaging and

Chapter 12: Best Practices in Licensing Administration

promotional materials to insure that the quality control provisions of the agreement are met;
- Wherever necessary, personally inspect the licensee's manufacturing facilities to insure that the quality control provisions are being complied with; and
- Collect all advances, guaranteed minimum royalty payments and actual royalty payments from licensees.

In short, the international agent should be tasked with doing everything that a vigilant property owner would do if it was overseeing the licensing program.

12.4.3 Selecting International Licensing Agents

There are licensing agents operating in virtually all key markets throughout the world. The first step in selecting the right international agent for the property begins by identifying those agents who have licensing expertise in the same or similar licensing category as your property. This can be done by asking friends and colleagues for recommendations or by accessing databases of international agents.

Most international agents typically have particular specialties, e.g., entertainment, brands, sports or celebrity properties. Most have their own individual "styles," and it is important that such style meshes well with the property the international agent will be representing.

The LIMA database (www.licensing.org) is an excellent way to obtain a roster of international agents. After landing on LIMA home page, click on the "LIMANET" tab, then click on "Licensing Agent" located at the top of the page. Agency listings typically will include the specific properties represented by the agency, and contact information.

Also highly useful are directories that provide listings of licensing agencies, which most often are listed on a country-by-country basis, and usually updated annually. Having just released its 22nd Edition, the directory we recommend using is the *Guide To The Licensing World* (www.licensingworld.co.uk). This directory offers a very comprehensive listing of international agents around the world, and provides the names of the properties that an agency represents, in addition to supplying all the necessary contact information. Simply because an agent has successfully represented one form of property, e.g., entertainment, brands or sports, does not mean that the agent will be equally successful with a different type of property, e.g., art, non-profit or music, as the agent may lack sufficient information (or relationships) with manufacturers outside of the agent's specialty.

12.4.4 International Agent Compensation

International agents are traditionally compensated through payment of a commission based on a percentage of the royalties generated from the international agent's territory. If they are retained directly by the property owner, the international agent's commission is usually calculated in much the same way as that of a licensing agent representing the property in the home territory. Therefore, the typical commission rate is anywhere from 25% to 35% of the royalty income paid by licensees.

If the international agent is retained by the property owner's master licensing agent (a licensing agent that controls worldwide representation of the property), the agent is considered a sub-agent. This can affect the international agent's level of compensation, as the total amount of available commission may be limited by the master licensing agent's commission rate. For example, if the master licensing agent had negotiated a commission rate of 40% for licenses obtained from the international market (to compensate for commissions paid to a sub-agent), the licensing agent and sub-agent might agree to a commission of 25% to 30% of the total licensing revenues from that country or region, with the master agent retaining 10% to 15% of the licensing revenues. If the master agent's commission rate is less, it is like to reduce the amount of commission available to pay the sub-agent.

Chapter 12: Best Practices in Licensing Administration

12.4.5 International Agent Exclusivity and Territory

Most international agents will demand exclusive representation of the property in their territory, which is a reasonable condition, as properties are usually ill-served by the use of multiple agents operating in the same market.

What must be clearly documented are the geographical boundaries of the international agent's territory. This benefits all parties, as it insures international agents that no other party can or will be offering the property for licensing within their territory. It also helps to protect the property owner (and licensees) from the situation of unknowingly licensing the same or similar rights to multiple licensees. The potential of this occurring is greatly increased if the geographical areas in which the international agent can freely operate are not well defined, as the markets in which the international agent has the right to represent the property would and should apply to where the area in which the licensed products can be distributed.

It should be noted that the formation of the European Union has created its own share of issues with respect to licensing, and it can impact the way licensing agents operate within the Union. Economically, the European Union is essentially one nation with individual states. Under European Union regulations, if a licensee acquires a license for one country within the Union, e.g., France, it has the ability to sell its products in other countries within the Union, irrespective of what the license agreement may provide or restrict. The EU has strictly enforced this requirement and will impose substantial fines if a party attempts to limit such territorial freedom. There are reports of manufacturers being fined as much as €1 million for violating these regulations.

There are, of course, ways to mitigate the impact of these restrictions. For example, in the category of publishing, licensors may limit the marketability of a published work by granting language-specific rights, e.g., an English language version, which can greatly impact the distribution of product. If distribution of the English version is obtained in other EU markets, and the same book has been licensed under different

Basics of Licensing: International Edition

language rights, these two different but similar products will not be direct competition.

Another consideration is the inclusion of language in all EU international agent representation agreements, that provides that agents must secure prior agreement from other agents in those EU markets in which the product will or is likely to be distributed, and that income generated in markets outside the agent's jurisdiction will be shared on an agreeable basis.

The right to free trade within the EU is an issue that property owners should be aware of. As this right can and has had an enormous impact on licensing and, more particularly, the work of agents and sub-agents within the EU block.

12.5 Ethics in Licensing

Some cynics who refer to licensing as the "last bastion of hucksterism" may think that the phrase "ethics in licensing" is an oxymoron — be assured it is not. With retail sales of licensed merchandise growing from $4.9 billion dollars in 1977 to $112.1 billion dollars at the end of 2012, licensing has become a very significant and important industry. Now more than ever, professionalism within the industry is important and that means that licensing professionals need to insure that ethical business practices are a top priority.

Webster defines "ethics" as the "principles of conduct governing an individual or a group." In the context of any professional group, "ethics" is typically considered to be:

- Honesty and candor, instead of gamesmanship and overreaching;
- Seeking enforceable, yet workable, business arrangements; and
- Protecting and enhancing the profession's reputation.

The International Licensing Industry Merchandisers' Association (LIMA) has adopted a Statement of Ethical Principles, addressing the manner in which licensing should be practiced. It states the following:

LIMA supports and encourages its members to conduct themselves in an ethical manner in the course

Chapter 12: Best Practices in Licensing Administration

of their business dealing involving licensing properties and licensed products.

A member of LIMA should respect the rights of others and should comply with all applicable local, national and international laws and regulations governing his or her business dealings.

A member should make fair representations as to the nature, quality and extent of the property being offered for license or of the capabilities of the company seeking a license. Any statement not supported by fact should be identified as opinion. A member should not engage in any misleading advertising or solicitation that could lead to false or exaggerated expectations as to the member's skill, experience or ability.

A member should not represent conflicting interests in the same transaction without the knowledge and consent of all parties involved.

A member should hold inviolate all confidences, whether written or implied.

12.6   Ensuring Social Compliance[4]

Social compliance is a relatively recent concern for many licensors due, in large measure, to negative media attention focused on working conditions in factories that produce licensed products, most notably in China and other international markets. The problem received national attention in the United States in 1996 as a result of a controversy involving Kathie Lee Gifford.

The news media and social activist groups around the world exposed the fact that some factories used to manufacture Ms. Gifford's licensed products were guilty of maintaining sub-standard working conditions, and some companies were employing prison and child labor to produce the products. This put pressure on the private sector to play a role in trying to improve such conditions.

---

[4] Based on a 2009 LIMA webinar presentation entitled *Social Compliance: Introduction and Overview* by Ian Spalding, President, InFact Global Partners, 16A, Dotcom House, 128 Wellington Street Central Hong Kong.

Basics of Licensing: International Edition

Make no mistake about it, this is a serious problem, which our industry must be aware of. Some factories blatantly violate their local laws, falsify their records and even bribe inspectors. To assume this is a way of life in "those" countries is to simply ignore these issues, which only acerbates the problem.

The private sector's reaction was the development of codes of conduct for these factories to abide by if they wanted to continue to work with those companies that pledged to honor those codes of conduct. The first code of conduct was actually adopted by Levi Strauss in 1991. In 1998, the Fair Labor Association was created, with White House support, and developed its own code.

Over the past decade, many licensors, retailers and trade associations have adopted social compliance standards, which they require their partners and suppliers to follow. The purpose of these codes is to raise the standards of working conditions in factories used by such partners and suppliers to manufacture their products (including licensed merchandise), in addition to promoting social responsibility as a shared effort.

While there are slight differences between many of these codes, in one form or another they all address the following issues:

- Maximum working hours for employees;
- Fair compensation of employees;
- Human working conditions
- Institution of child labor laws; and
- Social insurance that an employer must carry for its employees.

LIMA has its own Code of Business Practices, which may be found at http://www.licensing.org /about/business-practices.php.

Establishing standards is one thing—enforcing them is quite another. Progress is being made in this area, as today, very few licensors still simply ignore the issue. At the very least, most require their licensees to conform to some standard. While some licensors may not aggressively enforce such a requirement, they will reserve the right to terminate

Chapter 12: Best Practices in Licensing Administration

the licensee should it be determined that the licensee was non-compliant, and which should the very minimum that any licensor should do.

Most licensors actually go further and, do, in fact, actively look to enforce these standards by auditing factories of their licensees. This is done by either a licensor's internal auditors or by third parties who specialize in such audits. While some simply audit on a superficial basis and tend to look the other way when violations are found, there is an increasing number of licensors that require a non-conforming licensee to either correct the problems or face termination of their license agreement.

Some licensors will actually go the extra mile and work with licensees to make sure that their factories are in compliance with these standards. They have shifted focus from mere monitoring to actively promoting continuous improvement, even to the point where they are willing to share in the associated cost of reaching compliance. They have begun to emphasize education and capacity building, as opposed to simply conducting more audits. Longer-term corrective action plans are necessary and ultimately reinforce better business practices. Appropriately, a growing number of licensors today recognize the implications of non-compliance – the potential of seriously tarnish not only the attractiveness of the company's product lines, but also the erosion of its image and reputation.

Basics of Licensing: International Edition

APPENDIX

Appendix A:
Merchandising License Agreement

MERCHANDISING LICENSE AGREEMENT

THIS AGREEMENT is entered into this [*day*] day of [*month*], [*year*] by and between [*name of Licensor*], a [*place of incorporation of Licensor*] corporation with offices at [*address of Licensor*] ("LICENSOR"), and [*name of Licensee*], a [*place of incorporation of Licensee*] corporation with offices at [*address of Licensee*] ("LICENSEE").

WITNESSETH:

WHEREAS, LICENSOR is the sole and exclusive owner of the Property or Properties identified more fully in Schedule A attached hereto (the "Property"); and

WHEREAS, LICENSOR is the sole and exclusive owner of the trademark identified more fully in Schedule A attached hereto (the "Trademark"); and

WHEREAS, LICENSOR has the power and authority to grant to LICENSEE the right, privilege and license to use, manufacture and sell those types of products that incorporate or are otherwise based on the Property as identified in Schedule A attached hereto (the "Licensed Products") and to use the Trademark on or in association with such Licensed Products; and

WHEREAS, LICENSEE has represented that it has the ability to manufacture, market and distribute the Licensed Products in the countries identified in Schedule A attached hereto (the "Territory") and to use the Trademark on or in association with the Licensed Products; and

WHEREAS, LICENSEE desires to obtain from LICENSOR a license to use, manufacture, have manufactured and sell Licensed

Basics of Licensing: International Edition

Products in the Territory and to use the Trademark on or in association with the Licensed Products; and

WHEREAS, both LICENSEE and LICENSOR are in agreement with respect to the terms and conditions upon which LICENSEE shall use, manufacture, have manufactured and sell Licensed Products and to use the Trademark;

NOW, THEREFORE, in consideration of the promises and agreements set forth herein, the parties, each intending to be legally bound hereby, do promise and agree as follows.

1. LICENSE GRANT

A. LICENSOR hereby grants to LICENSEE, for the Term of this Agreement as recited in Schedule A attached hereto, the non-exclusive right and license to use, manufacture, have manufactured, sell, distribute and advertise the Licensed Products in the Territory. The license includes, but is not limited to, a license under any and all patents and copyrights and any applications therefore which have been filed or may be filed in the future with respect to the Property. It is understood and agreed that this license shall pertain only to the Licensed Products and does not extend to any other product or service.

B. LICENSOR hereby grants to LICENSEE for the Term of this Agreement as recited in Schedule A attached hereto, a non-exclusive license to use the Trademark on or in association with the Licensed Products in the Territory as well as on packaging, promotional and advertising material associated therewith.

C. LICENSEE may not grant any sublicenses to any third party without the prior express written consent of the LICENSOR which may be withheld for any reason.

2. TERM OF THE AGREEMENT

This Agreement and the provisions hereof, except as otherwise provided, shall be in full force and effect commencing on the date of execution by both parties and shall extend for a Term as recited in Schedule A attached hereto (the "Term").

Appendix

3. COMPENSATION

A. In consideration for the licenses granted hereunder, LICENSEE agrees to pay to LICENSOR during the Term of this Agreement a royalty in the amount recited in Schedule A attached hereto (the "Royalty") based on LICENSEE's Net Sales of Licensed Products.

B. In the event that LICENSEE grants any previously approved sub-licenses for the use of the Property in countries outside of the United States, LICENSEE shall pay LICENSOR FIFTY PERCENT (50%) of the gross income received by LICENSEE from such sub-licensees.

C. The Royalty owed LICENSOR shall be calculated on a quarterly calendar basis (the "Royalty Period") and shall be payable no later than thirty (30) days after the termination of the preceding full calendar quarter, i.e., commencing on the first (1st) day of January, April, July, and October with the exception of the first and last calendar quarters which may be "short" depending upon the effective date of this Agreement.

D. With each Royalty Payment, LICENSEE shall provide LICENSOR with a written royalty statement in a form acceptable to LICENSOR. Such royalty statement shall be certified as accurate by a duly authorized officer of LICENSEE, reciting on a country by country basis, the stock number, item, units sold, description, quantity shipped, gross invoice, amount billed customers less discounts, allowances, returns, and reportable sales for each Licensed Product. Such statements shall be furnished to LICENSOR whether or not any Licensed Products were sold during the Royalty Period.

E. LICENSEE agrees to pay to LICENSOR a Guaranteed Minimum Royalty in accordance with the terms of Schedule A attached hereto (the "Guaranteed Minimum Royalty"). As recited in Schedule A, a portion of the Guaranteed Minimum Royalty for the first year shall be payable as an Advance against royalties (the "Advance"). The actual royalty payments shall reflect the amount of all Guaranteed Minimum Royalty payments including any Advances made.

F. "Net Sales" shall mean LICENSEE's gross sales (the gross invoice amount billed customers) of Licensed Products, less discounts and allowances actually shown on the invoice (except cash discounts not deductible in the calculation of Royalty) and, further,

Basics of Licensing: International Edition

less any bona fide returns (net of all returns actually made or allowed as supported by credit memoranda actually issued to the customers). No other costs incurred in the manufacturing, selling, advertising, and distribution of the Licensed Products shall be deducted nor shall any deduction be allowed for any uncollectible accounts or allowances.

G. A Royalty obligation shall accrue upon the sale of the Licensed Products regardless of the time of collection by LICENSEE. For purposes of this Agreement, a Licensed Product shall be considered "sold" upon the date when such Licensed Product is billed, invoiced, shipped, or paid for, whichever event occurs first.

H. If LICENSEE sells any Licensed Products to any party affiliated with LICENSEE, or in any way directly or indirectly related to or under the common control with LICENSEE, at a price less than the regular price charged to other parties, the Royalty payable LICENSOR shall be computed on the basis of the regular price charged to other parties.

I. The receipt or acceptance by LICENSOR of any royalty statement, or the receipt or acceptance of any royalty payment made, shall not prevent LICENSOR from subsequently challenging the validity or accuracy of such statement or payment.

J. Upon expiration or termination of this Agreement, all Royalty obligations, including any unpaid portions of the Guaranteed Minimum Royalty, shall be accelerated and shall immediately become due and payable.

K. LICENSEE's obligations for the payment of a Royalty and the Guaranteed Minimum Royalty shall survive expiration or termination of this Agreement and will continue for so long as LICENSEE continues to manufacture, sell or otherwise market the Licensed Products.

L. All payments due hereunder shall be made in United States currency drawn on a United States bank, unless otherwise specified between the parties.

M. Late payments shall incur interest at the rate of ONE PERCENT (1%) per month from the date such payments were originally due.

Appendix

N. LICENSEE shall be responsible for any taxes on revenues received from sublicensing in countries outside the United States while LICENSOR shall be responsible for any taxes levied on the receipt of income in the United States. Any taxes foreign to United States taxes imposed on fees or royalties payable under this Agreement shall be paid by LICENSOR or deducted by LICENSEE from amounts due LICENSOR hereunder only if such taxes are allowable by the United States as a credit on LICENSOR's United States income tax return or would be allowable if the particular circumstance of the LICENSOR (such as that its profits are insufficient) causes disallowance. If not allowable, such taxes, if any, will be paid by the LICENSEE. Both parties will cooperate with one another to obtain the benefits of such double taxation agreements as may be applicable hereunder.

O. All fees payable hereunder shall be based on the official exchange rate on the date on which such payment is due and LICENSEE shall provide detailed conversion calculations with every payment submitted hereunder. If, by any reason of any governmental or fiscal restrictions effecting the convertibility, payment cannot be made in U.S. funds, then LICENSEE shall take such reasonable actions with respect to the payment due as LICENSOR shall direct.

4. AUDIT

A. LICENSOR shall have the right, upon at least five (5) days written notice and no more than once per calendar year, to inspect LICENSEE's books and records and all other documents and material in the possession of or under the control of LICENSEE with respect to the subject matter of this Agreement at a location in the United States. LICENSOR shall have free and full access thereto for such purposes and shall be permitted to make copies thereof and extracts therefrom.

B. In the event that such inspection reveals a discrepancy in the amount of Royalty owed LICENSOR from what was actually paid, LICENSEE shall pay such discrepancy, plus interest, calculated at the rate of ONE AND ONE-HALF PERCENT (1 1/2%) per month. In the event that such discrepancy is in excess of ONE THOUSAND UNITED STATES DOLLARS ($1,000.00), LICENSEE shall also reimburse LICENSOR for the cost of such inspection including any attorney's fees incurred in connection therewith.

Basics of Licensing: International Edition

C. All books and records relative to LICENSEE's obligations hereunder shall be maintained and kept accessible and available to LICENSOR for inspection in the United States for at least three (3) years after termination of this Agreement.

D. In the event that an investigation of LICENSEE's books and records is made, certain confidential and proprietary business information of LICENSEE may necessarily be made available to the person or persons conducting such investigation. It is agreed that such confidential and proprietary business information shall be retained in confidence by LICENSOR and shall not be used by LICENSOR or disclosed to any third party for a period of two (2) years from the date of disclosure, or without the prior express written permission of LICENSEE unless required by law. It is understood and agreed, however, that such information may be used in any proceeding based on LICENSEE's failure to pay its actual Royalty obligation.

5. WARRANTIES & OBLIGATIONS

A. LICENSOR represents and warrants that it has the right and power to grant the licenses granted herein and that there are no other agreements with any other party in conflict herewith.

B. LICENSOR further represents and warrants that the Property and/or Trademark do not infringe any valid right of any third party.

C. LICENSEE represents and warrants that it will use its best efforts to promote, market, sell and distribute the Licensed Products.

D. LICENSEE shall be solely responsible for the manufacture, production, sale, and distribution of the Licensed Products and will bear all related costs associated therewith.

E. It is the intention of the parties that LICENSEE shall introduce the Licensed Products in all countries in the Territory on or before the Product Introduction Date recited in Schedule A and commence shipment of Licensed Products in all countries in the Territory on or before the Initial Shipment Date recited in Schedule A. Failure to meet either the Product Introduction Date or the Initial Shipment Date shall constitute grounds for immediate termination of this Agreement by LICENSOR with respect to the particular

Appendix

country in which LICENSEE has failed to introduce or commence shipment as required herein. LICENSEE's rights with respect to all other countries will, however, survive such termination of a portion of this Agreement.

6. NOTICES, QUALITY CONTROL & SAMPLES

A. The licenses granted hereunder are conditioned upon LICENSEE's full and complete compliance with the marking provisions of the patent, trademark and copyright laws of the United States and other countries in the Territory.

B. The Licensed Products, as well as all promotional, packaging and advertising material relative thereto, shall include all appropriate legal notices as required by LICENSOR.

C. The Licensed Products shall be of a high quality which is at least equal to comparable products manufactured and marketed by LICENSEE and in conformity with a standard sample approved by LICENSOR.

D. If the quality of a class of the Licensed Products falls below such a production-run quality, as previously approved by LICENSOR, LICENSEE shall use its best efforts to restore such quality. In the event that LICENSEE has not taken appropriate steps to restore such quality within thirty (30) days after notification by LICENSOR, LICENSOR shall have the right to terminate this Agreement.

E. Prior to the commencement of manufacture and sale of the Licensed Products, LICENSEE shall submit to LICENSOR, at no cost to LICENSOR and for approval as to quality, six (6) sets of samples of all Licensed Products which LICENSEE intends to manufacture and sell and one (1) complete set of all promotional and advertising material associated therewith. Failure of LICENSOR to approve such samples within ten (10) working days after receipt hereof will be deemed approval. If LICENSOR should disapprove any sample, it shall provide specific reasons for such disapproval. Once such samples have been approved by LICENSOR, LICENSEE shall not materially depart therefrom without LICENSOR's prior express written consent, which shall not be unreasonably withheld.

F. At least once during each calendar year, LICENSEE shall submit to LICENSOR, for approval, an additional twelve (12) sets of samples.

G. The LICENSEE agrees to permit LICENSOR or its representative to inspect the facilities where the Licensed Products are being manufactured and packaged.

7. NOTICE & PAYMENT

A. Any notice required to be given pursuant to this Agreement shall be in writing and delivered personally to the other designated party at the above stated address or mailed by certified or registered mail, return receipt requested or delivered by a recognized national overnight courier service.

B. Either party may change the address to which notice or payment is to be sent by written notice to the other in accordance with the provisions of this paragraph.

8. PATENTS, TRADEMARKS & COPYRIGHTS

A. LICENSOR shall seek, obtain and, during the Term of this Agreement, maintain in its own name and at its own expense, appropriate trademark or copyright protection for the Property and Trademark in the United States. LICENSOR shall have no obligation whatsoever to obtain and/or maintain protection for the Property and/or Trademark in countries outside the United States.

B. In the event that LICENSEE requests that LICENSOR obtain trademark or copyright protection for a particular item or in a particular country where LICENSOR had not, heretofore, obtained such protection, LICENSOR agrees to take reasonable steps to obtain such protection, provided, however, that LICENSEE shall be obligated to reimburse LICENSOR for the cost of filing, prosecuting and maintaining same.

C. It is understood and agreed that LICENSOR shall retain all right, title and interest in the original Property as well as in any modifications or improvements made to the Property by LICENSEE.

D. The parties agree to execute any documents reasonably requested by the other party to effect any of the above provisions.

Appendix

E. LICENSEE acknowledges LICENSOR's exclusive rights in the Property and, further, acknowledges that the Property and/or the Trademark are unique and original to LICENSOR and that LICENSOR is the owner thereof. LICENSEE shall not, at any time during or after the effective Term of the Agreement, dispute or contest, directly or indirectly, LICENSOR's exclusive right and title to the Property and/or the Trademark or the validity thereof. LICENSOR, however, makes no representation or warranty with respect to the validity of any patent, trademark or copyright which may issue or be granted therefrom.

F. LICENSEE acknowledges that the Property and/or the Trademark have acquired secondary meaning.

G. LICENSEE agrees that its use of the Property and/or the Trademark inures to the benefit of LICENSOR and that the LICENSEE shall not acquire any rights in the Property and/or the Trademark.

9. TERMINATION

The following termination rights are in addition to the termination rights provided elsewhere in this Agreement:

A. *Immediate Right of Termination.* LICENSOR shall have the right to immediately terminate this Agreement by giving written notice to LICENSEE in the event that LICENSEE does any of the following:

(1) fails to meet the Product Introduction Date or the Initial Shipment Date as specified in Schedule A; or

(2) after having commenced sale of the Licensed Products, fails to continuously sell Licensed Products for three (3) consecutive Royalty Periods; or

(3) fails to obtain or maintain product liability insurance in the amount and of the type provided for herein; or

(4) files a petition in bankruptcy or is adjudicated a bankrupt or insolvent, or makes an assignment for the benefit of creditors, or an arrangement pursuant to any bankruptcy law, or if the LICENSEE discontinues its business or a receiver is appointed for the LI-

Basics of Licensing: International Edition

CENSEE or for the LICENSEE's business and such receiver is not discharged within thirty (30) days; or

(5) breaches any of the provisions of this Agreement relating to the unauthorized assertion of rights in the Property and/or the Trademark; or

(6) fails, after receipt of written notice from LICENSOR, to immediately discontinue the distribution or sale of the Licensed Products or the use of any packaging or promotional material which does not contain the requisite legal legends; or

(7) fails to make timely payment of Royalties when due two or more times during any twelve-month period.

B. *Immediate Right to Terminate a Portion.* LICENSOR shall have the right to immediately terminate the portion(s) of the Agreement relating to any Property and/or Licensed Product(s) and/or for any country in the Territory if LICENSEE, for any reason, fails to meet the Product Introduction Dates or the Initial Shipment Dates specified in Schedule A or, after the commencement of manufacture and sale of a particular Licensed Product in a particular country, ceases to sell commercial quantities of such Licensed Product in such country for three (3) consecutive Royalty Periods. In the event of such partial termination, all other non-terminated rights granted herein shall survive.

C. *Right to Terminate on Notice.* This Agreement may be terminated by either party upon thirty (30) days written notice to the other party in the event of a breach of a material provision of this Agreement by the other party, provided that, during the thirty (30) day period, the breaching party fails to cure such breach.

D. LICENSEE shall have the right to terminate this Agreement at any time on sixty (60) days written notice to LICENSOR. In such event, all moneys paid to LICENSOR shall be deemed non-refundable and LICENSEE's obligation to pay any guaranteed moneys, including the Guaranteed Minimum Royalty, shall be accelerated and any yet unpaid guaranteed moneys shall become immediately due and payable.

Appendix

10. POST TERMINATION RIGHTS

A. Not less than thirty (30) days prior to the expiration of this Agreement or immediately upon termination thereof, LICENSEE shall provide LICENSOR with a complete schedule of all inventory of Licensed Products then on-hand (the "Inventory").

B. Upon expiration or termination of this Agreement, except for reason of a breach of LICENSEE's duty to comply with the quality control or legal notice marking requirements, LICENSEE shall be entitled, for an additional period of three (3) months and on a nonexclusive basis, to continue to sell such Inventory. Such sales shall be made subject to all of the provisions of this Agreement and to an accounting for and the payment of a Royalty thereon. Such accounting and payment shall be due and paid within thirty (30) days after the close of the said three (3) month period.

C. Upon the expiration or termination of this Agreement, all of the rights of LICENSEE under this Agreement shall forthwith terminate and immediately revert to LICENSOR and LICENSEE shall immediately discontinue all use of the Property and the like, at no cost whatsoever to LICENSOR.

D. Upon termination of this Agreement for any reasons whatsoever, LICENSEE agrees to immediately return to LICENSOR all material relating to the Property including, but not limited to, all artwork, color separations, prototypes and the like, as well as any market studies or other tests or studies conducted by LICENSEE with respect to the Property, at no cost whatsoever to LICENSOR.

11. GOOD WILL

LICENSEE recognizes the value of the good will associated with the Property and acknowledges that the Property and all rights therein including the good will pertaining thereto, belong exclusively to LICENSOR.

12. INFRINGEMENTS

A. LICENSEE shall have the right, in its discretion, to institute and prosecute lawsuits against third persons for infringement of the rights licensed in this Agreement.

Basics of Licensing: International Edition

B. If LICENSEE does not institute an infringement suit within ninety (90) days after LICENSOR's written request that it do so, LICENSOR may institute and prosecute such lawsuit. Any lawsuit shall be prosecuted solely at the cost and expense of the party bringing suit and all sums recovered in any such lawsuits, whether by judgment, settlement or otherwise, in excess of the amount of reasonable attorneys' fees and other out of pocket expenses of such suit, shall be divided equally between the parties.

C. Upon request of the party bringing the lawsuit, the other party shall execute all papers, testify on all matters, and otherwise cooperate in every way necessary and desirable for the prosecution of any such lawsuit. The party bringing suit shall reimburse the other party for the expenses incurred as a result of such cooperation.

13. INDEMNITY

A. LICENSEE agrees to defend and indemnify LICENSOR, its officers, directors, agents, and employees, against all costs, expenses and losses (including reasonable attorneys' fees and costs) incurred through claims of third parties against LICENSOR based on the manufacture or sale of the Licensed Products including, but not limited to, actions founded on product liability.

B. LICENSOR agrees to defend and indemnify LICENSEE, its officers, directors, agents, and employees, against all costs, expenses and losses (including reasonable attorneys' fees and costs) incurred through claims of third parties against LICENSEE challenging the authenticity of the originally submitted Property provided, however, that such indemnity shall only be applicable in the event of a final decision by a court of competent jurisdiction from which no appeal of right exists and shall be limited up to the amount of the actual moneys received by LICENSOR under this Agreement. Further, this indemnity does not cover any modifications or changes made to the Property by LICENSEE nor does it cover any claims arising from countries outside the United States.

14. INSURANCE

LICENSEE shall, throughout the Term of the Agreement, obtain and maintain at its own cost and expense from a qualified insurance company licensed to do business in [*State*], standard Product Liability Insurance naming LICENSOR as an additional named insured. Such policy shall provide protection against any and all

Appendix

claims, demands and causes of action arising out of any defects or failure to perform, alleged or otherwise, of the Licensed Products or any material used in connection therewith or any use thereof. The amount of coverage shall be as specified in Schedule A attached hereto. The policy shall provide for ten (10) days notice to LICENSOR from the insurer by Registered or Certified Mail, return receipt requested, in the event of any modification, cancellation or termination thereof. LICENSEE agrees to furnish LICENSOR a certificate of insurance evidencing same within thirty (30) days after execution of this Agreement and, in no event shall LICENSEE manufacture, distribute or sell the Licensed Products prior to receipt by LICENSOR of such evidence of insurance.

15. JURISDICTION & DISPUTES

A. This Agreement shall be governed in accordance with the laws of the State of [*State*], United States of America.

B. Except as provided for herein, any dispute or disagreement which may arise between LICENSOR and LICENSEE in connection with either any interpretation of this Agreement or the performance or nonperformance thereof shall be settled by a board of three arbitrators without appeal under the rules of conciliation and arbitration of the International Chamber of Commerce. Unless otherwise agreed to by both parties, any arbitration shall be conducted in the city of New York, NY in the United States of America. The judgment upon any award rendered by the arbitration tribunal may be entered in any court having jurisdiction thereof, for the purpose of judicial enforcement.

16. AGREEMENT BINDING ON SUCCESSORS

The provisions of this Agreement shall be binding upon and shall inure to the benefit of the parties hereto, their heirs, administrators, successors and assigns.

17. WAIVER

No waiver by either party of any default shall be deemed as a waiver of prior or subsequent default of the same or other provisions of this Agreement.

18. SEVERABILITY

If any term, clause or provision hereof is held invalid or unenforceable by a court of competent jurisdiction, such invalidity shall not affect the validity or operation of any other term, clause or provision and such invalid term, clause or provision shall be deemed to be severed from the Agreement.

19. NO JOINT VENTURE

Nothing contained herein shall constitute this arrangement to be employment, a joint venture or a partnership.

20. ASSIGNABILITY

The license granted hereunder is personal to LICENSEE and shall not be assigned by any act of LICENSEE or by operation of law unless in connection with a transfer of substantially all of the assets of LICENSEE or with the consent of LICENSOR.

21. GOVERNMENTAL APPROVAL

As promptly as possible after execution of this Agreement, LICENSEE agrees to submit copies of this Agreement to any governmental agency in any country in the Territory where approval of a license agreement is necessary and agrees to promptly prosecute any such application diligently. This Agreement shall only become effective in such country or countries upon receipt of appropriate approval from the applicable governmental agency.

22. GOVERNING LANGUAGE

This Agreement is in the English language. No translation of this Agreement into any language other than English shall be considered in the interpretation thereof, and in the event that any translation of this Agreement is in conflict with the English language version, the English version shall govern.

23. BLOCKED CURRENCY

A. In the event that any payment required to be made to LICENSOR pursuant to this Agreement cannot be made when due because of the exchange control of any country in the Territory and such payment remains unpaid for twelve (12) months, LICENSOR

Appendix

may, by notice served to LICENSEE, elect any of the following alternative methods of handling such payment:

1. If the currency can be converted into currency other than U.S. Dollars for purposes of foreign remittance, LICENSOR may elect to receive such payment in any such currencies as it may specify and, in such case, the amount payable in the foreign currency so selected shall be determined by reference to the then existent legal rate of exchange which is most favorable to LICENSOR.

2. LICENSOR may elect to have payment made to it in the local currency, deposited to the credit of LICENSOR in a bank account in such country designated by LICENSOR, in which event LICENSEE shall furnish to LICENSOR evidence of such deposit.

3. LICENSOR may elect to receive payment in shares of stock in the LICENSEE corporation at such price as LICENSOR and LICENSEE may agree to at such time.

B. All expenses of currency conversion and transmission shall be borne by LICENSEE and no deduction shall be made from remittances on account of such expense. LICENSEE from time to time may prepare all applications, reports or other documents which may be required by the government of the applicable country in order that remittances may be made in accordance with this Agreement.

24. INTEGRATION

This Agreement constitutes the entire understanding of the parties, and revokes and supersedes all prior agreements between the parties, including any option agreements which may have been entered into between the parties, and is intended as a final expression of their Agreement. It shall not be modified or amended except in writing signed by the parties hereto and specifically referring to this Agreement. This Agreement shall take precedence over any other documents which may be in conflict with said Agreement.

IN WITNESS WHEREOF, the parties hereto, intending to be legally bound hereby, have each caused to be affixed hereto its or his/her hand and seal the day indicated.

[*Name of Licensor*]   [*Name of Licensee*]

Basics of Licensing: International Edition

SCHEDULE A

1. Licensed Properties
The following Licensed Properties form part of this Agreement:

2. Licensed Trademarks
The following Licensed Trademarks form part of this Agreement:

3. Licensed Products
The following Licensed Products form part of this Agreement:

4. Territory
The following countries shall constitute the Territory:

5. Term
This Agreement shall commence on the date executed by both parties and shall extend for an initial Term of:

[number] ([number]) YEARS

LICENSOR hereby grants LICENSEE two (2) separately exercisable options (the "Options") to renew this Agreement for additional two (2) year extended Terms on the same terms and conditions provided for herein, provided: a) LICENSEE provides written notice of its intention to exercise this Option within sixty (60) days prior to expiration of the then in-effect Term; and b) LICENSEE shall have paid LICENSOR total royalty income of at least [number] UNITED STATES DOLLARS ($ [number]) during the then in-effect Term.

6. Royalty Rate
LICENSEE shall pay the following royalty rate: [number] PERCENT ([number]%).

7. Guaranteed Minimum Royalty & Advance
LICENSEE agrees to pay LICENSOR an Advance of [number] UNITED STATES DOLLARS ($ [number]) upon execution of this Agreement.

LICENSEE agrees to and will pay LICENSOR a Guaranteed Minimum Royalty of [number] UNITED STATES DOLLARS ($

Appendix

[*number*]) for each calendar year during the Term of this Agreement.

8. Product Liability Insurance

[*number*] Million Dollars ($ [*number*]) combined single limit, with a deductible amount not to exceed [*number*] Dollars ($ [*number*]), for each single occurrence for bodily injury and/or for property damage.

9. Product Introduction/Initial Shipment

The Product Introduction Date for all Licensed Products in all countries in the Territory shall be [*insert date*].

The Initial Shipment Date for all Licensed Products in all countries in the Territory shall be [*insert date*].

Appendix B

Sub-Agent Agreement

THIS AGREEMENT is entered into this [*date*] by and between [*Name of Agent*] with offices at [*Address of Agent*] (the "Agent") and [*Name of Sub-Agent*], with offices at [*Address of Sub-Agent*] (the "Sub-Agent").

WITNESSETH:

WHEREAS, Agent, pursuant to an agent agreement dated [*date*] between [*Name of Property Owner*] (the "Owner") and the Agent (the "Agent Agreement"), the Property Owner has granted certain rights to the Agent to develop and conduct a licensing program for the property described in Schedule A attached hereto (the "Property"); and

WHEREAS, Agent would like to retain the services of Sub-Agent to commercialize or license the Property to third-party licensees in the Sub-Agent's territory as defined in Schedule A (the "Territory") for a line of licensed products (the "Licensed Products"); and

WHEREAS, Sub-Agent is willing to represent the Agent in such Territory with respect to the licensing of the Property within the Territory;

NOW, THEREFORE, in consideration of the promises and agreements set forth herein, the parties, each intending to be legally bound hereby, do promise and agree as follows.

1. SUB-AGENT APPOINTMENT

A. Agent hereby appoints the Sub-Agent, for the Term of this Agreement, its exclusive representative in the Territory for the purpose of commercializing or licensing the Property to third-party licensees, subject to the approval of Agent and the Owner.

B. In this regard, Sub-Agent shall be authorized to present, negotiate, and conclude licensing arrangements with third-party licensees using a form agreement approved by Agent and Owner

Appendix

and pursuant to terms and conditions previously approved by Agent and Owner.

C. All third-party license agreements shall be in the name of Owner and shall be signed by Owner, although Sub-Agent shall be a party to all such agreements as agent for Owner. All payments from third parties shall be directed to Sub-Agent.

D. It is understood and agreed that this Agreement shall relate only to the enumerated Property and to no other properties owned or controlled by Agent and/or Owner. Agent and Owner shall be free to commercialize such other properties to the exclusion of Sub-Agent.

E. Agent agrees not to retain the services of any third party to represent Agent with respect to the Property in the Territory. However, Agent may retain the services of other subagents with respect to merchandising of the Property in countries outside the Territory.

F. Sub-Agent agrees to refrain from licensing the Property to third party licensees who intend or are likely to sell the Licensed Products outside the Territory.

2. TERM OF THE AGREEMENT

This Agreement and the provisions hereof, except as otherwise provided, shall be in full force and effect commencing on the date of execution by both parties and shall extend for a Term as recited in Schedule A attached hereto (the "Term").

3. DUTIES AND OBLIGATIONS OF PARTIES

A. Subject to the conditions herein specified, Sub-Agent shall use reasonable efforts during the Term of this Agreement to find and conclude business arrangements with licensees for the Property that are advantageous to Agent and Owner and, thereafter, to reasonably service such arrangements during the term thereof. In furtherance of Sub-Agent's duties as herein specified, Sub-Agent will:

1. Periodically meet and confer with Agent to discuss the state of the merchandising industry;

Basics of Licensing: International Edition

2. Develop a merchandising plan for the Property in the Territory and provide a copy of same to Agent within thirty (30) days of the date of execution of this Agreement by both parties;

3. Implement the merchandising plan by contacting those prospective licensees best able to produce licensed products of the type and quality for the Property;

4. Negotiate all agreements with third party licensees in the name of the Owner and subject to the approval of Agent and Owner;

5. Provide record keeping and billing services to the licensees as reasonably requested by Agent and monitor and oversee the licensing program with such third-party licensees to ensure that the licenses, royalties, minimums, and sales reports are promptly submitted;

6. Make appropriate recommendations to the Agent with respect to seeking and maintaining appropriate intellectual property protection for the Property; and

7. Investigate all potential infringements of Owner's intellectual property rights in the Territory and report to Agent.

B. In addition to the foregoing, Sub-Agent shall be responsible for the enforcement of the quality control provisions of the third party license agreements which shall include periodic inspection of all Licensed Products and conducting personal visits to the third-party licensees' manufacturing facilities to ensure that the quality control provisions of the license agreements with the licensees are being complied with. Sub-Agent shall submit to Agent a written report after each of said reviews and visits.

C. Sub-Agent shall engage in other such activities as the parties may mutually agree and, in general, use its best efforts consistent with sound business practices to maximize revenue generated from the exploitation of the rights granted hereunder and to enhance the value and reputation of the Property.

D. While Sub-Agent is empowered to propose all necessary art, design, editorial, and other related approvals for the creation of the Licensed Products as well as to enforce the appropriately high standard of quality for all such Licensed Products created and pro-

Appendix

duced pursuant to licensing and promotional agreements entered into pursuant to this Agreement, Agent retains the right to grant final approval on art, design, and editorial matters. Sub-Agent agrees to submit to Agent, for final approval, drafts, prototypes and finished samples of all Licensed Products and any and all advertising, promotional and packaging material related to said Licensed Products. Agent will respond to Sub-Agent regarding approval within thirty (30) business days after receipt of such samples. Failure to respond within said period shall be deemed disapproval.

E. Sub-Agent shall oversee the payment by the licensees of all royalties and other payments due under this Agreement. If necessary, Sub-Agent shall conduct periodic royalty investigations of the licensee's books and records to ensure that all payments have been made. The cost of such royalty investigations shall be borne by Sub-Agent. However, any recoveries received as a result of such royalty investigation shall be applied against the cost of conducting such investigation.

F. It is understood that Agent and Owner may have concepts and properties other than the Property and such concepts and properties do not form part of this Agreement.

G. Agent recognizes that Sub-Agent performs similar services for its other clients and that Agent's retention of Sub-Agent is subject to such understanding.

H. Agent and Owner shall be solely responsible for all costs and expenses associated with the protection of the Property, including the costs for obtaining and maintaining patent, trademark, and copyright protection.

4. LICENSE AGREEMENTS

A. All proposed license agreements presented by Sub-Agent under this Agreement shall be subject to the express written approval of Agent and Owner, such approval not to be unreasonably withheld. It is understood that Sub-Agent will submit all such proposed agreements to Owner through Agent for consideration, approval, and execution and Agent will, thereupon, advise Sub-Agent within thirty (30) business days after receipt of the proposed agreement as to whether Agent and Owner agree or disagree to the terms thereof and whether Owner will execute same. Failure to act within said thirty (30) day period shall be deemed a disapproval of any

Basics of Licensing: International Edition

such agreement. No agreement shall be binding on Agent or Owner until signed by Owner.

B. All such license agreements with third-party licensees shall be between Owner and the third-party licensee presented by Sub-Agent. The basic form license agreement that is to be used by Sub-Agent in negotiating license agreements with third-party licensees has been deemed approved by Agent and Owner as in form only -- all prospective licenses, even if in this form, must be submitted for approval by Agent and Owner. Any and all additions, deletions and changes to this basic form agreement shall be subject to the absolute, unfettered express written approval of Agent and Owner and notification of approval or disapproval shall be provided to Sub-Agent within ten (10) business days after receipt of same by Agent. The lack of response from Agent within such ten (10) day period shall be deemed a disapproval of any proposed addition, deletion and/or change.

5. COMPENSATION

A. In consideration for the services rendered by Sub-Agent, Agent agrees to and shall pay Sub-Agent, during the Term of this Agreement, a commission in the amount recited in Schedule A attached hereto (the "Commission").

B. In addition to the Commission recited in Schedule A, Agent agrees to reimburse Sub-Agent for all reasonable expenses incurred on behalf of Agent, provided that such expenses have been previously approved by Agent.

C. Agent further agrees to pay Sub-Agent, during the Term of this Agreement, a Subagent Fee in the amount recited in Schedule A attached hereto.

D. "Gross Revenues" shall include all income generated as a result of any commercialization, sale, or licensing of the Property in the Territory (prior to deduction of Sub-Agent's Commission) from such third-party licensee(s), due solely to the efforts of Sub-Agent.

E. In the event that this Agreement should expire or terminate for reasons other than a breach of any provision herein by Sub-Agent, Sub-Agent shall be entitled to post-termination compensation based on gross income received by Owner from any third-party license agreement, for the life of such third party agreement, en-

Appendix

tered into through Sub-Agent during the Term of this Agreement and for which Sub-Agent would have received compensation had this Agreement not expired, subject to the schedule recited in Schedule A attached hereto.

F. Sub-Agent shall not be entitled to any post-termination compensation in the event that this Agreement is expressly terminated by Agent in the event of a material breach by Sub-Agent of the terms of this Agreement. Sub-Agent shall not be entitled to such post-termination compensation for any other agreements subsequently entered into by Agent or Owner.

G. All payments due hereunder shall be made in United States currency drawn on a United States bank, unless otherwise specified between the parties.

H. All fees payable hereunder shall be based on the official exchange rate on the date on which such payment is due and Sub-Agent shall provide detailed conversion calculations with every payment submitted hereunder. If, by any reason of any governmental or fiscal restrictions effecting the convertibility, payment cannot be made in U.S. funds, then Sub-Agent shall take such reasonable actions with respect to the payment due as Agent shall direct.

6. WARRANTIES AND INDEMNIFICATIONS

A. Agent represents and warrants that it has the right and power to enter into this agreement and, further, that it has not granted anyone else the right or authority to act for it in a manner that would conflict with Sub-Agent.

B. Agent hereby agrees to defend, indemnify, and hold Sub-Agent, its shareholders, directors, officers, employees, agents, parent companies, subsidiaries and affiliates, harmless from and against any and all claims, liabilities, judgments, penalties, and taxes, civil and criminal, and all costs and expenses (including, without limitation, reasonable attorney's fees) incurred in connection therewith, which any of them may incur or to which any of them may be subjected, arising out of or relating to a breach of Agent's representation and warranty or of any actions or inactions of Agent.

C. Sub-Agent hereby agrees to defend, indemnify, and hold Agent and any of its related entities harmless from and against any and all claims, liabilities, judgments, penalties, and taxes, civil and criminal, and all costs and expenses (including, without limitation, reasonable attorney's fees) arising out of or relating to a breach of Sub-Agent's representation and warranty or that may arise out of any action or inaction by Sub-Agent, other than as it may relate to Agent's warranty, as above stated.

D. Sub-Agent hereby agrees to comply with all laws and regulations in each country in the Territory.

7. STATEMENTS AND PAYMENTS

A. All payments from licensees based on agreements for the Property shall be paid directly to Owner. Within thirty (30) days after receipt by Agent of its commission from Owner, Agent shall transmit to Sub-Agent its Commission.

B. Agent agrees to keep accurate books of accounts and records at its principal place of business covering all transactions relating to the agreements with the licensees. Sub-Agent, through an independent certified public accountant acceptable to Owner, shall have the right, at all reasonable hours of the day and upon at least five (5) days' written notice, to examine Agent's books and records as they relate to the subject matter of this Agreement only. Such examination shall occur at the place where Agent maintains such records.

C. All books and records pertaining to the obligations of Sub-Agent hereunder shall be maintained and kept accessible and available to Agent for inspection for at least three (3) years after the date to which they pertain.

8. NOTICES

A. Any notice required to be given under this Agreement shall be in writing and delivered personally to the other designated party at the above-stated address or mailed by certified or registered mail, return receipt requested, or delivered by a recognized national overnight courier service.

B. Either party may change the address to which notice or payment is to be sent by written notice to the other under any provision of this paragraph.

Appendix

9. TERMINATION

A. This Agreement may be terminated by either party upon thirty (30) days' written notice to the other party in the event of a breach of a material provision of this Agreement by the other party, provided that, during the thirty (30) day period, the breaching party fails to cure such breach.

B. Agent shall have the right to terminate this Agreement immediately in the event that Sub-Agent fails to enter into at least _____ license agreements with third parties with _____ months after execution of this Agreement and generates at least _____ of licensing revenue from such third parties within _____ months after execution of this Agreement.

C. Sub-Agent shall have the right to terminate this Agreement for any reason on sixty (60) days' written notice to Agent subject to the post-termination compensation provisions of this Agreement.

D. This Agreement shall terminate automatically in the event that the Agent Agreement between Agent and Owner shall terminate or expire.

E. In the event that this Agreement shall terminate or expire, Sub-Agent shall turn over to Agent all records relating to each license entered into under this Agreement. All rights granted to Sub-Agent shall revert to Agent and Sub-Agent shall refrain from any further use of the Property.

10. JURISDICTION AND DISPUTES

A. This Agreement shall be governed in accordance with the laws of the State of [*State*], United States of America.

B. Except as provided for herein, any dispute or disagreement which may arise between Agent and Sub-Agent in connection with either any interpretation of this Agreement or the performance or nonperformance thereof shall be settled by a board of three arbitrators without appeal under the rules of conciliation and arbitration of the International Chamber of Commerce. Unless otherwise agreed to by both parties, any arbitration shall be conducted in the city of New York, NY in the United States of America. The judgment upon any award rendered by the arbitration tribunal may be entered in any court having jurisdiction thereof, for the purpose of judicial enforcement.

11. SUBORDINATION

The parties recognize that Agent's rights with respect to the Property are governed exclusively by the Agent Agreement. In the event there are conflicts between the Agent Agreement and this Agreement, the provisions of the Agent Agreement shall govern.

12. AGREEMENT BINDING ON SUCCESSORS

The provisions of the Agreement shall be binding on and shall inure to the benefit of the parties hereto, their heirs, assigns, and successors.

13. WAIVER

No waiver by either party of any default shall be deemed as a waiver of prior or subsequent default of the same or other provisions of this Agreement.

14. SEVERABILITY

If any term, clause, or provision hereof is held invalid or unenforceable by a court of competent jurisdiction, such invalidity shall not affect the validity or operation of any other term, clause, or provision and such invalid term, clause, or provision shall be deemed to be severed from the Agreement.

15. INDEPENDENT CONTRACTOR

Sub-Agent shall be deemed an independent contractor and nothing contained herein shall constitute this arrangement to be employment, a joint venture, or a partnership. Sub-Agent shall be solely responsible for and shall hold Agent harmless for any and all claims for taxes, fees, or costs, including but not limited to withholding, income tax, FICA, and workmen's compensation.

16. ASSIGNABILITY

This agreement and the rights and obligations thereof are personal to Sub-Agent and shall not be assigned by any act of Sub-Agent or by operation of law unless in connection with a transfer of

Appendix

substantially all of the assets of Sub-Agent or with the consent of Agent and Owner.

17. GOVERNMENTAL APPROVAL

Sub-Agent agrees to submit copies of this Agreement to any governmental agency in any country in the Territory where approval of this Agreement is necessary, and agrees to promptly prosecute any such application diligently. This Agreement shall become effective in such country or countries only upon receipt of appropriate approval from the applicable governmental agency.

18. GOVERNING LANGUAGE

This Agreement is in the English language. No translation of this Agreement into any language other than English shall be considered in the interpretation thereof, and in the event that any translation of this Agreement is in conflict with the English language version, the English version shall govern.

19. BLOCKED CURRENCY

A. In the event that any payment required to be made to Owner pursuant to this Agreement cannot be made when due because of the exchange control of any country in the Territory and such payment remains unpaid for twelve (12) months, Agent and/or Owner may, by notice served to Sub-Agent, elect any of the following alternative methods of handling such payment:

1. If the currency can be converted into currency other than U.S. Dollars for purposes of foreign remittance, Owner may elect to receive such payment in any such currencies as it may specify and, in such case, the amount payable in the foreign currency so selected shall be determined by reference to the then existent legal rate of exchange which is most favorable to Owner.

2. Owner may elect to have payment made to it in the local currency, deposited to the credit of Owner in a bank account in such country designated by Owner, in which event Sub-Agent shall furnish to Owner evidence of such deposit.

B. All expenses of currency conversion and transmission shall be borne by Sub-Agent and no deduction shall be made from remittances on account of such expense. Sub-Agent from time to time may prepare all applications, reports or other documents which may be required by the government of the applicable country in order that remittances may be made in accordance with this Agreement.

20. INTEGRATION

This Agreement constitutes the entire understanding of the parties, and revokes and supersedes all prior agreements between the parties and is intended as a final expression of their Agreement. It shall not be modified or amended except in writing signed by the parties hereto and specifically referring to this Agreement. This Agreement shall take precedence over any other documents that may conflict with this Agreement.

IN WITNESS WHEREOF, the parties hereto, intending to be legally bound hereby, have each caused to be affixed hereto its or his/her hand and seal the day indicated.

[AGENT]   [SUB-AGENT]

By: By:
Title: Title:
Date: Date:

SCHEDULE A

1. Licensed Property
The following Licensed Properties form part of this Agreement:

2. Territory
The following countries shall constitute the Territory:

3. Term
This Agreement shall commence on the date executed by both parties and shall extend for an initial Term of: [*number*] ([#]) YEARS

4. Commission
Agent shall pay the following Commission:

[*number*] PERCENT ([#]%) of the Gross Revenues received by Owner from the licensee(s) and/or third-party ancillary property licensees for the Property.

Appendix

5. Subagent Fee

Agent shall pay the following Subagent Fee:

[*number*] UNITED STATES DOLLARS ($[#]) per month during the Term of this Agreement, which shall be deemed as an advance against the Commission.

6. Post Termination Compensation

Sub-Agent may be entitled to continue to receive its full commission after termination or expiration of this Agreement (unless terminated as a result of Sub-Agent having breached any material provision of the Agreement), for the remaining term of any license agreement that its acquired during the Term of this Agreement.